The

Cook's Problem Solver

By Helen Kowtaluk

ACKNOWLEDGMENTS:
Special thanks to home economists Marilyn Meyer, Karen Miller and Carri Whitaker, and to Larry Pardun, amateur chef, for reading the manuscript. Their helpful suggestions, insights and encouragement are greatly appreciated.

A FIREBIRD PRESS BOOK

PELICAN PUBLISHING COMPANY
Gretna 1998

ISBN 0-88289-600-8

Manufactured in the United States of America

Published by Pelican Publishing Company, Inc.

1000 Burmaster Street, Gretna, Louisiana 70053

 *Contents*

Chapter 1 . . . . What's Your Problem?, 4
Chapter 2 . . . . Buying Food, 60
Chapter 3 . . . . Storing Food, 67
Chapter 4 . . . . Basic Cooking Methods, 77
Chapter 5 . . . . Using a Recipe, 104
Chapter 6 . . . . Milk, Cream, Yogurt, 119
Chapter 7 . . . . Cheese, 125
Chapter 8 . . . . Eggs, 129
Chapter 9 . . . . Grains, 138
Chapter 10 . . . . Thickeners, 144
Chapter 11 . . . . Seasonings, 155
Chapter 12 . . . . Fruits, 162
Chapter 13 . . . . Vegetables, 168
Chapter 14 . . . . Salads, 179
Chapter 15 . . . . Beverages, 182
Chapter 16 . . . . Soup, 186
Chapter 17 . . . . Meat, 191
Chapter 18 . . . . Poultry, 207
Chapter 19 . . . . Seafood, 218
Chapter 20 . . . . Baking Principles, 228
Chapter 21 . . . . Breads: Quick and Yeast, 243
Chapter 22 . . . . Cakes, 259
Chapter 23 . . . . Cookies, 271
Chapter 24 . . . . Pies and Pastries, 277
Index, 286

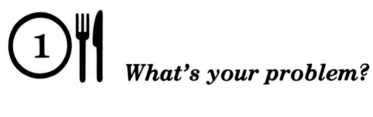

What's your problem?

CONVENTIONAL COOKING

A

ANGEL FOOD CAKE. See "FOAM CAKES."

ARROWROOT. See "THICKENERS."

B

BAKING, GENERAL. Also see "BISCUITS," "CHIFFON CAKES," "COOKIES," "CREAM PUFFS," "FOAM CAKES," "MUFFINS," "PIES," "QUICK LOAF BREADS," "SHORTENED CAKES" and "YEAST BREADS."

Whole grain flour difficult to put through sifter.
☐ Whole grain particles too large. 5-14

Whole grain flour has off flavor.
☐ Stored in warm area. 3-2, 3-3, 3-8, 20-2, 20-4.

Baked product is not done in the time specified in recipe.
☐ Oven not preheated. 20-33
☐ Oven thermostat not accurate. 20-33
☐ Substituted different shape or size of pan. 5-15, 22-11

Baked product overbakes or bakes too fast.
☐ Used dull metal, glass or ceramic pan. 20-30
☐ Oven thermostat not accurate. 20-33

Baked product sticks in pan and is difficult to remove.
☐ Pan not greased carefully, especially in corners. 20-31
☐ Pan greased with salted butter. 20-31
☐ Pan greased, but not floured. 20-31

Rich fruitcake sticks to pan that was well greased and floured.
☐ Pan bottom not lined with paper. 20-31

Baked product has off flavor.
☐ Did not use fresh, top-quality ingredients. 20-29

Recipe fails. See "RECIPES."

Baked product bakes unevenly.
☐ Pan placed in oven with one side too close to oven wall or another pan. 20-32

BEEF. See "MEAT."

BISCUITS. Also see "BAKING, GENERAL."

Biscuits are not flaky.
☐ Fat not cold. 21-5
☐ Oil substituted for solid fat. 20-16, 21-5
☐ Flour and fat undermixed or overmixed. 21-5
☐ Dough overmixed. 21-5
☐ Dough kneaded too long. 21-6, 21-7
☐ Leftover dough rerolled and cut. 21-7

Biscuits are dry.
☐ Not enough liquid. 5-8, 5-11, 20-5, 21-5
☐ Too much flour. 5-8 to 5-10, 20-1, 21-5
☐ Overbaked. 20-33, 21-7, 21-8

Biscuits have a poor color.
☐ Too much fat. 5-8 to 5-10, 5-14, 20-14, 21-5
☐ Undermixed. 21-5
☐ Pan placed too close to oven wall or to another pan. 20-32, 21-7

Biscuits have dark spots on crust.
☐ Too much baking soda. 5-10, 5-12, 20-7, 20-10, 21-5

Biscuits have a pale crust.
☐ Underbaked. 20-33, 21-7, 21-8

Biscuits have a dark brown crust.
☐ Overbaked. 20-33, 21-7, 21-8

Biscuits are tough.
☐ Too little fat. 5-8 to 5-10, 5-14, 20-14, 21-5
☐ Dough overmixed. 21-5
☐ Too much flour used in rolling. 21-7

5

Biscuits have a poor flavor.
☐ Dough undermixed. 21-5

Biscuits have poor flavor, texture and appearance.
☐ Ingredients not measured properly. 5-8 to 5-12, 5-14, 21-5

Biscuits are heavy.
☐ Too much fat. 5-8 to 5-10, 5-14, 20-14, 21-5
☐ Dough kneaded too long. 21-6, 21-7
☐ Underbaked. 21-7, 21-8

Biscuits have a coarse texture.
☐ Too much liquid. 5-11, 20-5, 21-5
☐ Dough kneaded too long. 21-6, 21-7

Biscuits have flour on the crust.
☐ Not enough liquid. 5-11, 20-5, 21-5
☐ Too much flour used in rolling out dough. 21-7

Biscuit crusts are not crisp or brown.
☐ Placed too close together on baking sheet. 21-7

Biscuits have uneven shapes.
☐ Too much fat. 5-8 to 5-10, 5-14, 20-14, 21-5
☐ Too much liquid. 5-11, 20-5, 21-5
☐ Dough overmixed. 21-5
☐ Dough kneaded too long. 21-6, 21-7
☐ Dough rolled out unevenly. 21-7
☐ Biscuit cutter twisted or turned when cutting. 21-7

BREADING

Breading does not stick to fried food.
☐ Food not completely dry before breading. 4-19
☐ Surface not completely coated. 4-19

BRAISING. See "MEAT" and "POULTRY."

BROILING, GENERAL. Also see "FISH," "FRUIT," "MEAT," "POULTRY" and "VEGETABLES."

Broiled meat is greasy.
☐ Broiler grid lined with foil. 4-21

Grease in broiler pan catches fire.
☐ Pan too close to heat. 4-21
☐ Broiler grid lined with foil. 4-21

BROWN SAUCE. See "SAUCES."

BUTTER CAKES. See "SHORTENED CAKES."

C

CHEESE

Ripened cheese has little flavor when served.
□ Served cold. 7-6

Cheese has too strong a flavor.
□ Wrong type purchased. 2-1, 2-8, 7-2, 7-4

Cheese doesn't melt when heated.
□ Wrong type purchased for cooking. 2-1, 2-8, 4-24, 7-2 to 7-4

Cooked cheese is tough, stringy or separates into small drops of grease.
□ Cooked too long or at too high a temperature. 4-24, 7-7

CHICKEN. See "POULTRY."

CHIFFON CAKES. Also see "BAKING, GENERAL."

Cake doesn't rise properly.
□ Eggs underbeaten. 8-15, 22-16
□ Batter overfolded or overmixed. 8-15, 22-16

Cake compact with uneven texture.
□ Eggs underbeaten. 8-15, 22-16

Cake soggy and coarse.
□ Batter underfolded or undermixed. 8-15, 22-16

Cake tough with uneven texture.
□ Batter overfolded or overmixed. 8-15, 22-16

CHOWDER. See "SOUP."

CLAMS. See "SHELLFISH."

COCOA. Also see "MILK."

Cocoa is lumpy.
□ Cocoa powder stirred into liquid. 15-12

COFFEE

Home-ground coffee has an off odor and off flavor.
□ Coffee grinder not cleaned properly. 15-3

Coffeemaker doesn't make good coffee.
☐ Wrong grind used. 2-1, 15-1
☐ Coffee grounds not fresh. 15-2
☐ Proper procedure not followed. 15-4

Freshly brewed coffee has off flavor.
☐ Coffeemaker not cleaned properly. 15-4

Coffee is too strong.
☐ Overcooked. 15-4
☐ Not diluted to desired strength. 15-4

Coffee is too weak.
☐ Ingredients not measured properly. 5-10 to 5-12, 15-4
☐ Wrong grind used. 2-1, 15-1
☐ Not cooked long enough. 15-4

Coffee is bitter.
☐ Boiled, not brewed. 15-4
☐ Cooked too long. 15-4
☐ Not enough grounds used. 15-4
☐ Reheated. 15-6

Iced coffee weak.
☐ Diluted by ice cubes. 15-5

COMMERCIAL CAKE MIX

Commercial cake mix fails.
☐ Package instructions not followed. 22-20
☐ Experimented with own variations. 22-20

COOKIES. Also see "BAKING, GENERAL."

Cookies spread out too much.
☐ Ingredients not measured properly. 5-8 to 5-12, 5-14, 23-7
☐ Eggs too large. 8-1, 8-2, 23-1
☐ Pan still warm from previous batch of cookies. 23-3
☐ Not dropped onto cookie sheet properly. 23-7
☐ Oven temperature too low. 20-33, 23-7

Cookies bake unevenly.
☐ Dough shaped unevenly on cookie sheet. 23-2
☐ Oven bakes unevenly. 23-4
☐ More than one cookie sheet in oven at one time. 23-4

Cookies do not brown properly.
☐ Not baked long enough. 23-7
☐ Wrong kind of pan used. 23-3
☐ Oven temperature too low. 20-33

Cookies are too brown.
☐ Baked too long. 23-4
☐ Oven temperature too high. 20-33
☐ Not removed from pan quickly enough. 23-4

Cookies are tough and dry.
☐ Eggs too small. 8-1, 8-2, 23-1
☐ Too much flour. 5-8 to 5-10, 20-1, 23-1, 23-11

Cookies are dry and crumble easily.
☐ Ingredients not measured properly. 5-8 to 5-12, 5-14, 23-8
☐ Baked too long. 23-5

Cookies are doughy.
☐ Not baked long enough. 23-7, 23-8
☐ Oven temperature too low. 20-33

Cookies are soggy.
☐ Cooled on solid surface instead of on cooling racks. 20-34, 23-5

Cookies stick to spatula as they are being removed from cookie sheet.
☐ Gummy cookie residue has built up on spatula. 20-34

Bar cookies have a hard, crusty top.
☐ Dough overmixed. 23-6

Bar cookies have an uneven shape.
☐ Dough spread unevenly in pan. 23-6
☐ Cookies cut with dull knife. 23-6

Cut edges on bar cookies compact and gummy.
☐ Cut while still warm. 23-6

Bar cookies crumble when cut.
☐ Cut while still warm. 23-6

Drop cookies have dark, crusty edges.
☐ Baked too long. 23-7
☐ Oven temperature too high. 20-33
☐ Baking sheet too large for oven. 23-7

Dough for molded cookies is difficult to shape.
☐ Not chilled before shaping. 23-8

Molded cookies lose their shape when baked.
☐ Dough not pressed together when shaped. 23-8

Molded cookies crumble.
☐ Dough not pressed together when shaped. 23-8

Pressed cookies do not hold shape.
☐ Dough too soft. 23-9

Pressed cookie dough difficult to force through cookie press.
☐ Dough too stiff. 23-9

Pressed cookies lose shape when baked.
☐ Oven temperature too low. 20-33, 23-9

Refrigerator cookies have an odd shape.
☐ Roll not shaped evenly. 23-11
☐ Roll too soft to slice. 23-11
☐ Dull knife used to slice cookies. 23-11

Rolled cookies are tough.
☐ Excess dough rerolled. 23-10

Flour shows on rolled cookies after baking.
☐ Too much flour used when rolling dough. 23-10

Crisp cookies soften in storage.
☐ Stored in container with loose cover. 23-19

CREAM PUFFS. Also see "BAKING, GENERAL."

Cream puffs do not rise properly.
☐ Flour-liquid combination cooked and stirred too long. 24-17
☐ Batter not beaten enough. 20-1, 24-16, 24-17
☐ Batter not shaped into high mounds. 24-17
☐ Dough too soft. 24-17
☐ Oven temperature too low. 20-33, 24-18

Cream puffs are too moist inside.
☐ Not baked long enough to dry out. 24-18, 24-19

Cream puffs have torn edge where cut in half.
☐ Knife not sharp enough. 24-19

CREAM SAUCE. See "SAUCES" and "THICKENERS."

CREAMED MIXTURES

Creamed mixtures curdle.
☐ Cooked too long. 6-12
☐ Cold milk added to hot food. 6-12
☐ Too much salt in mixture. 6-12
☐ Milk mixed with acid food. 6-12
☐ Mixture made with cream. 6-15

CREPES

Crepes are too thick.
☐ Too little liquid. 5-11, 21-2, 21-3

Crepes are doughy.
☐ Too little liquid. 5-11, 21-2, 21-3

Crepes are too dark.
☐ Cooked too long. 21-3

Crepes have dark, crisp crusts.
☐ Pan too hot. 21-3
☐ Cooked too long. 21-3

CUSTARD

Custard too thin.
☐ Not enough eggs. 10-16
☐ Eggs too small. 8-1, 8-2, 10-16
☐ Too much sugar. 5-8 to 5-12, 10-16
☐ Baked custard stirred while baking. 10-16

Custard too thick.
☐ Too many eggs. 10-16
☐ Eggs too large. 8-1, 8-2, 10-16

Custard curdles or "weeps."
☐ Overcooked. 10-14

D

DRIED BEANS. See "LEGUMES."

DRIED PEAS. See "LEGUMES."

E

EGG WHITES. Also see "MERINGUE."

Difficult to separate yolk from whites.
☐ Wrong grade purchased. 2-1, 8-1, 8-2
☐ Eggs too warm. 8-14

Yolk falls into bowl of egg whites when separating eggs.
☐ Didn't use separate dish when separating white from yolk.
8-14

Egg whites won't beat up to full volume.
☐ Bit of yolk in whites. 8-14
☐ Eggs too cold. 8-15
☐ Fat residue on bowls, beater or other equipment. 8-15

Beaten egg whites turn gray.
☐ Beaten in aluminum mixing bowl. 8-15

Beaten egg whites do not hold up but lose volume.
☐ Did not use cream of tartar. 8-15
☐ Salt added to egg whites. 8-15

Beaten egg whites fall apart.
☐ Overbeaten. 8-15

EGGS

Eggs, general

Eggs in storage container cracked.
☐ Didn't inspect eggs before buying. 8-2

Eggs stuck in cardboard storage container.
☐ Didn't inspect eggs when buying. 8-2, 8-3

Leftover yolks or whites spoil before they can be used.
☐ Improperly stored. 3-3, 3-4, 8-3, 8-4

Yolks break when cracking eggs open.
☐ Wrong grade purchased. 8-1, 8-2
☐ Eggs cracked too hard. 8-9
☐ Eggs cracked directly into skillet. 8-11

Frozen egg yolks are too thick to use.
☐ Improperly frozen. 3-4, 8-4

Cooked eggs are tough and rubbery.
☐ Overcooked. 4-24, 8-5

Cooked whites are tough and rubbery.
☐ Overcooked. 4-24, 8-5
☐ Frozen after being cooked. 8-4

Eggs cooked in the shell.

Egg shells crack when cooked whole in water.
☐ Cold eggs placed in warm or hot water. 8-6
☐ Shells not pricked with pin. 8-6

Hard-cooked eggs difficult to peel.
☐ Eggs too fresh. 8-8
☐ Eggs too hot. 8-8

Hard-cooked egg has dark ring around yolk.
☐ Not cooked properly. 8-5 to 8-7

Fried eggs

Fried eggs don't hold their shape.
☐ Wrong grade purchased. 8-1, 8-2
☐ Egg broken directly into skillet. 8-9, 8-11

Top of fried egg is not done.
☐ Egg not basted, turned or steamed. 8-11

Fried eggs have tough, brown crust.
☐ Skillet too hot. 8-11

Omelet

Omelet turns into scrambled eggs.
☐ Mixture stirred during cooking. 8-13

Omelet is hard to remove from pan.
☐ Wrong shape pan used. 8-13
☐ Cooked at too high a heat. 8-13
☐ Omelet not kept loose in pan. 8-13

Poached eggs

Poached eggs stick to pan.
☐ Pan not greased before adding water. 8-10

Eggs lose their shape during poaching.
☐ Wrong grade purchased. 8-1, 8-2
☐ Water boiling instead of simmering. 4-2, 4-3, 4-4, 8-10
☐ Eggs broken directly into liquid. 8-10

Tops of poached eggs are not done.
☐ Pan not covered. 8-10

Scrambled eggs

Scrambled eggs are tough and dry.
☐ Liquid not added to eggs before cooking. 8-12
☐ Overcooked. 8-12

Scrambled eggs are mushy.
☐ Stirred during cooking. 8-12

Green pepper and onions added to scrambled eggs did not cook completely.
☐ Vegetables not precooked. 4-15, 8-12, 13-17

F

FISH

Fresh fish has strong, fishy odor.
☐ Not fresh when purchased. 2-8, 19-4
☐ Not stored properly. 3-1, 3-3, 3-8, 19-8

Cooked fish is mushy and falls apart.
☐ Overcooked in liquid, moist heat or slow cooker. 4-1 to 4-9, 19-12, 19-13, 19-16, 19-21 to 19-23

Poached fish falls apart.
☐ Not placed in container or cloth to retain shape. 4-4, 19-22
☐ Boiled instead of simmered. 4-2 to 4-4, 19-22

Baked fish is dry and chewy.
☐ Oven temperature too high. 4-20, 4-24, 19-16 to 19-20, 20-33
☐ Cooked too long. 4-20, 4-24, 19-16 to 19-20

Broiled fish is dry.
☐ Fish too thin for broiling. 19-18
☐ Broiled too long or too close to heat. 4-20, 4-21, 19-18
☐ Not brushed with fat before broiling. 4-21, 19-18

Fried fish is dry.
☐ Fried too long. 4-15, 19-19
☐ Not breaded. 4-19, 19-19

Oven-fried fish is dry.
☐ Not breaded. 4-19, 4-20, 19-20
☐ Baked too long. 19-20

Cooked fish has a strong fish odor.
☐ Cooked too long. 19-22
☐ Didn't use an acidic food in recipe. 19-14, 19-22, 19-23

Difficult to get rid of fish odor on hands.
☐ Didn't rub with an acidic food such as lemon juice or vinegar. 19-14

FOAM CAKES (angel food or sponge cake). Also see "BAKING, GENERAL."

Batter overflows pan.
☐ Pan too small. 5-15, 22-17

Cake does not rise properly.
☐ Poor quality eggs used. 8-1, 20-27, 20-29, 22-15
☐ Egg whites either underbeaten or overbeaten. 8-15, 20-27, 22-15
☐ Egg whites beaten, not folded, with other ingredients. 8-15, 20-8, 22-16
☐ Too much liquid. 5-11, 20-5, 22-15
☐ Pan too large. 5-15, 22-17
☐ Pan either greased or it contains grease residue. 20-31, 22-17
☐ Oven temperature too low. 20-33, 22-18
☐ Not baked long enough. 22-18

Crust is pale.
☐ Pan too large. 5-15, 22-17
☐ Oven temperature too low. 20-33, 22-18
☐ Not baked long enough. 22-18

Crust is dark and sticky.
☐ Too much sugar. 5-8 to 5-10, 5-14, 20-20, 20-21, 22-15

Crust is dark and tough.
☐ Oven temperature too high. 20-33, 22-18
☐ Baked too long. 22-18

Cake has solid, compact texture.
☐ Too much flour. 5-8 to 5-10, 20-1, 22-15

Cake has solid, moist texture.
☐ Too much liquid. 5-11, 20-5, 22-15

Cake has dry texture.
☐ Not enough liquid. 5-11, 20-5, 22-15
☐ Oven temperature too high. 20-33, 22-18
☐ Baked too long. 22-18

Cake is tough.
☐ Not enough sugar. 5-8 to 5-10, 20-20, 20-21, 22-15

Cake is soggy.
☐ Oven temperature too low. 20-33, 22-18
☐ Not baked long enough. 22-18

Cake has streaks inside.
☐ Ingredients not mixed thoroughly during folding. 8-15, 22-16

Cake falls after baking.
☐ Pan not inverted when cooling. 20-34, 22-19
☐ Cake not completely cool when removed from pan. 22-19

FROSTING A CAKE

Crust forms on frosting in bowl.
☐ Frosting not covered. 22-21

Bits of cake crumbs mix with frosting as cake is being frosted.
☐ Crumbs not brushed from cake. 22-21
☐ Thin layer of frosting not spread over cake first. 22-21

Frosting at bottom of cake has ragged appearance.
☐ Wax paper not pulled out from under cake carefully enough. 22-21

FRUIT

Canned fruit too sweet
☐ Purchased fruit canned in sweetened syrup. 2-1, 2-2, 2-4, 2-8, 2-9, 12-2, 12-13

Fresh fruit will not ripen.
☐ Purchased immature. 12-1
☐ Stored in refrigerator. 12-6

Cherries spoil quickly in refrigerator.
☐ Overripe when purchased. 12-1
☐ Washed before storing. 3-1, 3-3, 12-6

Berries decay quickly in refrigerator.
☐ Overripe when purchased. 12-1
☐ Washed before storing. 3-1, 3-3, 12-6

Cantaloupe aroma permeates refrigerator and flavors other foods.
☐ Not wrapped properly for storage. 3-3, 12-6

Fresh fruit turns brown when cut.
☐ Doesn't have enough natural acid to prevent browning. 12-11

Frozen fruit is mushy when served.
☐ Allowed to thaw completely before serving. 3-4 to 3-6, 12-12

Baked apples split or explode while baking.
☐ Skin not slit before baking. 12-20

Broiled fruit falls apart.
☐ Wrong fruit chosen for broiling. 12-19
☐ Broiled too long. 4-21, 12-19

Broiled fruit dries out.
☐ Not protected from high heat. 12-19
☐ Overcooked. 12-19

Dried fruits are not plump when cooked.
☐ Not presoaked. 12-17

Dried fruits won't soften when cooked.
☐ Not presoaked. 12-17
☐ Too dry when purchased. 12-4

Dessert made with canned fruit is watery or too thin.
☐ Canned fruit not drained sufficiently. 12-13

Poached fruit shrivels and shrinks.
☐ Too much sugar added at beginning of cooking. 12-16

Poached fruit doesn't hold its shape.
☐ Acidic fruit juice not added to, or used as, cooking liquid. 12-16
☐ Sugar not added before cooking. 12-16
☐ Boiled instead of simmered. 4-1 to 4-4
☐ Cooked too long. 12-16

Fruit sauce is too lumpy.
☐ Sugar or acidic fruit juice added before cooking. 12-16

17

Sauteed fruit falls apart.
☐ Wrong kind selected for sauteing. 12-18
☐ Not handled carefully. 4-15, 12-18

FRYING. Also see "FISH," "FRUIT," "MEAT," "POULTRY" and "VEGETABLES."

Fat for frying foams.
☐ Food particles not removed from fat. 4-16

Fat for frying becomes discolored.
☐ Food particles not removed from fat. 4-16
☐ Overheated. 4-13

Fat bubbles over side of pan.
☐ Food pierced with fork. 4-16
☐ Food wet when added to fat. 4-16
☐ Pan too small. 4-16
☐ Fat heated too quickly. 4-16

Fat starts to smoke during frying.
☐ Overheated. 4-13

Fat for frying has off flavor.
☐ Food particles not removed from fat. 4-16
☐ Fat not clarified before reusing. 4-18
☐ Overheated. 4-13
☐ Not stored properly. 4-18, 20-19

Fried food is greasy.
☐ Fat not hot enough. 4-15, 4-16
☐ Food not drained properly before serving. 4-16

Fried food is brown but is not done inside.
☐ Fat too hot. 4-15, 4-16
☐ Cooked at high altitude. 5-3

Fried food is soggy.
☐ Too many pieces fried at one time. 4-15
☐ Food turned with a fork. 4-15

G

GELATIN

Unflavored gelatin congeals in lump when added to hot water.
☐ Not softened first in cold water. 10-17, 10-18

Gelatin mixture will not set.
□ Ingredients added that were not specified in recipe, such as acidic food, sugar, solid food. 5-4, 10-17.
□ Gelatin not completely dissolved. 10-17
□ Used fresh or frozen fruit or juice containing enzymes: pineapple, papaya, mango, figs. 10-17
□ Ingredients not measured properly. 5-8 to 5-12
□ Recipe not accurate. 5-1

Gelatin is gummy with cracks in the surface.
□ Put in freezer for short time to speed up gelling. 10-17

Gelatin is tough and rubbery.
□ Mixture frozen. 10-17

Fruits and vegetables float or sink in gelatin.
□ Mixture not thick enough before adding solid food. 10-19

Molded gelatin does not come out of mold.
□ Mold not oiled enough. 10-20
□ Not following recommended method for removing gelatin from mold. 10-20

Molded gelatin begins to melt as it is being removed from mold.
□ Mold held in warm water too long before removing gelatin. 10-20
□ Mold held in hot instead of warm water. 10-20

GRAINS. Also see "PASTA" and "RICE."

Can't get the right amount of a cooked grain for a recipe.
□ Started with wrong amount of raw product. 5-7

Grains get mushy and sticky when cooked.
□ Overstirred. 9-9

Whole grains get rancid quickly.
□ Storage area too warm. 3-2, 9-6
□ Stored too long. 3-2, 9-6

Grains stick to bottom of pan and scorch.
□ Not stirred while cooking. 9-9

GRAVY. Also see "THICKENERS."

Not enough drippings for gravy.
□ Overcooked. 17-14, 17-25

Gravy doesn't have a good flavor.
☐ Pan not deglazed. 11-21, 17-25
☐ Improperly seasoned. 11-1, 11-12

Gravy is lumpy.
☐ Flour or cornstarch added directly to liquid. 10-1, 10-3, 10-7, 10-9, 10-10, 17-25

Gravy has a floury flavor.
☐ Not cooked long enough. 10-3, 10-6, 10-7, 17-25

Gravy is too thin.
☐ Not cooked long enough. 10-3, 10-6, 10-7, 17-25
☐ Not enough thickener used. 10-2, 10-3, 10-5 to 10-7
☐ Overcooked. 10-2, 10-3

Skin forms on top of gravy.
☐ Not covered properly. 10-2

Frozen gravy separates when thawed.
☐ Wrong thickener used. 10-22, 10-30

GREASE FIRE

Grease fire spread and spattered.
☐ Didn't pour salt on it or use a fire extinguisher. 4-17.

GRIDDLE CAKES. See "PANCAKES."

H

HAM. See "MEAT."

HARD-COOKED EGGS. See "EGGS."

HIGH ALTITUDES

Baked goods rise too fast and have a coarse texture.
☐ Didn't allow for expansion of gases. 5-3.

Foods take longer to cook at high altitudes.
☐ Didn't allow for lower boiling temperature. 5-3

HOLLANDAISE SAUCE. See "SAUCES."

HONEY. See "SWEETENERS."

I-J-K-L

LAMB. See "MEAT."

LEGUMES

Dried legumes cook unevenly.
☐ Not uniform in size. 2-8, 2-10, 13-5
☐ Remainder in old package mixed with contents of newly purchased package. 3-2, 3-8, 13-9

Beans not cooked in time specified in recipe.
☐ Didn't presoak beans. 5-4, 13-22

LENTILS. See "LEGUMES."

LOBSTER. See "SHELLFISH."

M

MACARONI. See "PASTA."

MEAT

Meat, general

Raw meat has an off odor and off color.
☐ Didn't inspect package when buying. 2-8, 17-6, 17-10
☐ Meat not properly stored promptly after buying. 17-6, 17-7
☐ Stored too long in refrigerator. 3-3, 17-7, 17-10
☐ Improperly packaged for freezing. 3-4
☐ If frozen, defrosted at room temperature. 3-4, 17-8, 17-10
☐ If frozen, thawed completely and then refrozen. 17-9, 17-10

Meat didn't provide enough servings.
☐ Didn't consider amount of bone and fat. 17-6

Surface of raw hamburger is dark but the meat inside is pink.
☐ Surface exposed to air. 17-2

Meat isn't done in the time specified in the roasting chart.
☐ Not defrosted before roasting. 17-24
☐ Oven temperature too low. 20-33

Cooked meat, general

Cooked meat doesn't have much flavor.
☐ Lacks fat. 17-1, 17-3
☐ Improperly seasoned. 11-1, 11-12

21

Cooked meat is dry.
☐ Overcooked in dry heat. 4-20 to 4-24
☐ Lacks fat. 17-1, 17-3

Cooked meat is tough.
☐ Wrong cooking method used. 4-6, 4-20, 4-24, 17-1 to 17-5, 17-11

Cooked pork has red color.
☐ Reaction of pork to chemicals in other foods or to oven exhaust gases. 17-22

Braised meat

Braised meat is tough, dry and chewy.
☐ Liquid allowed to evaporate. 4-7, 17-20

Braised meat is mushy.
☐ Overcooked in moist heat. 4-6, 4-7, 17-11, 17-12, 17-13, 17-20

Braised meat cooks faster than expected.
☐ Acidic food added during cooking. 17-13, 17-20

Broiled meat. Also see "BROILING."

Broiled meat cooks but doesn't brown.
☐ Not wiped dry before broiling. 17-15
☐ Salted before broiling. 17-15
☐ Broiled while frozen. 17-15
☐ Too thin to broil. 4-21, 17-15

Broiled meat is not done inside.
☐ Too close to heat. 4-21, 17-15
☐ Not broiled long enough. 4-21, 17-12, 17-15

Broiled meat does not have a crisp crust.
☐ Pierced with fork during broiling. 4-21
☐ Salted before broiling. 17-15
☐ Not wiped dry before broiling. 17-15
☐ Broiled while frozen. 17-15

Broiled meat is tough.
☐ Wrong cut purchased for broiling. 4-20, 4-21, 17-1 to 17-5, 17-11, 17-15

Broiled meat is dry and chewy.
☐ Overcooked. 4-20, 4-21, 4-24, 17-11, 17-12, 17-15
☐ Too thin to broil. 17-15

Fat smokes excessively as meat broils.
☐ Excess fat not trimmed off. 17-15
☐ Water not placed in bottom pan. 17-15
☐ Meat too close to heat. 4-21, 17-15
☐ Grid covered with foil. 4-21

Meat curls while broiling.
☐ Didn't score fat and connective tissue around edge. 17-15

Fried Meat. Also see "FRYING."

Fried meat is soggy.
☐ Fat not hot enough. 4-15
☐ Too many pieces in skillet at one time. 17-18

Difficult to slice meat thin enough for stir-frying.
☐ Meat not partially frozen. 17-19

Panbroiled meat

Panbroiled meat curls as it fries.
☐ Fat and connective tissue around edges not scored. 4-14, 17-17

Panbroiled meat is greasy.
☐ Fat not drained frequently. 4-14, 17-17

Roast meat

Roast meat is tough and chewy.
☐ Overcooked. 4-20, 4-24, 17-11, 17-12, 17-14
☐ Wrong cut purchased for roasting. 17-1 to 17-6

Roast meat too dry.
☐ Cut too small for roasting. 5-2
☐ Overcooked. 4-20, 4-24, 17-11, 17-12, 17-14

Roast meat shrinks considerably during roasting and is dry.
☐ Roasting temperature too high. 4-24, 17-14

Roast meat does not have a crisp outer crust.
☐ Covered during roasting or cooked in plastic bag. 4-10, 4-20, 17-11, 17-14

Roast meat is overdone.
☐ Didn't check internal temperature with meat thermometer. 17-14
☐ Didn't allow for continued cooking from internal heat after roast removed from oven. 17-14

MERINGUE. Also see "EGG WHITES."

Meringue topping on pie has a tough, chewy "skin."
☐ Overbaked. 8-16

Meringue on pie shrinks.
☐ Didn't cover edge of pastry with meringue. 8-16

Meringue on pie "weeps."
☐ Pie filling allowed to cool before spreading meringue over it. 8-16

Meringue shell is sticky, not dry.
☐ Too much sugar. 5-8 to 5-10, 5-12, 8-16
☐ Egg whites not beaten properly. 8-15, 8-16
☐ Shells not allowed to dry out in oven. 4-20, 8-16, 20-33
☐ Weather humid. 8-16

METRICS

International recipe is written in the metric system.
☐ Convert amounts to standard measuring system. 5-5, 5-13

MILK

Milk, general

Container of milk accidentally froze in refrigerator.
☐ Refrigerator temperature too cold. 3-3, 6-5

Milk has an off flavor.
☐ Starting to spoil. 2-7, 3-1, 3-3, 3-8, 6-4
☐ Has picked up flavors from strong foods stored in refrigerator. 3-3, 6-4

Recipe calls for sour milk but milk spoils instead of souring.
☐ Pasteurization keeps milk from souring. 6-14

Nonfat dry milk cakes in package.
☐ Not stored properly. 6-6

Cooking milk

Milk boils over.
☐ Scum forms on top as it cooks. 6-11, 6-13

Mixture containing milk curdles. Also see "CREAMED MIXTURES."
☐ Too much salt. 6-12
☐ Milk mixed with an acid food. 6-12
☐ Temperature too high or cooked too long. 6-8, 6-12
☐ Cold milk added to hot food. 6-12
☐ Cooked in slow cooker. 4-8

Scum or skin forms on top of milk as it cooks.
☐ Milk not stirred or covered. 6-11

Milk scorches.
☐ Cooked at too high a temperature or too long. 6-8, 6-9

MOLASSES. See "SWEETENERS."

MUFFINS. Also see "BAKING, GENERAL."
Muffins have a tough texture.
☐ Not enough fat. 5-8 to 5-10, 5-14, 20-14, 21-9
☐ Too much flour. 5-8 to 5-10, 20-1, 21-9

Muffins are dry.
☐ Overbaked. 20-33, 21-10, 21-11

Muffins have a dry, crumbly texture.
☐ Too much flour. 5-8 to 5-10, 20-1, 21-9

Muffins have a moist, crumbly texture.
☐ Underbaked. 20-33, 21-10, 21-11

Muffins have tunnels.
☐ Not enough liquid. 5-11, 20-5, 21-9
☐ Too much flour. 5-8 to 5-10, 20-1, 21-9
☐ Batter overmixed. 21-9
☐ Muffin pans filled too full. 21-9
☐ Overbaked. 20-33, 21-10, 21-11

Muffins are heavy.
☐ Batter overmixed. 21-9

Muffins have an uneven color.
☐ Liquid ingredients not mixed well. 21-9

Muffins have a pale crust.
☐ Underbaked. 20-33, 21-10, 21-11

Muffins have a dark, tough crust.
☐ Overbaked. 20-33, 21-10, 21-11

Muffins have a dark, sticky crust.
☐ Too much sugar. 5-8 to 5-10, 20-20, 20-21, 21-9

Muffins have a smooth crust.
☐ Too much liquid. 5-11, 20-5, 21-9

Muffins have a tough, coarse crust.
☐ Liquid ingredients not mixed well. 21-9
☐ Batter overmixed. 21-9

Muffins have cracked tops.
☐ Oven temperature too low. 20-33, 21-10

Muffins have peaked tops.
☐ Batter overmixed. 21-9
☐ Oven temperature too low. 20-33, 21-10

Muffins have flat tops.
☐ Muffin pans filled too full. 21-9

Muffins have irregular shapes.
☐ Too much flour. 5-8 to 5-10, 20-1, 21-9
☐ Too much fat. 5-8 to 5-10, 5-14, 20-14, 21-9
☐ Too little liquid. 5-11, 20-5, 21-9
☐ Oven temperature too low. 20-33, 21-10
☐ Overbaked. 20-33, 21-10, 21-11

N

NOODLES. See "PASTA."

O

OIL

Cooking oil has an off flavor.
☐ Stored in warm area. 3-2, 3-3, 20-19
☐ Reached smoking point during cooking. 4-13

Oil gets thick and cloudy when refrigerated.
☐ Natural result of cold temperature. 20-19

OMELET. See "EGGS."

OUTDOOR COOKING

Meat sticks to grid of outdoor grill.
☐ Grid not rubbed with fat. 17-16

Grilled hamburgers don't brown well.
☐ Placed too close together on grid. 17-16

Food burns on outdoor grill.
☐ Cooked over flaming instead of glowing coals. 4-22
☐ Flareups not doused with water. 4-22

OYSTERS. See "SHELLFISH."

P

PANBROILING. See "MEAT."

PANCAKES

Pancakes are tough.
☐ Batter overmixed. 21-2

Pancakes are dry and hard.
☐ Overbaked. 21-3

PASTA

Homemade pasta doesn't hold its shape.
☐ Not made with semolina flour. 20-2, 20-3

Water foams up when cooking pasta.
☐ Oil not added to water. 9-8

Pasta sticks together when cooked.
☐ Pot too small. 9-8
☐ Water not boiling. 4-2, 9-8

Cooked pasta is gummy.
☐ Overcooked. 4-8, 9-8

Pasta sticks together when reheated.
☐ Reheated improperly. 4-9, 9-8

PIES

Dough is sticky.
☐ Too much water. 5-11, 24-1 to 24-3

Dough is soft and crumbly.
☐ Dough not kept cold enough. 24-1
☐ Too little water. 5-11, 24-1 to 24-3
☐ Dough not mixed enough to hold together. 24-3

Dough is difficult to roll out.
☐ Not chilled before rolling. 24-4

Dough splits as it is rolled out.
☐ Chilled too long before rolling. 24-4

Pie crust is too brown.
☐ Too much fat. 5-8 to 5-11, 5-14, 20-14, 20-17, 24-1, 24-2
☐ Dough rolled too thin. 24-4
☐ Oven temperature too high. 20-33, 24-13
☐ Baked too long. 24-13

Pie crust does not brown.
☐ Dough overhandled. 24-3
☐ Oven temperature too low. 20-33, 24-13
☐ Not baked long enough. 24-13

Pie bakes unevenly.
☐ Oven racks lined with foil. 24-13
☐ Pan placed on cookie sheet in oven. 24-13

Bottom pie crust is soggy.
☐ Dough overhandled. 24-3
☐ Crust not prebaked. 24-10
☐ Oven temperature too low. 20-33, 24-13
☐ Not baked long enough. 24-13

Pie shell puffs up as it bakes.
☐ Holes not pricked in shell before baking. 24-9

Pie crust is thick, soft and doughy.
☐ Rolled too thick. 24-4

Pie crust is solid, not flaky.
☐ Not enough fat. 5-8 to 5-10, 5-14, 20-14, 20-17, 24-1, 24-2
☐ Used hydrogenated lard instead of leaf lard. 20-17, 20-18
☐ Dough handled too much. 24-3
☐ Did not use all-purpose flour. 20-1, 20-2, 24-1, 24-2
☐ Oven not preheated. 20-33, 24-13

Pie crust is tough.
☐ Not enough fat. 5-8 to 5-10, 5-14, 20-14, 20-17, 24-1, 24-2
☐ Too much water. 5-11, 24-1, 24-2
☐ Dough rerolled. 24-4
☐ Too much flour used when rolling dough. 24-4
☐ Dough overhandled. 24-3

☐ Oven temperature too low. 20-33, 24-13
☐ Not baked long enough. 24-13

Pie crust is short and tender.
☐ Used butter or margarine instead of shortening. 20-14, 20-15, 20-17, 24-2

Pie crust is dry and mealy.
☐ Second half of fat cut in too fine. 24-3
☐ Too little water. 5-11, 24-1, 24-2

Pie crust falls apart.
☐ Too much fat. 5-8 to 5-11, 5-14, 20-14, 20-17, 24-1, 24-2
☐ Too little water. 5-11, 24-1, 24-2
☐ Dough not mixed enough. 24-3

Pie crust is brittle and breaks easily.
☐ Dough rolled too thin. 24-4

Pie crust shrinks as it bakes.
☐ Too much water. 5-11, 24-1, 24-2
☐ Dough not rolled out properly. 24-4
☐ Dough stretched as it is fitted into pie pan. 24-5

Pie filling boils over as pie bakes.
☐ Too much filling. 24-11
☐ Edge of pie not sealed properly. 24-8
☐ Slits not cut in top crust before baking. 24-12
☐ Oven temperature too hot. 20-33, 24-13
☐ Baked too long. 24-13

Filling runs out of the baked pie when it is cut.
☐ Pie cut while still hot. 20-34
☐ Filling not thickened properly. 10-2, 10-8, 10-9, 10-11, 10-12, 10-14, 10-15

Pie filling made with cornstarch is too thin.
☐ Filling overcooked. 10-8 to 10-10
☐ Food high in acid. 10-8, 10-10
☐ Too much sugar. 5-8 to 5-12, 10-8, 10-10

Tapioca pie filling is too thin.
☐ Not enough tapioca. 5-8 to 5-12, 10-11, 10-13

Tapioca pie filling is too thick.
☐ Too much tapioca. 5-8 to 5-12, 10-11, 10-13

Pie filling thickened with flour is too thin.
 □ Too much sugar. 5-8 to 5-10, 5-12, 10-2, 10-3
 □ Not enough flour. 5-8 to 5-10, 5-12, 10-2, 10-3
 □ Highly acidic fruit used. 10-2, 10-3

Pie filling thickened with flour is too thick.
 □ Too much flour. 5-8 to 5-10, 5-12, 10-2, 10-3

Lemon pie filling curdles after eggs are added.
 □ Eggs mixed with an acidic food. 10-14, 10-15
 □ Mixture overcooked. 10-14, 10-15

Cream pie spoils quickly.
 □ Not refrigerated. 3-1, 3-3, 24-26

PLASTIC BAG COOKING

Plastic bag bursts during roasting.
 □ Manufacturer's directions for using bag not followed. 4-10
 □ Did not use special cook-in-oven plastic bag. 4-10

POACHING. See "EGGS," "FISH" and "FRUIT."

PORK. See "MEAT."

POULTRY

Poultry, general

Uncooked poultry has off odor.
 □ Prepackaged. 18-4
 □ Fresh poultry improperly stored. 3-3, 3-4, 18-4
 □ Frozen poultry improperly stored. 2-11, 3-4 to 3-6, 18-5
 □ Frozen poultry improperly defrosted. 18-5

Poultry too fat.
 □ Didn't examine color of skin when purchasing. 18-3
 □ Bird is mature. 18-2, 18-3
 □ Characteristic of that type of poultry. 2-1, 2-8, 18-3

Frozen poultry has freezer burn.
 □ Package broken during freezer storage. 2-8, 2-11, 18-3

Cooked poultry, general

Cooked meat next to bones turns dark.
 □ Raw poultry was frozen. 18-17

Cooked poultry meat has pink color
☐ Chemical reaction between poultry and exhaust gases in oven. 18-16

Braised poultry

Braised poultry is mushy and lacks flavor.
☐ Overcooked. 4-6 to 4-8, 4-24, 18-1 to 18-3, 18-6, 18-12, 18-14

Braised poultry is tough and dry.
☐ Liquid allowed to evaporate. 4-7, 18-12

Braised poultry is not brown even though it is cooked.
☐ Not browned before cooking. 4-7, 18-12
☐ Cover left on pan during entire cooking time. 18-12

Broiled poultry

Broiled poultry is dry on the outside but not done on the inside.
☐ Pan too close to heat. 4-21, 4-24, 18-9

Broiled poultry is tough and dry.
☐ Wrong kind of poultry bought for broiling. 2-1, 2-8, 18-1 to 18-3
☐ Overcooked. 4-21, 4-24, 18-6, 18-9, 18-14

Fried poultry

Fried poultry is greasy.
☐ Fat not hot enough. 4-12, 4-15, 18-10, 18-11

Fried poultry is not crisp and brown.
☐ Fat not hot enough. 4-12, 4-13, 18-10
☐ Too many pieces fried at one time. 4-12, 4-15, 18-10
☐ Turned with fork. 18-10

Fried poultry is brown and crisp but not done inside.
☐ Cooked at too high a temperature. 4-15, 18-10

Roast poultry

Roast poultry is tough.
☐ Wrong kind of poultry bought for roasting. 2-1, 2-8, 18-1 to 18-3
☐ Overcooked. 4-20, 4-24, 18-6, 18-7, 18-14

Roast poultry has a dry, chewy skin.
☐ Not brushed with melted butter or basted during roasting. 18-7

Roast poultry did not brown evenly.
☐ Roasting rack not used. 18-7
☐ Excessively browned areas not protected. 18-7
☐ String tied around legs not cut near end of roasting time. 18-7

Cavity splits open as stuffed poultry roasts.
☐ Too much stuffing used. 18-7, 18-8
☐ Cavity not closed securely. 18-7

Thread used to sew or tie roast poultry melts or burns.
☐ Made of synthetic fiber. 18-7

Poultry stuffing is too moist.
☐ Did not consider liquid added by poultry juices during roasting. 18-8

Poultry roasted in foil is overdone.
☐ Did not allow for shorter cooking time. 4-6, 18-7

Stewed poultry

Vegetables in poultry stew are overcooked.
☐ Vegetables added too soon. 4-5, 13-12, 13-15, 18-13

Stewed poultry is mushy and lacks flavor.
☐ Overcooked. 4-5, 4-8, 4-24, 18-1 to 18-3, 18-6, 18-13, 18-14

Q

QUICK LOAF BREADS. Also see "BAKING, GENERAL."

Bread doesn't rise properly.
☐ Not enough liquid. 5-11, 20-5, 21-9
☐ Oven temperature too low. 20-33, 21-10

Bread has an uneven color.
☐ Liquid ingredients not mixed well. 21-9

Bread has a tough texture.
☐ Not enough fat. 5-8 to 5-10, 5-14, 20-14, 21-9
☐ Too much flour. 5-8 to 5-10, 20-1, 21-9

Bread has a dry, crumbly texture.
☐ Too much flour. 5-8 to 5-10, 20-1, 21-9

Bread has a coarse texture.
☐ Batter overmixed. 21-9

Bread is dry.
☐ Overbaked. 20-33, 21-10, 21-11

Bread has a moist, crumbly texture.
☐ Underbaked. 20-33, 21-10, 21-11

Bread is heavy.
☐ Batter overmixed. 21-9

Bread has tunnels.
☐ Too much flour. 5-8 to 5-10, 20-1, 21-9
☐ Not enough liquid. 5-11, 20-5, 21-9
☐ Overbaked. 20-33, 21-10, 21-11

Bread has an irregular shape.
☐ Overbaked. 20-33, 21-10, 21-11

Bread has rounded or flat top without a crack.
☐ Batter overmixed. 21-9

Bread has a pale crust.
☐ Underbaked. 20-33, 21-10, 21-11

Bread has a dark, tough crust.
☐ Overbaked. 20-33, 21-10, 21-11

Bread has a dark, sticky crust.
☐ Too much sugar. 5-8 to 5-10, 20-20, 20-21, 21-9

Bread has a tough crust.
☐ Liquid ingredients not mixed well. 21-9
☐ Batter overmixed. 21-9

Bread has a smooth crust.
☐ Too much liquid. 5-11, 21-9

Bread is difficult to slice.
☐ Not allowed to cool completely before slicing. 20-34, 21-11

R

RECIPES

Recipe fails.
☐ Recipe may contain errors. 5-1

☐ Did not use standard measuring equipment. 5-8 to 5-12, 5-14
☐ Did not follow recipe instructions carefully. 5-1, 5-4, 22-2
☐ Did not measure accurately. 5-8 to 5-14, 22-2
☐ Made substitutions in ingredients. 5-4, 5-6, 22-22 (Also see specific food being prepared.)
☐ Increased or decreased recipe. 5-2

RICE

Brown rice has an off flavor.
☐ Not stored properly. 3-2, 9-1, 9-6

Rice ring falls apart.
☐ Wrong kind of rice used. 2-1, 9-1, 9-2

Cooked rice is gritty and tough to chew.
☐ Undercooked. 9-7

Cooked rice is soft and sticky.
☐ Wrong kind purchased. 9-1, 9-2
☐ Cooked too long. 4-8, 9-7
☐ Stirred while cooking. 9-7

Rice turns slightly yellow when cooked.
☐ Water is very hard. 9-7

ROASTING. See "MEAT" and "POULTRY."

S

SALADS

Salad has a poor flavor.
☐ A variety of greens not used. 14-1
☐ Wrong kind of dressing used. 14-5
☐ Not properly seasoned. 11-1, 11-12, 11-16, 11-19, 11-20

Difficult to separate lettuce leaves to make lettuce cups.
☐ Lettuce not cleaned and cored properly. 13-6

Greens turn brown at edges.
☐ Cut greens allowed to stand too long before serving. 14-4

Greens wilt.
☐ Not fresh when purchased. 13-2
☐ Improperly stored. 3-3, 13-6
☐ Dressing added too far ahead of serving. 14-6

Fresh fruit salad is gritty.
☐ Fruits not properly washed. 12-10

Salad dressing overpowers salad.
☐ Too much dressing. 14-6
☐ Wrong kind of dressing used. 14-5

Dressing won't cling to greens but settles at bottom of bowl.
☐ Greens and other vegetables not dried thoroughly. 14-3

Dressing turns watery after it is poured over greens.
☐ Greens not properly dried after washing. 14-3

SALT. See "SEASONINGS."

SAUCES. Also see "THICKENERS."

Sauces, general

Sauce is lumpy.
☐ Thickener added without being dispersed. 10-1, 10-2

Skin forms on top of sauce.
☐ Not covered properly. 10-2

Sauce is opaque instead of clear.
☐ Used flour instead of cornstarch. 10-1, 10-2, 10-8
☐ Cornstarch mixture not cooked long enough. 10-9

Frozen flour-base sauce separates when thawed.
☐ Wrong thickener used. 10-21, 10-22, 10-30

Sauce thickened with cornstarch is too thick.
☐ Too much cornstarch. 5-8 to 5-12, 10-8, 10-10

Leftover sauce has an off flavor.
☐ Not stored properly. 3-1, 3-3, 3-4, 3-8, 3-9, 10-30

Brown sauce is too thin.
☐ Not enough flour. 10-3, 10-5 to 10-7

Sauce thickened with eggs curdles.
☐ Eggs added to hot liquid. 10-14, 10-15
☐ Eggs mixed with an acidic food. 10-14, 10-15.
☐ Mixture overcooked. 10-14, 10-15

White Sauce

White sauce is too thin.
□ Wrong proportions of flour and liquid used. 5-8 to 5-12, 5-14, 10-2 to 10-4, 10-6, 10-7
□ Flour browned. 10-2, 10-4 to 10-7
□ Acidic food added. 10-2 to 10-4, 10-6, 10-7
□ Overcooked. 10-2, 10-4, 10-6, 10-7

White sauce is too thick.
□ Wrong proportions of flour and liquid used. 5-8 to 5-12, 10-2, 10-4, 10-7

White sauce has a brown color.
□ Fat-flour mixture overcooked. 10-4

White sauce has a pasty or floury flavor.
□ Not cooked long enough. 10-4

Frozen white sauce curdles when thawed.
□ Wrong kind of thickener used. 10-22

SCALLOPED FOODS

Vegetables in scalloped vegetable dish are not cooked.
□ High-fiber vegetables not precooked. 4-15, 13-17, 13-21

Scalloped potatoes curdle. See "CREAMED MIXTURES."

SCALLOPS. See "SHELLFISH."

SCRAMBLED EGGS. See "EGGS."

SEASONINGS

Seasonings, general

Dried herbs lose their flavor quickly in storage.
□ Old when purchased. 11-2
□ Improperly stored. 11-3 to 11-5

Fresh herbs wilt before they can be used.
□ Improperly stored. 11-6 to 11-10

Fresh herbs lose color and flavor when they are dried.
□ Overdried. 11-8

Frozen fresh herbs difficult to use when defrosted.
□ Mushy when thawed. 3-6, 11-10

Cooking with seasonings

Seasoning added to food, but food has no flavor.
☐ Used same amount of fresh herbs as dried. 11-11
☐ Seasoning too old. 11-2 to 11-5
☐ Not enough seasoning used. 11-11, 11-12
☐ Herbs not crushed before using. 11-16
☐ Wrong seasoning used. 11-1
☐ Overcooked. 11-14
☐ Herbs added after cooking is completed. 11-12

Food overseasoned.
☐ Too much added. 11-11, 11-12
☐ Increased amount of seasoning when recipe increased. 11-13
☐ Ingredients not properly measured. 5-8 to 5-12
☐ Liquid cooked down, accenting flavor. 4-2, 11-22
☐ Commercial soup used in recipe along with additional salt. 16-10

Whole herbs in mixture difficult to remove.
☐ Herbs not put in separate container. 11-15

SHELLFISH

Cooked shellfish is tough and rubbery.
☐ Overcooked in liquid. 4-1 to 4-9, 19-12, 19-21 to 19-23

Clam chowder is gritty.
☐ Clams not cleaned properly. 19-13

Shucked clams or oysters have a sour or unpleasant odor.
☐ Not fresh when purchased. 2-8, 19-5
☐ Not stored properly. 3-3, 3-8, 19-8

Cooked shrimp has a black strip along its back.
☐ Not deveined. 19-5, 19-13

SHORTENED CAKES. (Made with butter, margarine or other solid fat.) Also see "BAKING, GENERAL."

Cake does not rise properly.
☐ Recipe instructions not followed. 5-1, 5-4, 22-1, 22-2, 22-9, 22-10
☐ Too much fat. 5-8 to 5-10, 5-14, 20-14, 22-2, 22-3
☐ Eggs either underbeaten or overbeaten. 22-9

☐ Butter and sugar not creamed thoroughly. 22-9
☐ Butter and sugar creamed too much. 22-9
☐ Baking soda dissolved in liquid. 20-10, 22-7
☐ Not enough leavening. 5-8, 5-10, 5-12, 20-7, 20-10, 22-7
☐ Too much liquid. 5-8, 5-11, 20-5, 22-2, 22-8
☐ Batter undermixed. 22-9, 22-10
☐ Pan too large. 5-15, 22-11
☐ Oven not preheated. 20-33, 22-12
☐ Not baked long enough. 22-12, 22-13
☐ Oven temperature too high. 20-33, 22-12

Batter overflows pans.
☐ Pans too small. 5-15, 22-11

Top of cake has a peak.
☐ Too much flour. 5-8 to 5-10, 20-1, 22-2, 22-6
☐ Oven temperature too high. 20-33, 22-12

Top of cake cracks.
☐ Too much flour. 5-8 to 5-10, 20-1, 22-2, 22-6
☐ Oven temperature too high. 20-33, 22-12

Cake falls during baking.
☐ Not enough flour. 5-8 to 5-10, 20-1, 22-2, 22-6
☐ Too much baking powder. 5-8, 5-10, 5-12, 20-7, 20-10, 22-2, 22-7

Cake sinks in center.
☐ Too much fat. 5-8 to 5-10, 5-14, 20-14, 22-2, 22-3
☐ Too much sugar. 5-8 to 5-10, 5-14, 20-20, 20-21, 22-2, 22-4
☐ Not enough liquid. 5-8, 5-11, 20-5, 22-2, 22-8
☐ Oven temperature too low. 20-33, 22-12

Crust is pale.
☐ Not enough sugar. 5-8 to 5-10, 20-20, 20-21, 22-2, 22-4
☐ Oven not preheated. 20-33, 22-12
☐ Oven temperature too low. 20-33, 22-12
☐ Not baked long enough. 22-12, 22-13

Crust is too brown.
☐ Too much sugar. 5-8 to 5-10, 5-14, 20-20, 20-21, 22-2, 22-4
☐ Oven temperature too high. 20-32, 22-12

Crust is too brown and hard.
☐ Baked too long. 22-12, 22-13

Cake has coarse texture.
☐ All-purpose flour substituted for cake flour. 5-6, 20-1 to 20-3, 22-2, 22-6
☐ Unbleached flour used. 2-1, 2-8, 20-2
☐ Butter and sugar not creamed thoroughly. 22-9
☐ Butter and sugar creamed too much. 22-9
☐ Too much baking powder. 5-8, 5-10, 5-12, 20-7, 20-10, 22-7
☐ Liquid added last to batter in conventional method. 5-4, 22-1, 22-2, 22-9
☐ Batter undermixed. 22-9, 22-10
☐ Batter overmixed. 22-9, 22-10

Cake is heavy.
☐ Used leaf lard instead of hydrogenated lard. 20-17, 20-18
☐ Batter undermixed. 22-9, 22-10

Cake is compact.
☐ Eggs either underbeaten or overbeaten. 22-9
☐ Recipe instructions not followed. 5-4, 22-1, 22-2, 22-9, 22-10

Cake is tough and compact.
☐ Too much flour. 5-8 to 5-10, 20-1, 22-2, 22-6
☐ Batter overmixed. 22-9, 22-10

Cake is gummy and compact.
☐ Too little flour. 5-8 to 5-10, 20-1, 22-2, 22-6
☐ Too much liquid. 5-8, 5-11, 20-5, 22-2, 22-8

Cake is soggy and compact.
☐ Too much fat. 5-8 to 5-10, 5-14, 20-14, 22-2, 22-3

Cake has soggy texture.
☐ Oven temperature too low. 20-33, 22-12
☐ Not baked long enough. 22-12, 22-13

Cake has soggy top layer.
☐ Honey substituted for part or all of sugar. 20-22

Cake has soggy bottom.
☐ Allowed to cool in pan. 20-34, 22-14

Cake is not tender.
☐ Too little fat. 5-8 to 5-10, 5-14, 20-14, 22-2, 22-3

Cake has tunnels.
☐ Too many eggs. 5-4, 20-27, 22-2, 22-5
☐ Eggs too large. 2-1, 8-1, 8-2, 20-27, 22-5
☐ Batter undermixed. 22-9, 22-10

Cake has a dry texture with tunnels.
☐ Not enough sugar. 5-8 to 5-10, 5-14, 20-20 to 20-22, 22-4

Cake is dry.
☐ Too few eggs. 5-4, 20-27, 22-2, 22-5
☐ Eggs too small. 2-1, 8-1, 8-2, 20-27, 22-5
☐ Pan too large. 5-15, 22-11
☐ Baked too long. 22-12, 22-13

Cake crumbles easily.
☐ Too much sugar. 5-8 to 5-10, 5-14, 20-20 to 20-22, 22-4

Cake has an off flavor.
☐ Ingredients not fresh or top quality. 20-29
☐ Too much baking powder or baking soda. 5-8, 5-10, 5-12, 20-7, 20-10, 22-2, 22-7

Cream-filled cake spoils quickly.
☐ Not refrigerated. 3-1, 3-3, 3-9, 22-34

Non-cream cake stales quickly.
☐ Stored in refrigerator. 3-3, 3-9, 22-35

SHRIMP. See "SHELLFISH."

SOUFFLE. Also see "EGGS."

Souffle didn't rise.
☐ Egg whites not beaten properly. 8-15
☐ Egg whites beaten or stirred with other ingredients. 8-15
☐ Oven temperature too low. 20-33

SOUP. Also see "STOCK."

Chilled soup does not set or gel.
☐ Wrong kind of bones used. 17-1

Cream soup curdles. Also see "CREAMED MIXTURES."
☐ Milk old. 16-13
☐ Too much salt. 16-13
☐ Soup held too long before serving. 16-13

SPAGHETTI. See "PASTA."

SPONGE CAKE. See "FOAM CAKES."

STEW. See "FISH," "MEAT" and "POULTRY."

STOCK

Flavor of stock is too mild.
☐ Wrong proportion of ingredients used. 16-1
☐ Meat and vegetables not cut into small pieces. 16-3
☐ Too much of meat was browned. 16-3
☐ Only light-colored meat used. 16-3
☐ Wrong kind of ingredients used. 16-1, 17-1 to 17-6
☐ Stock not reduced. 16-6

Stock flavor is too strong.
☐ Only beef used. 16-3
☐ Reduced too much. 16-6

Stock is too highly seasoned.
☐ Cured meat used in stock. 16-1
☐ Wine used as flavoring. 16-2
☐ Too much seasoning added. 16-2
☐ Stock cooked down. 16-2, 16-6

Stock is cloudy.
☐ Starchy food used in stock. 16-1
☐ Not clarified. 16-7

Stock contains bone particles and other ingredients.
☐ Not strained. 16-4

Stock is too fat.
☐ Not degreased. 16-5

Stock sours during storage.
☐ Starchy vegetables used in cooking. 16-1
☐ Improperly stored. 16-8

STUFFING. See "POULTRY."

SUGAR. See "SWEETENERS."

SWEETENERS

Honey crystallizes when stored in refrigerator.
☐ Natural result of cold temperature. 20-26

Recipe doesn't turn out when molasses is substituted for sugar.
☐ Didn't make other modifications in recipe necessary when substituting molasses. 20-23

Molasses has a sulfur flavor.
☐ Did not read label when purchasing. 2-1, 2-8, 20-23

Brown sugar is hard and lumpy.
☐ Improperly stored. 5-14, 20-26

T

TEA

Tea has little or no flavor.
☐ Tea leaves improperly stored. 3-2, 15-7
☐ Package directions not followed. 2-1
☐ Not steeped long enough. 15-8
☐ Not brewed properly. 15-8

Tea has a bitter flavor.
☐ Brewed in metal pot. 15-8
☐ Brewed too long. 15-8

Tea has a light film over its surface.
☐ Brewed in metal pot. 15-8
☐ Water very hard. 15-9

Tea is cloudy.
☐ Water very hard. 15-8
☐ Iced tea chilled in a refrigerator. 15-10

THICKENERS

Mixture thickened with arrowroot is too thin.
☐ Stirred too much. 10-22

Cornstarch is substituted for flour but the mixture is too thick.
☐ Too much cornstarch. 10-8, 10-10

Tapioca pudding is too thick.
☐ Too much tapioca. 5-8 to 5-12, 10-11, 10-13

Tapioca pudding is thick and sticky.
☐ Overstirred. 10-13

Stew thickened with pureed vegetables is too thin.
☐ Vegetables low in starch. 4-5, 10-21, 13-1
☐ Not enough vegetables added. 10-21
☐ Not cooked long enough to soften vegetables thoroughly. 10-21

TURKEY. See "POULTRY."

U-V

VEAL. See "MEAT."

VEGETABLES

Vegetable storage

Fresh vegetables do not ripen in storage.
☐ Purchased underripe. 13-2

Onions get moldy.
☐ Stored in damp area. 3-2, 13-6
☐ Stored next to potatoes. 13-6

Sweet potatoes get moldy.
☐ Improperly stored. 3-2, 13-6

Potatoes get moldy.
☐ Not stored in dark, cool, dry place. 3-2, 13-6
☐ Stored next to onions. 13-6

Skin on potatoes is green in spots.
☐ Exposed to light during storage. 13-6
☐ Not inspected carefully when purchased. 13-2

Potatoes sprout.
☐ Not stored in cool, dry place. 3-2, 13-6
☐ Not inspected carefully when purchased. 13-2
☐ Stored next to onions. 13-6

Carrots and beets wilt quickly in storage.
☐ Purchased fresh with tops. 13-2
☐ Starting to sprout. 13-2
☐ Improperly stored. 3-2, 13-6

Vegetables, cooking and serving

Fresh vegetable snacks are gritty.
☐ Improperly cleaned before serving. 13-11

Cooked vegetables are mushy and lack flavor and color.
☐ Overcooked. 4-2, 4-3, 4-8, 4-9, 13-12 to 13-16

Cooked vegetables are slimy.
☐ Cooked in very hard water. 13-12
☐ Baking soda added when cooked. 13-12

43

White vegetables turn yellow when cooked.
☐ Cooked in hard water or with baking soda. 13-13
☐ Overcooked. 4-2, 4-3, 4-9, 13-12, 13-13, 13-15, 13-16

Green vegetables turn olive green when cooked.
☐ Overcooked. 4-2, 4-3, 4-9, 13-12, 13-13, 13-15, 13-16
☐ Cooked with an acidic food. 13-13

Red vegetables turn blue or green when cooked.
☐ Cooked in hard water or with baking soda. 13-12, 13-13, 13-15, 13-16

Strong-flavored vegetables such as cabbage get even stronger when cooked.
☐ Too little water used in cooking. 13-14
☐ Overcooked. 4-2, 4-3, 13-12, 13-13, 13-15

Vegetables in stew are not cooked although meat is done.
☐ Added too late. 17-21
☐ Acidic food used in stew. 13-12

Vegetables in stew are overcooked but meat not done.
☐ Added too early. 17-21

Fresh vegetables are gritty after cooking.
☐ Improperly cleaned before cooking. 13-11

Potatoes turn dark when cooked.
☐ Stored in refrigerator or extremely cold area. 13-6

Broiled tomatoes dry and shrivel.
☐ Overbroiled. 4-21, 13-20
☐ Tops not protected from heat. 4-21, 13-20

Baked potatoes have soft instead of crispy crusts.
☐ Baked in aluminum foil. 13-19
☐ Not baked long enough. 13-19

Sauteed vegetables are brown and tough.
☐ Heat too high. 4-15, 13-17
☐ Cooked too long. 4-15, 13-17

Stir-fried vegetables do not cook evenly.
☐ Not cut evenly. 13-18
☐ Not cooked separately according to cooking time. 4-15, 13-18

Stir-fried vegetables are cooked before the meat is done.
☐ Meat not cooked first. 4-15, 13-18

W

WAFFLES

Waffles are tough.
☐ Batter overmixed. 21-2

Waffles are limp.
☐ Too much liquid. 5-11, 20-5, 21-2, 21-4
☐ Baking temperature too low. 21-4
☐ Not baked long enough. 21-4

WHIPPING CREAM

Whipping cream won't whip.
☐ Bought wrong kind of cream for whipping. 2-1, 6-2
☐ Cream is too warm to whip. 6-16

Whipping cream turns into thick globs of fat while being whipped.
☐ Overbeaten. 6-16

X-Y-Z

YEAST BREAD. Also see "BAKING, GENERAL."

Yeast dough

Yeast dough is difficult to handle.
☐ Not enough flour. 5-8 to 5-10, 20-1, 21-15

Yeast dough does not become smooth, shiny and elastic after kneading.
☐ Improperly kneaded. 21-6, 21-17

Yeast dough does not rise properly.
☐ Self-rising flour used. 20-2, 20-3
☐ Whole-grain flour used. 21-18
☐ Soy flour added to recipe or substituted for part of flour. 21-26
☐ Wheat germ added to recipe. 21-26
☐ Too much flour. 5-8 to 5-10, 20-1, 21-15
☐ Dry ingredients too cold. 21-16
☐ Cold liquid added to dough. 21-16
☐ Yeast softened in liquid other than water. 21-14

□ Liquid for softening yeast too cool. 21-14
□ Liquid for softening yeast too hot. 21-14
□ Rising temperature too cool. 21-18
□ Dough not kneaded properly. 21-6, 21-17
□ Dough not kneaded long enough. 21-17
□ Dough overkneaded. 21-6, 21-17
□ Dough divided by tearing instead of cutting. 21-20
□ Rapid mix method only: too much flour used in first stage of mixing. 5-4, 5-8 to 5-10, 21-14
□ Standard recipe converted to rapid mix method but not enough water used. 5-4, 5-11, 21-14

Dough rises too fast.
□ Rising temperature too warm. 21-18

Top of dough dries out during rising.
□ Top not greased and covered with plastic. 21-18

Dough is difficult to shape.
□ Overkneaded. 21-6, 21-17

Yeast bread, baking

Bread does not rise as it bakes.
□ Dough rising temperature too high. 21-18
□ Dough allowed to rise too long. 21-18

Bread sinks in middle as it bakes.
□ Dough not kneaded enough. 21-6, 21-17

Bread falls during baking.
□ Dough allowed to rise too long during final rising. 21-18

Bread rises unevenly when baking.
□ Dough shaped unevenly. 21-20
□ Pans not placed in oven properly. 20-32, 21-23

Sides of bread do not brown.
□ Too many loaves baked at one time. 20-32, 21-23

Top of loaf cracks.
□ Too much flour. 5-8 to 5-10, 20-1, 21-15
□ Dough not kneaded enough. 21-6, 21-17
□ Baked loaf cooled too quickly. 21-25

Top of loaf pops up or "mushrooms" as it bakes.
□ Oven temperature too high. 20-33, 21-22

Top of loaf does not brown.
☐ Pan too large. 5-15, 21-21

Baked bread has a thick crust.
☐ Too much flour. 5-8 to 5-10, 20-1, 21-15
☐ Dough did not rise for proper length of time. 21-18
☐ Baked in glass pan. 20-30
☐ Oven temperature too low. 20-33, 21-22

Crust is too brown.
☐ Baked in glass pan. 20-30
☐ Oven temperature too high. 20-33, 21-22

Crust is soft.
☐ Wrapped for storage while still warm. 21-25

Coating of flour on baked crust.
☐ Too much flour used when shaping loaf. 21-20

Loaf has irregular shape.
☐ Dough not shaped evenly. 21-20
☐ Pan too small. 5-15, 21-21

Loaf is small and compact.
☐ Rising temperature too low. 21-18

Bread is tough.
☐ Too much flour. 5-8 to 5-10, 20-1, 21-15, 21-17, 21-20

Bread is heavy and compact.
☐ Only whole-grain flour used. 20-1
☐ Too much flour. 5-8 to 5-10, 20-1, 21-15
☐ Dough did not rise required amount of time. 21-18

Bread is moist and coarse.
☐ Dough did not rise required amount of time. 21-18
☐ Oven temperature too low. 20-33, 21-22

Bread is crumbly.
☐ Too much flour. 5-8 to 5-10, 20-1, 21-15, 21-17
☐ Dough not kneaded enough. 21-6, 21-17
☐ Rising temperature too high. 21-18

Bread is dry.
☐ Too much flour. 5-8 to 5-10, 20-1, 21-15, 21-17
☐ Dough not kneaded enough. 21-6, 21-17

Bread is coarse.
□ Used unbleached flour. 2-1, 2-8, 20-2
□ Dough not kneaded enough. 21-6, 21-17
□ Dough allowed to rise too long. 21-18

Bread has large holes.
□ Dough overkneaded. 21-6, 21-17
□ Dough allowed to rise too long. 21-18
□ Air not pressed out as dough was shaped. 21-20
□ Air trapped as dough was shaped into roll. 21-20

Bread has dark streaks.
□ Dough not kneaded enough. 21-6, 21-17
□ Bowl oiled or greased too heavily for first rising. 21-18
□ Top of dough allowed to dry out during first rising. 21-18

Bottom of loaf is soggy.
□ Not cooled on cooling rack. 20-34, 21-25

Bread has a sour flavor.
□ Dough rising temperature too high. 21-18

Bread has a yeasty smell and sour flavor.
□ Dough allowed to rise too long. 21-18

Whole grain bread has an off flavor.
□ Whole grain flour rancid. 3-2, 3-3, 20-4

Bread gets moldy in storage.
□ Stored in warm, humid area. 3-2, 3-3, 3-8, 21-30

Bread gets stale quickly.
□ Stored in refrigerator. 3-2 to 3-4, 3-8, 21-30

YOGURT

Yogurt separates in storage.
□ Natural occurence. 6-7

CONVECTION OVEN

Food is not done in the time specified.
□ Glass pan used. 4-28C
□ Pan with high sides used. 4-28C

Food cooks unevenly.
- ☐ Pan not placed properly in oven. 4-29 C
- ☐ Rack not properly placed in oven. 4-30C
- ☐ Rack covered with foil. 4-30C

Food has a thick, brown crust.
- ☐ Oven temperature too high. 4-27C

Outside of roast is done but inside is not cooked.
- ☐ Oven temperature too high. 4-27C

Casserole cooks in same amount of time as in a conventional oven.
- ☐ Contains food high in moisture. 4-26C, 4-32C
- ☐ Baked in pan with high sides. 4-28C

Frozen convenience foods overcook in convection oven.
- ☐ Thawed before being cooked. 4-31C

MICROWAVE OVEN

GENERAL

Food boils over.
- ☐ Pan too small. 4-43MW
- ☐ Power too high. 4-37MW
- ☐ Oven has hot spots. 4-38MW
- ☐ Cooked too long. 4-40MW

Food cooks too slowly.
- ☐ Container is absorbing some of the microwaves. 4-43MW
- ☐ Oven not plugged into a separate grounded circuit. 4-37MW
- ☐ Electric current flowing into home fluctuates. 4-37MW
- ☐ Oven not clean. 4-37MW

Cloth napkins melt in oven.
- ☐ Made of synthetic fiber. 4-43MW

Plastic bag explodes in oven.
- ☐ Bag not pierced before cooking. 4-51MW
- ☐ Bag closed too tightly. 4-51MW

Plastic container explodes in oven.
☐ Lid on tight. 4-43MW

Plastic container damaged in oven.
☐ Not heat resistant. 4-43MW

Plastic wrap used to cover dish bursts.
☐ Plastic not pierced. 4-45MW

Paper napkin flames up in oven.
☐ Made from recycled paper. 4-45MW
☐ Contains synthetic fiber. 4-45MW

Newspaper flames up in oven.
☐ Ink attracts microwaves. 4-56MW

BEVERAGES

Beverages boil over.
☐ Container too small. 4-43MW, 15-13MW
☐ Hot spots in oven. 4-38MW
☐ Power too high. 4-49MW

Beverage explodes when reheated in microwave.
☐ Not stirred before reheating. 4-51MW, 15-14MW

Difficult to heat beverage to proper drinking temperature.
☐ Temperature probe not used, if available. 15-15MW
☐ Oven has hot spots. 4-38MW

BREADING

Breading is soggy.
☐ Pan covered during microwaving. 4-47MW, 4-55MW, 19-31MW

Breading is gummy.
☐ Flour used in breading. 18-25MW

CAKES

Cake baked in microwave oven fails.
☐ Adapted standard recipe to microwave oven without making necessary adjustments. 4-64MW, 22-23MW
☐ Cake mix: didn't read package directions. 22-24MW

Cake batter overflows pan.
☐ Pan not large enough for microwaving. 4-43MW, 22-25MW

Corners dry on cake baked in square or rectangular pan.
☐ Wrong pan used. 4-43MW, 22-26MW
☐ Corners not shielded. 4-48MW, 22-26MW

Top of cake does not set.
☐ Covered during baking. 4-55MW, 22-28MW
☐ Container not elevated during baking. 22-29MW

Surface of baked cake has puddles of liquid.
☐ Too much liquid. 5-8, 5-11, 5-12
☐ Moisture does not evaporate in microwave oven. 4-53MW
☐ Cake not covered at end of cooking time. 22-28MW

Center of baked cake is not done.
☐ Cake batter was not "hollowed out" in center before baking. 22-29MW
☐ Pan of batter was not placed on an inverted pan in the oven. 22-29MW

Cake bakes unevenly.
☐ Pan not rotated. 4-42MW, 22-30MW
☐ Oven has hot spots. 4-38MW
☐ Wrong pan used. 4-43MW, 22-26MW

Cake is tough, chewy and hard.
☐ Overbaked. 4-36MW to 4-38MW, 4-40MW, 4-41MW, 4-44MW, 4-64MW, 22-31MW

Baked cake has gummy bottom.
☐ Pan was floured. 4-64MW, 20-36MW, 20-37MW

Baked cake has soggy bottom.
☐ Pan not lined with paper towel. 4-45MW, 22-27MW

Baked cake does not come out of pan easily.
☐ Pan not lined with paper towel. 22-27MW
☐ Pan not sprinkled with sugar. 22-27MW
☐ Cooled in pan too long. 22-32MW

Surface of cake tears easily as it is frosted.
☐ Microwaved cake lacks crust. 22-33MW

COOKIES

Cookies fail in microwave oven.
☐ Adapted standard recipe to microwave oven without making adjustments. 23-15MW

Cookies burn in center.
☐ Overbaked. 23-16MW

Baked cookies are crumbly.
☐ Not enough egg. 23-18MW

Cookies bake unevenly.
☐ Cookies uneven in size. 23-14MW
☐ Baked in wrong kind of pan. 23-14MW
☐ If square or rectangular pan used, corners not shielded. 23-13MW

CUSTARD

Custard does not set.
☐ Stirred instead of rotated during baking. 4-42MW, 10-28MW

EGGS

Cooked eggs are tough and rubbery.
☐ Overcooked. 4-38MW, 8-19MW
☐ Not covered during cooking. 8-20MW
☐ Scrambled eggs overbeaten. 8-22MW

Eggs cook unevenly.
☐ Not covered during cooking. 8-20MW
☐ Not turned or stirred. 4-42MW
☐ Eggs cooked whole. 8-17MW
☐ Oven has hot spots. 4-38MW

Whole eggs explode in oven.
☐ Eggs cooked without removing shell. 4-51MW, 8-18MW
☐ Yolk not pierced. 8-21MW
☐ Whole cooked egg reheated without first being chopped. 8-21MW, 8-24MW

Poached eggs "jump around" during cooking.
☐ Yolk attracts more microwave energy than white. 8-17MW, 8-23MW

FRUIT

Fruit does not cook evenly.
☐ Oven has hot spots. 4-38MW
☐ Not covered during cooking. 4-55MW, 12-22MW
☐ Not stirred during cooking. 4-42MW

Poached fruit is mushy.
☐ Overcooked. 4-41MW, 4-44MW, 4-49MW, 4-50MW, 12-21MW

GELATIN

Unflavored gelatin does not set.
☐ Not softened and properly dissolved. 10-29MW

GRAINS

Grains boil over when cooked.
☐ Pan too small. 4-43MW, 9-12MW
☐ Not stirred during cooking. 4-42MW, 9-12MW

GRAVY

Gravy is too thin.
☐ Not microwaved long enough. 4-38MW, 4-40MW, 4-41MW, 4-44MW, 10-25MW

Gravy is lumpy.
☐ Not stirred enough. 4-42MW, 10-24MW

Gravy has a floury flavor.
☐ Not cooked long enough. 4-38MW, 4-44MW, 10-25MW

MILK

Milk boils over.
☐ Pan too small. 6-19MW
☐ Overcooked. 6-19MW

Milk scorches.
☐ Cooked too long. 6-18MW

MEAT

Meat cooks unevenly.
☐ Frozen meat cooked without thawing first. 17-26MW
☐ Cut of meat has uneven shape. 2-14MW, 17-27MW
☐ Meat not turned properly during cooking. 4-42MW, 17-27MW
☐ Oven has hot spots. 4-38MW

Roast does not have a brown, crisp outer crust.
☐ Moisture does not evaporate from oven during cooking. 4-47MW, 17-28MW

Meat is tough.
☐ Salted before cooking. 4-58MW
☐ Wrong cut of meat selected for roasting. 17-1 to 17-6, 17-32MW
☐ Cooked at incorrect power. 4-49MW

Fat spatters when meat is cooking.
☐ Meat not covered during cooking. 4-55MW, 17-29MW

Meat doesn't cook as fast as it should.
☐ Drippings not removed from pan frequently. 4-44MW, 17-36MW
☐ Not covered during carryover cooking. 4-41MW, 17-34MW
☐ Low power. 4-37MW
☐ Oven has hot spots. 4-38MW
☐ Bought wrong cut. 17-32MW

Edges of meatloaf overcook.
☐ Wrong kind of pan used. 4-43MW, 17-35MW
☐ Incorrect shape. 17-35MW

Regular meat thermometer doesn't work.
☐ Not compatible with microwaves. 17-30MW

Pot roast and stew meats are tough.
☐ Not cooked long enough for moisture to soften connective tissue. 17-1, 17-32MW

Sausage casing splits.
☐ Not pierced before cooking. 4-51MW
☐ Overcooked. 17-33MW

Bacon cooks unevenly.
☐ Different curing processes can affect cooking. 17-37MW
☐ Pieces not rearranged during cooking. 17-37MW
☐ Oven has hot spots. 4-38MW

PASTA

Pasta is hard and chewy when cooked.
☐ Not enough liquid used. 9-10MW
☐ Not cooked long enough. 9-10MW

PIES

Pie crust sticks to the pie pan.
☐ Pan not greased. 4-39MW, 24-22MW

Bottom crust is not done.
  □ Bottom crust not precooked. 4-39MW, 24-23MW

Pie crust is not brown.
  □ Color not added. 4-36MW, 4-59MW, 24-25MW

Bottom crust is not done when frozen pie is baked.
  □ Pie not defrosted before baking. 24-21MW

POULTRY

Poultry defrosts unevenly.
  □ Not turned and separated during thawing. 4-42MW, 18-18MW
  □ Oven has hot spots. 4-38MW

Poultry cooks unevenly.
  □ Legs and wings not tied close to body. 18-19MW
  □ Shielding not used. 4-48MW, 18-27MW
  □ Poultry not covered during cooking. 4-55MW, 18-26MW
  □ Poultry not turned. 4-42MW, 18-23MW
  □ Roasting rack not used. 18-21MW

Roast poultry does not brown enough.
  □ Not basted with browning sauce. 4-59MW, 18-28MW

Whole poultry cooks too slow in microwave.
  □ Drippings not removed from pan frequently. 4-44MW, 18-29MW
  □ Not covered during carryover cooking. 4-41MW, 18-31MW
  □ Low power. 4-37MW
  □ Oven has hot spots. 4-38MW

Poultry cavity breaks open as bird roasts.
  □ Used too much stuffing. 18-32MW

Vegetables in poultry stuffing are not completely cooked.
  □ Not precooked before adding to stuffing. 4-15, 18-32MW

Stuffing is too moist after cooking.
  □ Did not allow for lack of evaporation in microwave oven. 18-32MW

String used to tie poultry burns or melts.
  □ Made of synthetic fiber. 4-43MW, 18-19MW

Poultry skin bubbles and bursts.
  □ Skin not pierced before cooking. 4-51MW, 18-20MW

Black spots on poultry skin.
☐ Salted before microwaving. 4-58MW, 18-22MW

Poultry pieces cook unevenly.
☐ Not arranged properly in pan. 4-43MW, 18-24MW
☐ Oven has hot spots. 4-38MW

Breaded poultry is gummy.
☐ Flour used in breading. 18-25MW

Chicken livers explode.
☐ Not pierced before cooking. 4-51MW, 18-30MW

PUDDING

Pudding does not set.
☐ Nonfat dry milk used as an ingredient. 6-20MW

RICE

Rice is hard and grainy after cooking.
☐ Not enough liquid in recipe. 9-10MW
☐ Not cooked long enough. 9-10MW

SAUCES

Flour-base sauce has a floury flavor.
☐ Not microwaved long enough. 4-38MW, 4-44MW, 10-24MW

Flour-base sauce is too thin.
☐ Not microwaved long enough. 4-38MW, 4-40MW, 4-41MW, 4-44MW, 10-24MW

White sauce is lumpy.
☐ Not stirred enough. 4-42MW, 10-24MW

White sauce does not thicken.
☐ Nonfat dry milk used dry as an ingredient. 6-20MW

Egg-base sauce curdles.
☐ Allowed to boil. 4-37MW, 10-26MW
☐ Not stirred. 4-42MW, 10-26MW
☐ Oven has hot spots. 4-38MW

Hollandaise sauce curdles.
☐ Butter too hot. 10-27MW
☐ Lemon juice added to milk. 10-27MW

SEAFOOD

Cooked seafood is too moist.
☐ Covered during microwaving. 4-45MW, 4-55MW, 19-30MW
☐ Not dried well before microwaving. 19-26MW

Seafood cooks as it defrosts.
☐ Defrosted in microwave oven too long. 19-25MW
☐ Oven has hot spots. 4-38MW
☐ Not turned. 4-42MW

Seafood cooks unevenly.
☐ Not defrosted before cooking. 19-25MW
☐ Not placed in pans properly. 4-43MW, 19-27MW
☐ Oven has hot spots. 4-38MW
☐ Not turned. 4-42MW

Cooked seafood is dry and tough with a strong odor and flavor.
☐ Overcooked. 4-44MW, 4-49MW, 19-24MW, 19-29MW, 19-32MW, 19-33MW
☐ Oven has hot spots. 4-38MW

SEASONING

Herbs dried in the microwave oven lose color and flavor.
☐ Overdried. 4-62MW, 11-23MW

SOUP

Cream soup curdles.
☐ Temperature selected on temperature probe is too high. 16-19MW
☐ Power too high. 4-37MW, 4-38MW

Canned soup explodes when being heated.
☐ Not removed from can before heating. 4-43MW, 16-16MW
☐ Not stirred before reheating. 4-51MW, 15-14MW, 16-18MW

Soup erupts during cooking.
☐ Not stirred during cooking. 4-42MW, 4-51MW, 16-17MW

VEGETABLES

Cooked vegetables are tough, chewy and dry.
☐ Overcooked. 4-36MW, 4-38MW, 4-40MW, 4-41MW, 4-44MW, 13-24MW, 13-26MW, 13-28MW

Vegetables cook unevenly.
- ☐ Not stirred or turned during cooking. 4-42MW
- ☐ Uneven sizes. 13-28MW
- ☐ Oven power uneven. 4-37MW
- ☐ Oven has hot spots. 4-38MW
- ☐ Wrong pan used. 4-43MW

Cooked vegetables have brown specks.
- ☐ Salt added directly to vegetables. 4-58MW, 13-25MW

Can of vegetables explodes in oven.
- ☐ Vegetables not removed and put in another container before reheating. 13-34MW

Vegetable carton used to cook vegetables leaves an ink imprint on the oven bottom.
- ☐ Oven bottom not protected. 13-33MW

Head of cauliflower takes long to microwave.
- ☐ Not cut into small even pieces. 4-36MW

Sweet potatoes don't microwave evenly.
- ☐ Not cooked properly. 13-32MW
- ☐ Have an odd shape. 2-14MW, 13-28MW
- ☐ Oven has hot spots. 4-38MW

Frozen vegetables in plastic bag explode during microwaving.
- ☐ Bag not pierced. 4-51MW, 13-30MW

Baked potatoes explode when microwaved.
- ☐ Skins not pierced before cooking. 4-51MW, 13-29MW

Skin shrivels when potatoes are microwaved.
- ☐ Overbaked. 13-31MW

Creamed vegetables curdle.
- ☐ Overcooked. 4-40MW, 4-41MW, 13-26MW, 13-27MW
- ☐ Oven has hot spots. 4-38MW
- ☐ Not stirred. 4-42MW
- ☐ Wrong kind of container used. 4-43MW

YEAST BREAD

Yeast breads do not rise properly.
- ☐ Liquid for yeast at incorrect temperature. 21-28MW

Reheated yeast rolls soggy.
□ Reheated without wrapping in paper towel. 4-45MW, 21-29MW

Reheated sweet roll warm but filling too hot.
□ Sugar attracts more microwaves. 4-44MW

Reheated yeast rolls are tough.
□ Reheated too long. 21-29MW

Buying food

2-1. Food labels. According to federal law, certain important information must appear on food labels in specific locations. The front of the label gives the following:

• The usual or common name of the product, such as "sliced peaches."

If the food is a mixture, the foods in the product name must be listed in order, beginning with the food present in the greatest amount by weight. If the label reads "beef and gravy," the container has more beef than gravy. But if it reads "gravy with beef," the container has more gravy by weight than beef.

Some packaged foods call for the addition of other foods before they can be eaten. In that case, the front label must include a statement of the ingredients that have to be added such as, "Add chicken to complete the recipe" or "To be used in preparing hamburger casserole."

• Net contents or net weight.

The following information must appear on the side panel of the label:

• Ingredients. Ingredients must be listed in order, beginning with the one present in the largest amount and ending with the least. Additives must be included.

There's one exception. Foods prepared according to federal standards of identity need not have a list of ingredients on the label. A standard of identity specifies the ingredients that can be used in a common food such as jelly or catsup. However, if any foods other than those specified are used, the ingredients must be listed on the label.

• The name and place of business of the manufacturer, packer or distributor.

• Nutrition information must be listed for certain foods. See 2-2, "Nutrition labels."

Other information, such as the following, may also appear on the label:

• An accurate photograph or drawing of the contents.
• Perishable foods must include instructions for storing, such as "Store in refrigerator" or "Keep frozen."
• Some labels may show the grade of the food.
• Directions may be given for preparing, using or serving the food, including recipes. If an illustration shows a completed recipe or serving suggestion, it must be clearly stated so you'll know it's not an illustration of just the food in the container.

2-2. Nutrition labels. Although many food manufacturers are putting nutrition labels on their products voluntarily, federal law requires that nutrition labels appear on the following:

• Foods that are fortified or have nutrients added to them.
• Foods that make a nutrition claim, such as "one glass gives you a day's supply of Vitamin C."
• Foods that are labeled "low calorie," "reduced calorie," "sugar free," "diet" or "dietetic."

Nutrition labels must give the following information:

• Serving size. The size is based on the average amount of the food eaten by one person as part of a meal. If you eat a larger quantity, you'll get more nutrients than the amounts listed on the label.
• Servings per container. The number of servings is based on the average serving size. You may get more or fewer servings, depending on your eating habits. Even so, this information can help you decide how much to buy.
• Calories. If you're watching your weight, this information will help you to count and compare calories.
• Grams of proteins, carbohydrates and fat. Some products may also include information on fatty acids, cholesterol and sodium.
• Percentage of U.S. Recommended Daily Allowances. The label gives the percentage that one serving of the product supplies of the following nutrients:

• proteins
• carbohydrates
• fats
• thiamin
• riboflavin
• niacin

- vitamin A   • calcium
- vitamin C   • iron

Nutrition labels can be a big help when you shop. Use them to find out which foods are good sources of the nutrients you need. Compare different brands of the same product to find out which one gives you the most nutrients for your money. If different brands have the same nutrients, the least expensive is your best buy.

Pay particular attention to nutrition labels if you're choosing foods for special diets, such as low-sodium.

2-3. Labels for imitation foods. Federal law requires that the following information appear on labels for imitation foods:

• If the imitation food is not as nutritious as the food it replaces, the word "imitation" must be used on the label.

• If the product is similar to the real food and is just as nutritious, the word "imitation" need not be used. But the product cannot be called by the same name as the real food—it must be given a new name. For example, imitation sausage can be called "breakfast links." Imitation fruit juice can be called a "drink" or "beverage" but not "juice." The name must be followed by an accurate description of the product, such as "Farmer Sam's Breakfast Patties . . . textured vegetable protein."

2-4. Labels for diet foods. Diet foods must have the following information on the labels:

• A statement as to whether the food is "low calorie" or "reduced calorie."

A "low-calorie" food must have no more than 40 calories per serving.

A "reduced-calorie" food must have one-third fewer calories than the regular food it is to replace. It must tell on the label the basis on which the claim is made. For example: "Artificially sweetened peaches packed in water, 60 calories a serving, 59% less than Brand X peaches in heavy syrup." The "reduced-calorie" food must have the same kind and number of nutrients as the regular food.

• A complete nutrition label. See 2-2, "Nutrition labels."

If a "diet" food does not meet the above requirements, the label must clearly state this fact, such as "not a reduced-calorie food" or "not for weight control."

2-5. Unit pricing. Many stores have adopted unit pricing to help their customers. The unit price is the price for one unit of each product, such as an ounce. Usually, the unit price appears on the price tag attached to the shelf below the food or it may be on a separate tag.

Sometimes the unit price is given in such small type that it's almost impossible to read. To solve this problem, carry a small magnifying glass with you when you shop.

2-6. Price per serving. Because some foods, such as meat, poultry and fish, have varying amounts of waste, they don't give the same number of servings per pound. Even if you compare prices on the package, you still don't have a true picture of the cost involved. For a more realistic comparison, figure out the price per serving. For instance, lean, boneless meat gives more servings per pound than meat with fat or bones. Even though the boneless meat may cost more per pound, it may cost less per serving than the "cheaper" cuts.

To figure out the cost per serving, divide the number of servings into the cost of one pound of the food. For example, a pound of hamburger gives about 4 servings per pound, at a cost of $1.69 a pound. Divide $1.69 by 4 to get the price per serving, which in this case is a little over 42 cents.

For the number of servings in a pound, see the following sections: Eggs, 8-2, "Hints for buying eggs"; Meat, 17-5, "Names of cuts"; Poultry, 18-2, "Tenderness"; Seafood, 19-2, "Forms of fish" and 19-3, "Forms of shellfish."

2-7. Open dating. Open dating is a date stamped on the packages of perishable foods such as baking powder, processed meats, dairy foods, bakery goods and refrigerated doughs. It generally tells you the last date the product should be sold or used.

Open dating does not guarantee freshness. If the food has been stored improperly or mishandled before the consumer buys it, its freshness may be lost long before the open date is reached.

Rely on your own judgment as well as the date stamped on the package. If you bring a food home and discover it is spoiled, even though the open date indicates it should be fresh, take it back to the store.

2-8. General buying guidelines.
Make up a shopping list and buy only the food you need. But be flexible enough to make changes if you find a food on sale that you can substitute for one of the foods on your list.

Avoid impulse buying. Stick to the items on your shopping list.

Save money wherever you can—buy on sale or use coupons. But don't buy an item you don't need just because it's a bargain. You may never use it and what started out as a bargain will turn into a loss.

Don't shop when you're hungry. Studies prove that hungry people buy more food than they intend, even though they have a shopping list.

Buy only clean containers of food. Dust could mean the container has been on the shelf a long time. Dirty containers or those with food residues attract harmful germs, rodents and insects.

Avoid crush, dented, broken or otherwise damaged containers. They may be advertised as a bargain, but the food inside could be damaged or contaminated.

The large "economy" size isn't always the most economical. Check prices carefully. Sometimes a smaller size is a better buy.

Read the labels. It takes time but in the long run it's well worth it. Compare nutrients, grades and ingredients.

Become familiar with consumer aids offered by the store, such as unit pricing (see 2-5, "Unit pricing"), recipes and menus.

You pay a price for convenience. Whenever another step is added to processing food, the cost of that step is added to the price you pay. Bulk cheese, for instance, costs less per pound than the same amount sliced or grated.

Whenever possible, cook from scratch instead of using convenience foods. Generally, you'll save money and get more nutrients and fewer additives.

If you have enough freezer space, cook your own frozen dinners. Make up a double portion of a meal and freeze the extra for future use (see 3-4, "Freezer storage").

Figure out the price per serving to compare prices of different brands and products (see 2-6, "Price per serving").

Take advantage of seasonal foods that are priced relatively low.

Buy locally grown foods whenever possible. Prices are usually lower and overall quality better.

Many stores prepackage fruits and vegetables. If the amount in the package is more than you need, ask one of the clerks to open the package so you can select the amount you need.

Keep track of how much you're spending as you shop. If necessary, invest in a small automatic counter to help you. Experiment with generic foods and house brands. They're usually lower in price than regular brands.

When you've finished shopping, bring the food home and store perishables immediately. If you stop to do errands on the way home, perishable food may get too warm and start to spoil.

2-9. Buying canned food. Buy the form of canned food most suitable for your needs. Whole fruits and vegetables generally cost more than pieces because they must be handled more carefully during processing to keep their shape. If you need canned tomatoes for stew, don't buy the more expensive whole tomatoes.

Don't buy bulging cans. If could mean the contents have spoiled. If you have accidentally bought a bulging can or if a can starts to bulge on your storage shelf, report it to your local FDA office or public health department.

2-10. Buying packaged food. Don't open the package to examine the contents. Food packages are sealed to protect the food from germs, rodents and insects. If you open the package and put it back on the shelf, the food can become contaminated. Opened packages are usually thrown away by stores, but the loss is added to the store's operating costs and passed on to consumers.

Food packages are usually fragile. Don't put them on the bottom of your shopping cart and pile heavy items on top of them.

2-11. Buying frozen food. Packages should be frozen solid.

Ice coating on a package usually indicates the package has thawed and refrozen. This could mean the contents are not as high quality as they should be.

Breaks or tears in the package could mean the food has "freezer burn" (see 3-4, "Freezer storage").

If you have the freezer space, buy large-size plastic bags of fruits or vegetables. They generally cost less and are more convenient than the smaller packages. Pour out the amount you need, refasten the bag with a plastic tie and store the remainder in the freezer immediately.

2-12. Salt in processed food. Salt is a form of sodium,

a common mineral found in most foods and essential to good health. Too much sodium, however, can create health problems.

If you want to cut down on sodium in your diet, don't just look for the word "salt" listed in the ingredients. Because many additives contain sodium, check for any ingredients using the word "sodium" such as sodium ascorbate, sodium benzoate, monosodium glutamate, sodium propionate or sodium bicarbonate or baking soda.

2-13. Sugar in processed food. Many different types of sugars are used to sweeten processed foods. If you want to cut down on the amount of sugar you eat, read labels carefully. Sugars can be listed under many different names such as sugar, corn syrup, corn sweeteners, cane syrup, caramel, natural sweeteners, invert sugar, dextrose, fructose, lactose, molasses, sucrose, glucose and honey.

BUYING FOOD FOR MICROWAVE COOKING

2-14MW. Shape and size of food. (See 4-44MW, "Cooking time.") When you buy food for microwaving, be especially conscious of its shape. Even, rounded shapes cook the most evenly in microwave ovens.

Buy meat in a block or square shape rather than a thin, long piece.

Avoid irregular pieces, such as potatoes that are thick in the middle and taper to long, narrow ends. The ends will overcook before the center is done. Instead, buy rounded potatoes.

Buy several smaller sizes of the same food rather than one large one. The smaller ones will cook faster than one large piece.

Storing food

3-1. Enzymes and microorganisms spoil food. Enzymes, present in all food, speed up chemical changes, causing loss of flavor, color and texture.

Microorganisms include bacteria, yeasts and molds. Many are helpful, but others are harmful and can spoil food.

Bacteria are microorganisms that grow rapidly by dividing in half. One can multiply into over 2,000,000 in just 7 hours under ideal conditions. The human body can usually cope with limited amounts of harmful bacteria, but large amounts can cause serious illness.

Bacteria give off waste products known as toxins, many of which are poisonous. The deadliest is the botulism toxin, which may be present in improperly canned low-acid foods such as vegetables, fish, meat and poultry.

Bacteria are especially fond of protein foods such as milk, eggs, poultry, seafood and meat. They also like rich foods such as cream pies; custards; ham, fish, poultry and potato salads; rich sauces and gravies; and stuffings.

Molds are microscopic plants that grow as fuzzy patches on food. Some like cold temperatures and will grow on refrigerated food that is kept too long. Molds give food an unpleasant odor and flavor.

Yeasts are small plants that multiply by sending out buds. They can spoil some food by causing it to ferment.

Microorganisms are found everywhere. They float in the air, are present in food and are carried on pets, pests, people and objects.

All microorganisms need moisture and food. Although a few prefer cold temperatures, most microorganisms grow fastest at room temperature. To discourage them, serve hot food HOT and cold food COLD. Serve the food quickly and put the remainder in the oven to keep warm or refrigerate it to keep it cool. Never let cooked food cool down at room temperature before freezing it—bacteria will grow quickly.

Heat and cold affect enzymes and microorganisms. Cold temperatures slow them down but don't kill them. That's why food can be stored in a refrigerator or freezer for only a limited time. Hot temperatures over 140°F kill most microorganisms and enzymes.

Storing food properly can save you money and food. Proper food storage retards enzyme activity, slowing down the loss of color, flavor and texture. It also helps keep microorganisms out of food and prevents those already in the food from multiplying. Good storage helps preserve nutrients by protecting food from light, heat, air and moisture.

The average home generally has three main storage areas—dry storage, refrigerator and freezer. Each should be used to store only certain kinds of food. Whichever storage area is used, the food must be properly wrapped for maximum protection.

3-2. Dry storage. Dry storage is a dry, cool, dark area, away from light, heat and moisture, such as closed cabinets, a pantry or a clean area in the basement. Temperatures should be cool but not freezing, about 50°F to 70°F.

Heat causes processed foods to lose quality and nutrients. A canned food stored at 85°F will lose its quality twice as fast as the same product stored at 67°F for the same length of time. If you don't have a cool storage area and plan to keep the food for a while, store it in the refrigerator.

Don't store food in cabinets above the refrigerator or range or near a radiator or furnace outlet. These areas are too warm for safe food storage. Use them for other items, such as utensils and dishes.

Don't store food under the sink. Because openings around pipes usually cannot be completely sealed, insects and other pests may crawl through. Water leaking from pipes will damage cans and food packages and spoil potatoes and onions. Use the under-sink area for storing household cleaning supplies.

Use the dry storage area for foods which are not highly perishable. These include breads, crackers, grains and grain products, sweeteners, oils, seasonings and unopened cans and jars that do not need refrigeration. Also store onions, potatoes and sweet potatoes in the dry storage area.

Reseal opened packages tightly to keep out dirt, dust and pests. If a package cannot be resealed, put the contents into a clean, tightly closed container.

Check canned goods regularly for bulges, leaks or weak seams. These could be warning signals for possible food poisoning. Contact your local FDA office or public health department.

Never use canned foods that show signs of spoilage, spurting liquid, off odor or mold. Never taste such foods. They could be harmful to your health.

Don't store food next to household cleaners or chemicals— you could be inviting disaster. You might accidentally contaminate the food with the chemicals.

How long can foods be kept in dry storage?

• Use canned foods within a year. After that time, they may be safe to eat but have lost some quality and nutrients.

• Most grain products and dried beans and peas can be stored up to two months. If you plan to keep them longer, refrigerate them.

• Because whole grain products such as whole wheat flour or brown rice contain oil, they turn rancid at room temperatures. If you cannot use whole grain products quickly, refrigerate them.

3-3. Refrigerator storage. To keep food properly, refrigerator temperatures should be between 36°F and 40°F. Check the temperature in your refrigerator with a refrigerator thermometer and adjust the setting, if needed.

In frostless and semi-defrosting refrigerators, the temperatures are usually the same throughout the inside, including door shelves.

If your refrigerator is the type that must be defrosted manually, inside temperatures may vary. The coldest area is usually the chill tray below the freezer. The bottom of the cabinet and the door shelves are generally the warmest. Store dairy foods, meat, poultry, fish and leftovers in the coldest part near the freezing compartment. Store produce in the lower part to keep ice crystals from forming.

Don't cover refrigerator shelves with foil or other material to keep them clean. Covered shelves keep the cold air from circulating inside the refrigerator. As a result, parts of the refrigerator may be too warm for safe storage.

Store the following foods in the refrigerator:

• Perishable foods such as fresh fruits and most vegetables, dairy products, eggs, fresh and cured meats, poultry, seafood and cooked foods.

• Canned food if refrigerator storage is specified on the label.

• Leftover canned food.

• Honey and syrup for long-term storage.

• Food containing oil, such as peanut butter, margarine and bacon grease.

• Cooking and salad oils for long-term storage.

• Shelled nuts and seeds.

• Dried fruits.

• Baked goods with custard or cream fillings.

• Grain products that are to be kept more than two months.

To store food in the refrigerator:

• Cover all food tightly. Air circulating in the refrigerator will dry out uncovered food.

• Sort fruits and vegetables before storing. Don't store produce that is bruised, damaged or starting to decay. The softened tissues allow bacteria to enter, causing spoilage. Produce that is starting to decay can make other produce decay. Cut away inedible areas and use the produce immediately.

• Don't store food in opened metal cans. Some food can develop a metallic flavor if stored in opened cans. Transfer it to another container, such as a covered dish or jar or a plastic container with a tight-fitting lid.

• Don't refrigerate large pots filled with food, such as a large pot of soup or spaghetti sauce. It could be hours before the food in the center of the pot cools down, giving bacteria plenty of time to grow. Instead, divide large quantities of food into several smaller containers for refrigeration.

• Don't overload the refrigerator. Leave space between containers for air circulation. Otherwise, parts of the refrigerator may be too warm for safe food storage.

• Read the owner's manual to learn to use any special features your refrigerator may have.

How long will food keep in the refrigerator?

• Use meat, produce and leftovers in 3-5 days.

• Use fish, poultry and hamburger in 1-2 days.

70

3-4. Freezer storage. The temperature in the freezer should be 0°F or below. Low temperatures are needed to freeze fresh food completely. Otherwise, food will lose quality and nutrients.

There are two types of freezers:

● Freezer. This appliance comes in two styles—an upright or vertical freezer and a chest freezer.

● Refrigerator-freezer. You can recognize this appliance easily—it has two outside doors, one for the refrigerator and one for the freezer.

A conventional refrigerator has only one outside door, but it has a frozen food compartment inside. Don't attempt to freeze fresh food in the frozen food compartment—the temperatures are not low enough to freeze the food completely and quickly. However, you can use the compartment for storing already frozen food for about two weeks.

Store the following food in the freezer:

● Store-bought frozen foods.

● Fresh meat, poultry and seafood that must be kept longer than a few days.

● Butter that is to be kept longer than 2 weeks.

● Home-cooked food for future use.

● Fresh produce for future use.

● Infrequently used foods such as nuts, herbs, spices and grains.

● Breads, cakes, cookies, pies.

Don't freeze bananas, gelatin, lettuce, custard, mayonnaise, cream (except whipped), cooked egg white, ready-to-eat cold cuts or any mixtures containing these foods. They don't freeze well.

Produce loses its crispness when frozen. Freeze only those vegetables you plan to cook.

Store-bought frozen food should be stored in its original package.

Freeze food in small batches. If you try to freeze large quantities at one time, the temperature inside the freezer may get too high and already frozen food may begin to thaw.

Food to be frozen must be packaged in moisture-vapor-proof wrapping or containers. Suitable materials include heavy-duty foil, plastic-coated freezer paper, heavy-duty freezer bags and rigid plastic or plastic-coated containers with tight-fitting lids. Don't use waxed paper, regular-weight foil, thin plastic storage bags, milk cartons or lightweight plastic cheese, cream or margarine containers—they are not heavy enough and the food will lose quality. Small containers give better results than larger ones because the food freezes faster.

Improperly packaged food develops freezer "burn" or loss of moisture—it dries out, becomes tough, loses texture and develops an off flavor.

To keep fruits from discoloring, use ascorbic acid or an acidic juice such as orange or lemon juice. Sugar also keeps fruits from discoloring, but most fruits have enough natural sugar and don't need additional sweeteners.

To stop enzyme action, fresh vegetables must be blanched or held in boiling water for a few minutes. Drain the vegetables and plunge them into ice water immediately to stop further cooking. When the vegetables are cool, drain and package them immediately.

If you're cooking meals for future use, undercook the food slightly. It will finish cooking when reheated. If cooked completely before freezing, it may overcook when you reheat it.

Food expands as it freezes. When packing food into containers, allow about an inch of head space at the top for expansion.

When you wrap food for freezing, squeeze as much air out of the package as possible. Air left in packages causes freezer burn. Seal packages tightly with freezer tape.

Label packages and containers with the name of the food, whether the food is raw or cooked, the portion size and the date.

Organize the freezer so the same foods are all in one area.

Keep a freezer inventory. Make a list of the foods in the freezer, the date and amount. List the foods in the same order as they are arranged in the freezer. This will make it easier for you to locate them. As you remove food, change the amount on the inventory. You'll know exactly what you have in the freezer and how much. Attach the list to the freezer door with magnets. Also attach a pencil on a string to the magnet so you can keep your inventory up to date. Use packages with the earliest dates first.

How long will food keep in the freezer?

- **Fresh meat**
  Beef, lamb roasts and steaks: 8 to 12 months
  Veal and pork roasts: 4 to 8 months
  Chops, cutlets: 3 to 6 months
  Ground beef, veal, lamb: 3 to 4 months

Ground pork: 1 to 3 months
Stew meat: 3 to 4 months
Organ meats: 3 to 4 months
Sausage: 1 to 2 months
• **Fresh game**
Birds: 6 to 7 months
Animals: 6 to 9 months
• **Cured, smoked and ready-to-serve meats**
Ham, bacon, corned beef, frankfurters: 1 to 2 months
Ready-to-eat cold cuts: don't freeze well.
• **Cooked meat**
Cooked meat and main dishes: 2 to 6 months
• **Fresh poultry**
Chicken, turkey: 12 months
Duck, goose: 6 months
Giblets: 3 months
• **Cooked poultry**
Covered with broth or gravy: 6 months
Fried: 4 months
Plain cooked pieces or slices: 1 month
• **Fresh seafood**
Lean fish: 6 to 9 months
Fatty fish: 2 to 3 months
Shrimp: 3 to 4 months
Most shellfish: 2 months
• **Commercially frozen seafood**
All types: 1 month
• **Cooked seafood**
All dishes: 3 months
• **Fruits and vegetables**
Most fruits and vegetables: 6 to 12 months
Citrus fruits and juices: 4 to 6 months
French fried or stuffed potatoes, partially cooked: 2 to 3
months
• **Milk products**
Cheese, 1 lb. or less, not more than 1 inch thick: 6 months or
less
Butter and margarine: 2 months
Frozen milk desserts, commercial: 1 month
• **Prepared foods**
Yeast bread dough, pie shells: 1 to 2 months
Baked yeast bread: 2 to 8 months
Cakes: 4 to 12 months

Cookies: 4 to 6 months
Combination main dishes: 3 to 6 months
Pies: 3 to 6 months
Sandwiches: 2 to 4 WEEKS
Soups: 6 months
NOTE: The length of time frozen food will keep in YOUR freezer depends on the following: the temperature in the freezer, the quality of food when frozen, how carefully you packaged it and how quickly it froze.

3-5. If the power fails.
Keep refrigerator and freezer doors closed.
If the door is not opened, a fully loaded freezer will keep foods frozen for two days. A half-full freezer will only keep food cold for a day.
Put dry ice in the freezer to keep food cold. Handle dry ice carefully with tongs or with protective gloves—dry ice burns bare hands. Also be sure you have adequate ventilation since vapors from dry ice can be harmful. Put heavy cardboard directly on the packages of frozen food and then put the dry ice on top of the cardboard. A 10-cubic-foot freezer, fully loaded, needs 25 pounds of dry ice to keep foods frozen for up to three full days. Find out in advance where to buy dry ice and how much you may need. The yellow pages of your telephone directory may list sources for dry ice.
Never use dry ice in the refrigerator. Add REGULAR ice to the refrigerator to keep food cold. The more ice you use, the longer the food will keep cold. Put pans in the refrigerator to catch drip water from the melting ice.
When power is restored, find out if any food has thawed. Get rid of food that is off color or has an off odor. Never taste food if you suspect it may be spoiled.

3-6. Refreezing thawed foods. As a general rule, partially thawed foods that still contain ice crystals can be refrozen immediately.
Fruits can be refrozen even if they have completely thawed. Relabel the foods, indicating that they have been refrozen, and use them as soon as possible. Refreezing foods causes some loss of nutrients, quality, flavor and texture.
If fresh-frozen foods other than fruits have completely thawed and have no off odor or off color, use them immediately. Or, cook them and then refreeze them.
Already cooked frozen foods that have thawed and have no

74

off odor or off color must be heated and eaten immediately or discarded.

3-7. Keep storage areas clean. Follow the manufacturer's recommendations, found in your owner's manual, for cleaning the refrigerator and freezer regularly.

Make sure all storage cabinets, shelves and drawers are washed regularly.

Wipe off tops of cans, jars and packages before storing to remove dust and dirt. To be on the safe side, wipe them off again before opening the container to keep dust from falling into the food.

Wipe up food spills immediately—they attract microorganisms and pests.

3-8. Special tips for storing food.

When you return from a food shopping trip, store the food immediately in this order:

a) First, unless you plan to use it immediately, store frozen food in the freezer so it will not thaw.

b) Next, refrigerate all foods that need refrigeration, such as milk and cream, eggs, cheese, meat, poultry, seafood and perishable canned food.

c) Next, wash fresh vegetables, if necessary, and refrigerate.

d) Wash all fresh fruits, except citrus fruits, cherries, grapes and berries and refrigerate immediately. If fruits are not fully ripe, keep them at room temperature until ripe and then refrigerate.

e) Store onions, potatoes and sweet potatoes in dry storage.

f) Finally, store canned and packaged foods in a cool, dry cabinet.

If you reuse glass jars and plastic containers, first clean them thoroughly. Wash them in warm sudsy water, rinse well and let them air dry completely.

When storing food, whether it's in the dry storage area, refrigerator or freezer, don't push older food to the back of the shelf and put the newly purchased food at the front. Instead, store recent purchases behind older food items. Mark the purchase date on containers with a black felt marker. Use older food first.

Every time you open the refrigerator or freezer door, warm air rushes in and raises the inside temperature. If you open the door frequently within a short time, the inside temperature may not be cold enough for safe food storage. In addition, as the temperature increases, the motor turns on to cool it. This means extra energy is being used. Plan your trips to the refrigerator and freezer to get all the food you need in one trip instead of opening the door countless times. Work quickly so the door is open for as short a time as possible.

If you use only a portion of a frozen package, store the remainder before it has a chance to thaw. Seal the package tightly before you return it to the freezer.

3-9. Storing leftovers. Refrigerate or freeze leftovers as soon as possible. Don't cool them at room temperature—harmful bacteria will grow.

Store leftovers in plastic containers or jars with tight-fitting lids. Or put them in a bowl or dish and wrap tightly with foil or plastic. Wax paper allows moisture to evaporate, drying the food. Airtight containers not only prevent drying but they also keep odors from escaping into the refrigerator or freezer.

Leftovers frequently wind up at the back of the refrigerator shelf and eventually discarded. Food is too costly to waste, so make a list of the leftovers stored in the refrigerator and freezer. Attach the lists to the refrigerator door with magnets. Include an idea for using the leftovers in the next day or two.

Basic cooking methods

CONVENTIONAL COOKING

4-1. Cooking in liquid. This means the food is covered with liquid. Boiling, simmering, poaching and stewing are all methods of cooking food in liquid.

4-2. Boiling. Water normally boils at 212°F. Boiling is the highest temperature to which water can be heated in a normal cooking process.

When a liquid boils, the air bubbles rise up from the bottom of the pan continuously and break the surface of the liquid. As the bubbles break the surface, steam escapes. Eventually, as steam continues to escape, the amount of liquid is reduced.

Because boiling creates a vigorous, rolling action, solid pieces of food bump against each other and break up.

Boiling is desirable for certain kinds of cooking but undesirable for others.

Don't boil tender foods such as fruits, vegetables and fish—they break apart and lose texture, color and flavor. Tender foods overcook because of the high temperature.

The boiling temperature is high enough to toughen protein foods such as eggs, poultry and meat.

Soup stock is often boiled to evaporate some of the liquid, giving the stock a more concentrated flavor. This is generally done after the meat or poultry is cooked and removed from the stock.

Pasta—such as spaghetti—must be boiled because it is starchy. The boiling action of the water keeps the pasta from sticking together.

The combination of high heat, large amount of liquid and

vigorous rolling action is destructive to nutrients. Boiling causes the greatest loss of vitamins and minerals, especially if the food is overcooked.

4-3. Simmering. To simmer means to cook in liquid at temperatures just below boiling, 185°F to 210°F. You can easily notice the difference between simmering and boiling. When a liquid simmers, the air bubbles come up to the surface slowly but do not break the surface. Although the temperature is lower than boiling, it is still high enough to cook most foods within a reasonable length of time.

Simmering is usually the preferred method of cooking food in liquid. Fewer nutrients are lost by simmering than by boiling. The lower temperatures keep tender protein foods such as eggs from toughening. Because simmering liquid does not have a vigorous, rolling action, simmered foods tend to hold their shape, texture and flavor. Foods cooked at simmering are less apt to be overcooked.

Older recipes often instruct you to "boil" vegetables but they actually mean "simmer." A "boiled dinner" of meat and vegetables must be simmered to retain flavor, color, texture and nutrients.

4-4. Poaching. To poach food, simmer it whole in a small amount of liquid so it retains its shape. If the liquid is allowed to boil, the food breaks up and loses its shape. Poaching is generally used for tender foods such as fish (19-22, "Cooking fish in liquid"), eggs (8-10, "Poaching eggs") and fruit (12-16, "Poaching and stewing fruit").

4-5. Stewing. To stew food, simmer it in a covered pan with enough liquid to cover the food. This method is used frequently for fruit (12-16, "Poaching and stewing fruit" and 12-17, "Cooking dried fruit") and less-tender cuts of meat (17-21, "Stewing meat") and poultry (18-13, "Stewing poultry"). Large pieces are usually cut into smaller ones to speed up cooking.

4-6. Cooking in moist heat. This method differs considerably from cooking in liquid. To cook in moist heat, use a pan with a tight-fitting lid and a small amount of liquid. When the liquid simmers, it creates steam or moist heat, which cooks the food. The moisture helps to tenderize the food as it cooks. Moist heat methods include braising, steaming, using a pres-

78

sure cooker, wrapping food in foil and roasting in a plastic cooking bag.

4-7. Braising. Usually food to be braised is left in large pieces, such as a pot roast or pork chops. If you wish, brown the food on all sides in a small amount of fat. Browning gives a characteristic flavor and color to the food and gravy. Add seasoning and a small amount of liquid—just enough to cover the bottom of the pan about a quarter-inch deep. Be sure the liquid flows under the food. Cover the pan with a tight-fitting lid to hold in the steam.

If you're cooking on top of the range, bring the liquid to a boil. Then lower the heat so the liquid bubbles just enough to create steam. If steam escapes around the edges of the pan lid, the liquid is boiling too vigorously. Cut down on the amount of heat or the liquid may boil down to nothing and the food will scorch.

If you're braising the food in the oven, use the temperature guide given in the recipe. Generally, 325°F is used for long, slow cooking.

Check the pan for moisture occasionally. Lift up the food to allow liquid to flow under it and keep it from scorching. If more liquid is needed, add a small amount of HOT liquid. Don't add cold liquid—it slows down the cooking.

Braising is generally used for large, less tender cuts of meat (17-20, "Braising meat") and poultry (18-12, "Braising poultry"). Whole vegetables such as parsnips, carrots and potatoes are often braised along with meat and poultry.

4-8. Slow cooker. Slow cookers generally have two temperatures: HIGH, or 300°F, and LOW, or 190°F. As a rule, combinations of uncooked meat and vegetables will take about 8 hours to cook on LOW.

Some foods do not give satisfactory results when cooked for that long a time, even at low temperatures. Seafood, frozen vegetables and fresh mushrooms, for instance, fall apart and lose their flavor. Rice and pasta sometimes become gummy. Sour cream and milk may curdle. Seasonings generally lose their flavor. As a rule, those foods should be added during the last hour of cooking.

If you'd like to adapt some of your favorite recipes for a slow cooker, find a similar recipe that has already been tested in the slow cooker. Follow the cooking procedure outlined in that recipe.

4-9. Steaming. Food cooks in steam, not in water. Use a pan with a perforated insert to hold the food out of the water. The perforations allow the steam to reach the food and cook it. The pan must also have a tight-fitting lid to contain the steam.

The water level in the pan should be slightly below the insert. As the water boils, it should not touch the food. If it does, the food will boil and overcook.

Let the water boil hard enough to create steam but not so vigorously that the pan will boil dry.

Steaming is used for fish, meat, poultry, vegetables, puddings and some breads such as Boston brown bread.

4-10. Roasting in a plastic cooking bag. Use only the special plastic cooking bags and follow directions very carefully. Otherwise, the bag may burst, spatter hot grease and food in the oven, and catch fire.

Plastic cooking bags are generally used for less-tender cuts of meat and poultry. Because the food is enclosed in a vapor-proof bag, it cooks in moist heat.

4-11. Pressure cooker. A pressure cooker cooks food in steam under pressure. The combination of heat and high pressure cooks food more quickly than conventional methods.

All pressure cookers work a little differently, so follow the manufacturer's directions carefully.

Pressure cookers are usually used for foods that take long to cook, such as whole potatoes and carrots and less-tender cuts of meat and poultry. Tender foods that normally cook in a small amount of time will be overdone to the mushy stage in a pressure cooker.

4-12. Cooking in fat. Several methods are used to cook food in fat—you can panbroil, panfry, saute, stir-fry or French fry. Either solid fat or oil can be used.

When you're cooking in fat, work carefully to avoid grease fires (4-17, "Grease fires").

Often food to be fried is breaded (4-19, "Breading food for frying"). Besides adding flavor, the breading protects the food from the high temperature of the fat so it doesn't dry out. It also helps to keep the fat from soaking into the food.

Some people believe the characteristic flavor of fried food comes from the fat. Actually, most of the flavor comes from the high temperature at which the food cooks. Since fat can be heated to higher temperatures than water, fried food browns and develops a crisp, flavorful outer coat.

With the flavor and crispness come extra calories. Every Tablespoon of fat absorbed by the food adds 125 calories. A medium-size potato has about 100 calories. But cut into strips and French fried, that same potato has between 400 and 500 calories.

If you enjoy the crispness and flavor of fried foods but want fewer calories, follow some of these suggestions for lower-calorie "fried" foods:

• Before eating fried food, remove the coating since it contains most of the absorbed fat.

• Use a skillet with a non-stick surface for frying. You can fry with a minimum of fat by merely putting a few drops of oil on a paper towel and wiping the oil very lightly on the non-stick surface.

• Bake or broil some of your favorite "frying" foods such as chicken and fish. Breaded and baked, these foods can be just as delicious as the fried version, but much lower in calories.

• Don't add fat but use the natural fat in food such as meat, poultry and some fish. The natural fat in these foods helps them to brown as they cook, without adding more fat.

4-13. Smoking point of fat. Fats and oils have a smoking point—the temperature at which they begin to break down and smoke. At that point, nutrients are destroyed, an off flavor develops and the color may darken. Fats and oils which have started to smoke should not be used for further cooking.

To keep fat from reaching the smoking point, use low or medium heat.

Butter has the lowest smoking point while oil has the highest. To raise the smoking point of butter so you can use it for frying, mix it with a little oil.

4-14. Panbroiling. Foods that cook quickly, such as bacon and thin cuts of tender meat, can be panbroiled.

To panbroil, use a heavy skillet but don't add fat. Heat the skillet. If the meat is lean, cut a small piece of fat from the meat and rub it over the bottom of the skillet as it warms so the meat will not stick. Add the meat, let it brown quickly and turn it to brown on the other side. As the fat accumulates, pour it off to keep the food as fat-free as possible.

When panbroiling, don't use such a high heat that the fat in the pan begins to smoke.

4-15. Panfrying, sauteing, stir-frying. These three words mean the same cooking method in three different languages. Americans panfry, the French saute and the Chinese stir-fry.

To panfry, cut the food in uniform pieces, if possible, so it will cook evenly. Use only a small amount of fat—a Tablespoon or two—just enough to lightly cover the bottom of the pan. Heat the pan so the fat is hot enough to sear the food when it is added.

Have the food at room temperature. If it is cold, it will cool the pan.

The food must be dry since moisture mixed with hot fat can create problems. Wet food cools the fat. As moisture comes in contact with hot fat, it spatters. Wet food also creates steam, which prevents proper browning. If necessary, wipe the food dry with paper toweling. Breading or flouring helps to keep food dry but it also adds calories.

Keep the temperature of the fat just hot enough to cook the food quickly. If the fat is too hot, the food will brown quickly but won't cook inside.

Don't fry too much food at the same time. Overcrowding can create steam, which prevents browning and gives a soggy rather than crisp crust.

Use tongs or a slotted spoon to turn the food. Do not pierce it with a fork—juices will be released, creating steam. Pour off excess fat as needed.

If the food pieces vary in size and thickness, such as chicken, they will cook at different rates. Remove smaller pieces as soon as they are done. Continue to cook larger pieces until done, turning to prevent overbrowning. If necessary, lower the heat to keep large pieces from overbrowning.

4-16. French frying. (Also called deep-fat frying.) To French fry, use a deep 3- to 4-quart pan. As food is added, fat bubbles up. The pan must be large enough to hold the fat and food and still allow plenty of space for bubbling. If fat bubbles up over the edges of the pan, it could catch fire.

Use enough fat or oil to cover the food—about 3 pounds of shortening or 6 cups of oil. Don't fill the pan more than half full of fat.

Heat the fat gradually to the proper temperature, using medium heat. If you heat it too quickly, it may bubble up. Use a deep-fat thermometer to be sure the fat is at the proper temperature, as given in your recipe. If the fat is not hot enough, the food will cook too slowly and absorb fat. If the fat is too hot, the food will overcook on the outside but the inside won't be done.

Dry the food well. Moisture creates bubbling and spattering and also cools the fat.

Use a basket to hold small pieces of food in the fat. Fry larger pieces without a basket and turn them with tongs or a slotted spoon. Never turn food by piercing it with a fork—you'll release juices, which will lower the temperature of the fat. The juices may also cause the fat to bubble over.

Remove fried food and drain on paper toweling to remove as much excess fat as possible.

Let the fat heat to the required temperature before adding more food.

With a large spoon, remove bits of food floating in the fat. They cause foaming, create off flavors and discolor the fat.

4-17. Grease fires. If you have a grease fire, DON'T POUR WATER ON IT. WATER WILL ONLY MAKE THE FLAMING GREASE SPATTER AND SPREAD.

To put out a grease fire, turn off the heat. Put a lid on the pan if the fire is inside the pan. NEVER TRY TO MOVE A BURNING PAN. Pour salt over the burning grease.

Whenever you fry food, keep a large container of salt handy for emergencies. Also keep a home-size fire extinguisher in the kitchen.

4-18. Reusing fat for frying. Clarify used fat before storing it for future use. Clarifying eliminates some of the off flavors.

To clarify used fat, add about 5 to 6 slices of potatoes for every cup of fat. The potatoes will absorb off flavors. Fry until the potatoes are brown, then remove them. Cool the fat so you can handle it safely. Strain the cooled fat through a cheesecloth, pour into a container, cover tightly and refrigerate until needed.

Some chemists don't recommend reusing fats for frying. Their studies have shown that as fats and oils are reused over a period of time, they decompose. When reused, the fats may leave traces of possibly harmful decomposition products in the fried food.

4-19. Breading food for frying. Foods for frying are often coated with breading. Besides adding flavor, the breading protects the food from the high heat of the fat so it doesn't get tough and dry. Breading helps to keep the food dry, thus keeping grease from spattering.

Before coating food, be sure it is dry or the coating may not stick. If the entire surface is not coated thoroughly, the coating will fall off.

To flour or bread food that is not fragile, such as meat or chicken pieces, put the breading in a plastic bag. Add the food, close the bag and shake until the food is well coated.

Beaten egg is often used as a binder to hold the breading to the surface of some foods, such as fish. For this method of breading, line up 3 dishes, pans, or pie plates—any containers large enough to hold one piece of the food at a time. In the first container place seasoned flour. In the second container, slightly beat an egg with a teaspoon of oil. In the third container put seasoned fine crumbs. Pat the food dry with a paper towel, if necessary.

Place one piece of food in the container holding the flour. Pat the flour onto the food, making sure it's completely covered. Shake off the excess. If any part is not covered with flour, pat more on and shake off the excess.

Gently put the floured piece into the egg mixture. Spoon the egg mixture onto the food, making sure it's completely covered. Using tongs or a slotted spoon, lift up the piece and let the excess egg drain off into the egg mixture.

Place the egg-covered food into the crumbs. Using your hands, pat the crumbs onto the surface of the food, making sure it is completely covered. Lift and shake off the excess. If any part is not covered, pat more onto the surface. Shake off the excess. Handle the coated piece gently and place it on a rack or dish covered with wax paper.

4-20. Cooking in dry heat. To cook food in dry heat, do not cover it and do not add liquid. Dry heat cooking is used for tender cuts of meat such as T-bone steaks, chops, roasts and poultry.

As a rule, don't attempt to cook less-tender cuts of meat in dry heat—the meat will get tough, dry and stringy.

Dry heat cooking methods include oven roasting, broiling and cooking on an outdoor grill.

Cooking in dry heat gives meat a characteristic crisp, brown outer crust with a pleasant flavor. Properly cooked meat remains tender and juicy on the inside.

4-21. Broiling. Food to be broiled is placed on a broiler pan, which usually slides under the heating unit. The broiler pan has two parts: the top is a grid with slots and fits over the bottom pan. Food is placed on the grid and is cooked by the direct heat which flows down on it. As the food broils, fat drains through the slots into the bottom pan. Because the fat drains away, broiling is a healthful, low-calorie cooking method.

Don't line the broiler grid with foil—the fat can't drain away and the food fries instead of broiling. As fat accumulates on the foil, it may catch fire.

The broiler does not have a thermostat for controlling the heat. You control the cooking in two ways: (1) by placing the pan a specific distance from the heat and (2) by broiling the food for a certain amount of time, depending on the doneness desired.

Thick pieces of food should be placed farther from the heat than thin pieces. This gives them time to cook inside without overcooking on the outside. Generally, place thin, quick-cooking foods about 2 to 3 inches from the heat. Place thicker foods or those which burn easily 3 to 5 inches from the heat.

Read the broiling instructions in the owner's manual for your range. It'll give you general instructions, including timing and position of the broiler pan.

Broiling is generally limited to foods that cook quickly, such as tender cuts of meat, young poultry, fish and some fruits. Most of those foods have enough natural fat to protect them from drying out under the high heat of the broiler. However, foods lacking in natural fat, such as lean fish, fruits and vegetables, should be brushed with a light coating of fat to keep them from drying out.

To broil, put the food on the cold broiler grid. Turn thick pieces about halfway during the broiling time. Use tongs or two large spoons held together to turn the food. Avoid piercing foods with a fork since juices may escape. Juices create steam and keep the food from browning and developing a crisp crust.

Watch the food carefully. Because broiling is a quick method of cooking, food can overcook easily. As you near the time when the food should be done, test it frequently.

See the following for specific broiling information and doneness tests: fruit, 12-19, "Broiling fruits"; meat, 17-12, "Degree of doneness," and 17-15, "Broiling meat"; poultry, 18-9, "Broiling poultry," and 18-14, "Doneness tests"; and seafood, 19-16, "Test seafood for doneness," and 19-18, "Broiling fish."

4-22. Outdoor grill. Cooking on an outdoor grill is similar to broiling, except that the heat source is below the food rather than above it. The main part of the grill is the fire bowl—a metal container shaped like a box or a bowl, which holds the burning charcoal. A metal grid fits over the top of the fire bowl to hold the food over the hot coals. As the food cooks, the fat and juices drip down onto the coals.

Gas and electric grills are available if you prefer not to use burning charcoal.

On some grills, the grid can be raised or lowered, giving you a little control over the amount of heat that reaches the food.

Covered grills retain heat and usually have a temperature control, making it possible to grill large pieces of meat slowly and evenly.

Tender cuts of meat, poultry and fish are the most popular for grill cookery. However, other foods can also be cooked. Less-tender cuts of meat can be marinated to help tenderize them, wrapped in heavy-duty foil, and cooked over the coals. Skillets and pans can also be used on the grid to cook foods such as vegetables and to warm rolls and breads.

When using an outdoor grill, keep safety uppermost in mind. A moment of carelessness can turn your cookout into a tragedy.

Here are general instructions for cooking on an outdoor grill, but be sure to read and follow the manufacturer's instructions. Your grill may have special procedures that must be followed for safe and proper cooking.

Wear a heavy-duty apron. Avoid dangling clothing that may catch fire such as sashes, ruffles, long sleeves and shirttails. Don't wear plastic aprons—some ignite easily. If you wear long hair, tie it back in a ponytail to keep it from catching fire.

Use the grill out in the open, away from any structure that might catch fire. If the grill is movable, place it so the wind will not blow smoke or hot ashes toward you as you work.

Never use an outdoor grill or hibachi indoors or in a garage. Burning charcoal gives off carbon monoxide, a deadly odorless gas. Even if you keep a window open, enough fumes can accumulate in an inside area to kill you.

To cook properly, the charcoal briquets must be glowing, not burning. You can't see the glow because, at this point, the briquets are covered with a gray ash. Once ignited, charcoal briquets take about 45 minutes to reach the glowing stage, so be sure to allow extra time for this process. Don't try to cook food over flaming coals—the food will burn.

Keep a work table close to the grill to hold food and tools. Also keep a bowl of water and baster handy for flareups, which occur when fat drippings accumulate on the hot coals and ignite. To douse the flames, squirt water on them with the baster. If you don't douse the flames, the food will burn.

Pile the charcoal briquets in the bowl of the grill. Barbecue experts recommend stacking the briquets in a pyramid so they burn more quickly. However, follow the manufacturer's directions for positioning the coals.

Ignite the coals, using long wooden matches. In humid weather, the briquets may have absorbed moisture from the air and may take considerably longer to ignite.

Briquets will heat up more rapidly if you ignite each one. Don't be concerned if you don't see a visible flame. Under normal conditions, the fire does not flame but creeps around the surface of the briquets to form a gray ash. A strong wind or draft, however, will make the briquets flame.

A fire starter will help the briquets ignite more quickly, but it's dangerous to use. Keep other people, especially children, away from the grill. Saturate the briquets with the fire starter, but don't flood them. Allow a minute or two for the fluid to soak into the briquets. Use a long fireplace match to ignite the briquets. NEVER USE GASOLINE, KEROSENE, ALCOHOL OR CIGARETTE LIGHTER FLUID TO START A FIRE—THEY FLARE UP EASILY.

Once some of the briquets have been ignited, never apply more fire starter. It could explode.

If you buy an electric fire starter, be sure it has the UL (Underwriters' Laboratories) safety seal of approval.

For an added smoky flavor, sprinkle wood chips over the coals. Hickory and oak chips are available but be sure to follow package directions. Some chips must be soaked in water before using.

Use long-handled tongs or a spatula to turn food.

Keep pets away from the outdoor cooking area. They can easily knock over the grill or the work table.

Never leave a fire unattended. If you must step away, ask someone to take over until you return.

When you're through cooking, let the briquets cool in the grill. Briquets retain their heat for a long time, so don't dump them in an area where people or animals might walk on them. Never put hot briquets in a combustible box such as cardboard or plastic—it could ignite.

Never remove the grid from the grill until it is cool enough to handle with bare hands. If you place a hot grid on the ground, someone walking barefoot could step on it and suffer serious burns.

When you serve food outdoors, keep hot food hot and cold food cold. Remember, food left outdoors on a warm day quickly reaches the ideal temperature for the growth of harmful microorganisms. For more information, see 3-1, "Enzymes and microorganisms spoil food." Bring out only enough food to serve everyone once and keep the rest stored at the proper temperatures, either indoors or in insulated food keepers. Bring out more food as second helpings are requested.

4-23. Cooking in a conventional oven. Food cooked in the oven is generally baked or roasted. Baking usually refers to cakes, breads, pies and cookies. Roasting refers to meat, although a roasted ham is generally called a "baked" ham.

For true roasting, meat, poultry and fish must be cooked in an uncovered pan without any added liquid. If you add liquid or use a cover, you will cook the food in moist heat, not dry heat. (See 4-20, "Cooking in dry heat," and 4-6, "Cooking in moist heat.")

For specific information, see the following: meat, 17-14, "Roasting meat"; poultry, 18-7, "Roasting poultry," and 18-8, "Stuffing for poultry"; fish, 19-17, "Baking fish."

For information on baking, see Chapter 20, "Baking Principles"; Chapter 21, "Breads: Quick and Yeast"; Chapter 22, "Cakes"; Chapter 23, "Cookies"; and Chapter 24, "Pies and Pastries."

4-24. Protein cooking. Protein foods include meat, poultry, fish, eggs, milk and cheese. All protein foods have one characteristic in common—they are highly heat sensitive. This means protein foods generally must be cooked at lower temperatures for just the right amount of time.

If you cook protein foods in dry heat at too high a temperature or too long, they will be tough, chewy and dry. Be especially careful when you broil protein foods. If left in the broiler even a few minutes too long, they'll overcook.

If overcooked in liquid or moist heat, protein foods become mushy. If boiled, they may get tough or fall apart.

Since protein foods are generally the most expensive items on your menus, cook them with care so you don't waste your money.

CONVECTION OVEN

4-25C. The difference between a conventional oven and a convection oven. Both types of ovens use either gas or electricity as a heat source.

The heat source in a conventional oven is located at the bottom of the oven. The heated air rises slowly and gently circulates throughout the oven. As the heated air circulates, the heat is transferred to the food and cooks it. A sensing element in the oven is connected to the thermostat. As the temperature of the oven reaches the degrees selected on the thermostat, the heat automatically lowers or shuts down. As the oven begins to cool, the heat turns back on. Generally, temperatures in an oven fluctuate about 25 to 30 degrees above to 25 to 30 degrees below the temperature selected on the thermostat.

In a convection oven, a fan circulates the heated air continuously at a high velocity. The heated air hits all food surfaces at the same time. For this reason and because temperatures in the convection oven are more even than those in the conventional oven, the cooking time for many foods is faster.

Unless otherwise instructed, it is not necessary to preheat a convection oven.

Cooking methods will vary, depending on the brand and type of convection oven. Therefore, follow the instructions in the owner's manual. While it's not necessary to learn new cooking methods, it may be necessary to reduce the cooking time and temperature for some foods. (See 4-26C, "Cooking time," and 4-27C, "Cooking temperatures.") The amount will depend on the brand of the oven, the size, whether the oven uses gas or electric heat and whether it is a countertop oven, one in a standard size range or a combination oven.

4-26C. Cooking time. Generally, foods will cook up to 30% faster. On the average, cooking time is midway between conventional cooking and microwave cooking. But there are exceptions.

Some moist foods, such as baked goods and casseroles, which are baked in pans with high sides, require low cooking temperatures. Therefore they will probably take just as long to cook in the convection oven as they do in a conventional oven.

4-27C. Cooking temperatures. Depending on the food, cooking temperatures generally need to be lowered, sometimes by as much as 75°F. The amount varies with the food and type of oven, so follow the instructions in the owner's manual. If you use conventional oven temperatures when baking instead of the recommended convection oven temperatures, the outer surfaces will be cooked before the interior is done. Outer surfaces of cakes and other soft desserts overbrown easily and may even develop a hard crust.

4-28C. Types of pans. Any pan that can be used in a conventional oven is usable in a convection oven.

Metal pans brown foods more evenly and quickly than glass pans because metal is a better conductor of heat. If the pans are covered or have high sides, the food will cook more slowly because the circulating air cannot reach it. Using glass pans or pans with high sides may increase total cooking time.

4-29C. Pan placement. Pans must be placed in the convection oven so the heated air has space to circulate. Place pans so they don't touch the oven walls, sides, door or each other. Allow a 1-inch air space between pans and between pans and oven walls.

If you're using just one pan, place it in the center of the oven.

4-30C. Rack position. For best cooking results, oven racks must be positioned as specified in the owner's manual. Since heated air is circulated by a fan, air flow depends on the location of the fan. If the fan is at the top, the heated air flows down and around the food. If the fan is at the back or the side, the heated air flows from that direction around the food. Placement of racks may vary depending on the type of food being cooked.

Don't cover the racks with foil or any other material to keep them clean. Covering the racks cuts off the air flow and keeps the oven from baking and roasting properly.

4-31C. Frozen prepared foods. Don't thaw frozen prepared foods. Follow package directions regarding use of the package for cooking, such as removing the foil cover. However, follow instructions in your owner's manual for times and temperatures, which will probably be lower than those given on the frozen food package.

4-32C. Casseroles, stews, less-tender cuts of meat. These foods need moist heat and slow cooking. Cover stews and braised meats to retain moisture. Use a crumb topping on casseroles to keep them from drying out.

Follow the owner's manual for time and temperature. Generally, these foods require the same time and temperature, whether cooked in a conventional or convection oven.

4-33C. Roasting in a convection oven. As a rule, in a countertop convection oven the roast is placed right on the oven rack. In a standard oven and combination ovens, a roasting rack and pan must be used. Follow the instructions in the owner's manual.

The higher, more constant heat in the convection oven sears in more juices, which means less shrinkage. It also means less pan juices for gravies. Since the forced heated air circulates around meat held on a rack, basting and turning are not needed.

4-34C. Broiling in a convection oven. In most countertop ovens, food is broiled on both sides at the same time because of the circulating action of the forced heated air. Generally, the food is placed directly on the oven rack.

The process differs for standard and combination ovens. Follow the instructions in your owner's manual for broiling times and temperatures.

4-35C. Adapting conventional recipes to the convection oven. The most simple method is to find a food or recipe in your owner's manual that corresponds with your recipe. Adjust the time, temperature and rack position according to the directions in the owner's manual.

As a rule, cooking times are shortened by about 30%, except for baked goods. To start, reduce temperatures by 25°F for roasting and 50°F for baking. You may have to experiment several times before you achieve the results you want.

MICROWAVE COOKING

4-36MW. How microwave cooking differs from other methods. In both conventional and convection ovens, the food is cooked by circulating heated air. (See 4-25C, "The difference between a conventional oven and a convection oven.") As the food heats on the outside, the heat penetrates the food, moving toward the center.

In a microwave oven, the food is cooked by invisible waves of energy called microwaves. The energy is generated by a magnetron tube located in the oven. The microwaves bounce off the oven walls and bottom to the food.

Microwave energy makes food molecules vibrate against each other, producing friction. The friction creates heat and cooks the food.

Generally, microwaves penetrate food to a depth of about an inch from the surface on all sides, cooking food quickly. The center portions of large pieces of food are cooked more slowly by heat which is conducted from the hot portions to the center of the food. Therefore, one large piece of food will take longer to cook than the same weight of food cut into smaller pieces.

4-37MW. Cooking power. Cooking power is the amount of energy the oven uses to generate microwaves. The energy is expressed in terms of "watts" of electricity. Since the cooking power of microwave ovens varies, check your owner's manual to find out the cooking power of your oven. Most ovens fall within the range of 500-700 watts of cooking power.

Some ovens have only one power setting while others have a number of settings. The owner's manual tells you the amount of power supplied by each setting.

Generally, the higher the cooking power, the faster the food cooks. The lower the power, the more slowly the food cooks. Some delicate foods, such as eggs and milk, give better results when cooked on lower power settings.

Plug the microwave oven into a separate grounded 110-volt circuit. If other appliances are on the same circuit, they draw power away from the microwave oven if used at the same time. The oven will be less efficient and take longer to cook.

You can test the cooking power of your microwave oven by cooking a cup of water. One cup of water should boil in 2½ to 3 minutes, on the average. If it takes longer or shorter, make a comparable time adjustment in recipes.

The amount of electric current coming into your home can fluctuate and affect the cooking power of the oven. Less power coming into your home means slower cooking. In some areas, lower power occurs regularly at certain times of the day.

Check with your local electric utility and make a note of these times. If you cook during low-power periods, increase the cooking times to make up for the lower power. Keep the oven clean. Food spatters absorb microwaves and lower the efficiency of the oven.

4-38MW. Oven hot spots. Because microwaves bounce off the walls and oven bottom onto the food, cooking power may not be evenly distributed, especially in older ovens. Generally, food will cook the slowest in the center of the oven. Whenever possible, arrange food in a circle or doughnut shape. For mixtures, place a glass in the center of the dish to keep the food around the edges. If you're placing more than one dish in the oven, arrange them in a circle. Arrange large pieces of food so the thicker or heavier parts extend toward the edges of the oven rather than into the center.

Because certain parts of a microwave oven may have more power than other parts, each oven has its own cooking pattern. You can determine the power pattern in your oven with the following test: Place several sheets of wax paper on the oven bottom. Arrange about a dozen large marshmallows on the wax paper, spaced evenly apart. Turn the oven on high power for several minutes. Turn on the oven light and watch the marshmallows. Those in the areas with the most power will puff up and brown more quickly than those in other areas.

Use this information to your advantage when placing food in the oven. If you want foods to cook more quickly, place them in the high power areas.

4-39MW. Cooking with microwaves. Cooking in a microwave oven differs considerably from cooking in a conventional oven. Proper timing and special microwave techniques are essential.

Take time to read the owner's manual and become familiar with the operation of your microwave oven. Begin with simple foods and master the microwave techniques. The results will more than make up for the little extra time and effort this step requires.

Don't try to guess or use the same methods you use for conventional cooking. You'll waste time, food and money. Many foods, when overcooked in a conventional oven, become soft and mushy, but they're still edible. When overcooked in the microwave oven, foods often become tough, dry and inedible.

4-40MW. Microwave time. Two kinds of time are essential to microwave cooking: microwave time and carryover time. Microwave time is the actual time the food cooks with microwave energy. Most microwave recipes give a range of microwave time, such as 2 to 3 minutes. Always choose the lowest amount of time and check the food for doneness at the end of that period. If necessary, continue microwaving.

Keep your own chart of microwave times for your favorite foods and recipes.

Microwave times for combination ovens will vary. Check your owner's manual.

4-41MW. Carryover time. When the microwave power is turned off and the food is removed from the oven, the food continues to cook until it cools slightly. This cooking, called "carryover time" or "carryover cooking" is an important step in microwave cooking. It is also called "standing," "holding" or "rest" time. Microwave recipes include carryover cooking as part of the recipe.

Generally, remove foods from the microwave oven when they are just slightly undercooked. Carryover time completes the cooking. If foods are removed when completely cooked, they will probably begin to toughen and dry by the time they are served because of the carryover cooking.

If you test a food and it is not done, hold the food for the carryover period before you add more microwave time. If the food still needs cooking, microwave it for a short time, hold, and test. If necessary, microwave again for a short time. Two or three additional but brief microwave cookings, followed by carryover cooking, are much safer than one long additional microwaving. You can always add a short microwave time, but once food is overcooked, there's not much you can do.

The amount of time allowed for carryover cooking varies, depending on the size, volume, moisture content and density of the food. Here is a general guide for carryover cooking:

1 to 3 minutes—small or individual items.

5 minutes—most vegetables, sauces, baked goods.

10 minutes—main dishes, except large roasts.

15 minutes—large dense foods such as meats and poultry.

Generally, if the food is cooked uncovered, cover it with plastic wrap during the standing time to prevent heat loss. If moisture begins to condense, uncover it for a short time.

Some foods cool more quickly than others. If a food cools too much during the carryover period, plan to add a final 1 to 2 minutes of cooking just before serving so it is piping hot. Don't confuse the carryover time in microwave cooking with the resting time called for in some conventional meat and poultry recipes. Roasts prepared in conventional and convection ovens are often allowed to rest for 10 or 15 minutes after removal from the oven so they will be easier to carve.

4-42MW. Turning and stirring. Because the energy in some microwave ovens may be uneven, food must be turned or stirred to help it cook evenly. However, follow the instructions given in your owner's manual since newer microwave ovens may not require this step.

There are two ways to turn food. One way is to rotate the container either one-fourth or one-half turn at least once during cooking. Usually, this is done halfway through the cooking period. Follow the directions in your owner's manual or in the recipe. As a reminder, set the timer for half the total cooking time and then reset it for the remaining time. Usually, turning is used for large or solid foods which cannot be stirred.

Food can also be turned over in the cooking pan. Occasionally recipes for large cuts of meat include this instruction. These foods will also have to be rotated.

Liquids and some mixtures such as vegetables and soups can be stirred rather than rotated. Stirring helps to distribute the heated food so the cold portions heat up faster.

Some recipes may instruct you to rotate or stir the food more than once. Follow the directions carefully.

If your oven has a turntable, don't rotate the food during cooking unless your owner's manual instructs differently.

4-43MW. Containers for microwave cooking. Metal reflects microwaves, so never use metal pans in a microwave oven. Metal pans can prevent cooking, cause slow or uneven cooking and damage the oven.

Use glass, glass-ceramic, china, pottery, some types of plastic and paper. Microwaves pass through these materials to heat only the food, not the container. Some glass-ceramic dishes cannot be used in the microwave oven—check the labels for warnings. Avoid china with metal trim, such as gold or silver.

Use heat-resistant containers. Even though the microwaves do not heat the containers, heat from the food is tranferred to the containers. If the food cooks for only a few minutes, there may not be time for heat to transfer to the container. But if the food cooks for a longer time or has a high fat, sugar or moisture content, it could give off enough heat to damage containers which are not heat resistant. Plastic made especially for microwave cooking is usually heat resistant.

Don't reuse plastic containers from dairy foods, margarine or take-out foods. Some of the plastics are made with polyvinyl chloride (PVC), polystyrene or other materials unsuitable for heating food. If food is heated in these plastics, poisonous materials may leach out into the food. Use only plastic containers that are labeled safe for microwave ovens.

Glazes used on some dishes and pottery contain metals. These absorb microwaves, slowing down the cooking process. To test whether or not a dish is usable, place the empty dish in the microwave oven. Fill a 1-cup glass measuring cup with water and place it in the oven next to the empty dish. Heat on full power for 1 minute, 15 seconds. Check the temperature of the dish and the water in the cup. If the dish is absorbing microwaves, it will be hot and the water will be warm. Don't use the dish for microwave cooking. If the dish is not absorbing microwaves, it will remain cool to the touch and the water in the cup will be hot. The dish can be used for microwave cooking.

Don't use lead crystal or antique glass—it may contain metal or impurities. It may also crack from the heat of the food.

Don't use wood or straw in the microwave oven. It can dry out and may eventually crack or char.

Natural fiber cloths may be used, such as cotton or linen. Don't use any synthetic fiber cloths such as nylon or polyester —some may melt.

Don't use tight-fitting lids on plastic containers—they could explode as inside pressure builds up. Instead, cover the container with plastic wrap or wax paper.

The shape of the pan affects cooking results. Food in round pans cooks more evenly. Food in square or rectangular pans may overcook in the corners. If you must use a square or rectangular pan, shield the corners. See 4-48MW, "Aluminum foil."

If you don't have the size of pan recommended in the recipe, use a larger size—never a smaller one. Food in a smaller pan may boil over. If you don't have a larger size pan, divide the food into several smaller portions. When you use a larger size, you may have to change the cooking time. Check the food about three-fourths through the cooking period. Remember to add carryover time before continuing with the cooking.

If you're using plastic cooking bags, don't use ties containing metal. Cut a small strip of plastic from the open end of the bag. Tie the bag loosely with the plastic strip so steam can escape.

4-44MW. Cooking time. In a microwave oven, cooking time is affected by the following:

• *Size of food.* Small, even pieces cook more quickly than one large piece of the same food. Thin pieces cook more quickly than thick ones.

• *Shape of food.* Square, chunky pieces cook more slowly than long, thin ones. A regular shape cooks more evenly than an odd, irregular shape. Round pieces cook more evenly than irregular or square shapes.

• *Beginning temperature of the food.* Food just removed from the refrigerator will take longer to cook than food at room temperature.

• *Density.* Porous foods, such as breads and rolls, cook faster than denser foods, such as meats. The more solid and compact the food, the longer it takes to cook.

• *Quantity.* If quantity is increased, the food will take longer to cook. As a general rule, if a recipe is doubled, it will take almost twice as long to cook. Begin to check the food about three-fourths of the way through the cooking time. Add carryover time before continuing with the cooking.

• *Moisture content.* The higher the moisture content, the longer the cooking time.

• *Fat and sugar content.* The more fat and sugar a food contains, the faster it cooks and the hotter it gets. Pour off fat as it accumulates. Because fat attracts microwaves, the rest of the food cooks more slowly. Be especially careful when you're warming sweet breads, rolls or pies with sugary fillings or toppings. While the bread or pastry may be just warm to the touch, the sugary filling or frosting may get hot enough to burn you severely when you bite into it.

• *Pan size.* If you use a different pan size, adjust the cooking time. (See 4-43MW, "Containers for microwave cooking.")

• *Pan material.* Plastic cooks the fastest, glass next fastest, and glass-ceramic the slowest.

4-45MW. Paper toweling, wax paper and plastic wrap. Paper toweling, wax paper and plastic wrap are essential accessories in microwave cooking. Each serves a specific purpose:

• Paper toweling or paper napkins retain some heat and absorb excess moisture. Don't use paper toweling that contains synthetic fibers such as nylon—it could flame up. Don't use paper toweling, napkins or other paper products made from recycled paper. They may contain substances that will ignite in the microwave oven.

• Wax paper retains heat and allows some moisture to evaporate.

• Plastic wrap retains both heat and moisture and is similar to placing a lid on the pan. Be sure to use a plastic wrap that is microwave safe. Some brands melt when the food gets extremely hot, such as a meat or casserole. When you cover a pan or dish with plastic, pierce it in several spots so steam can escape. Otherwise the plastic will burst.

If instructions call for a cover on a pan and you have none, use plastic wrap, or use a plate as the cover.

4-46MW. Preparing a meal. If the microwave oven has a rack which permits two layers of food to cook at the same time, follow instructions in your owner's manual. But remember, the more food in the oven, the longer the cooking time.

As a rule, cook foods for a meal in sequence according to the time they take to cook. Begin with the food that takes longest to cook and end with the one that needs the shortest cooking.

First prepare any food that must cool before being served, such as dessert. Next, cook the meat or main dish, then potatoes, vegetables and gravy or sauce. Then warm the bread or rolls and, finally, heat the beverage.

Carryover cooking will keep most foods warm until they are served. If necessary, reheat them quickly just before serving.

If fish is the main dish, cook it last. It cooks quickly and may overcook if you have to reheat it before serving.

4-47MW. Lack of crispness. Foods cooked in the microwave oven will not be crisp. To develop a crisp brown crust, foods need dry circulating heated air. The microwave oven is a sealed compartment, which keeps moisture from evaporating.

If you want a crisp skin on baked potatoes, a crisp crust on roasts, or a flaky, browned pie crust, use the conventional oven.

4-48MW. Aluminum foil. Don't use aluminum foil unless

your owner's manual instructs you to do so. However, you can generally use very small pieces of foil as a shield for uneven areas that may overcook, such as ends of roasts, poultry wings and drumsticks, and corners of square and rectangular pans. Cover only the area to be protected with a small piece of smooth aluminum foil. If necessary, secure the foil to the food with a wooden toothpick. Remove the foil halfway through the cooking time.

Don't allow the foil to touch the metal parts of the oven. It could cause arcing (lightning-like sparks) which can damage the oven.

4-49MW. If food overcooks regularly. If you have problems with food consistently overcooking in the microwave oven, try any of the following methods.

• Reduce the power. If you have only one power, try turning the power off and on at regular intervals during the cooking time. You will probably have to experiment several times to get the results you want.

• Reduce the cooking time.

• Make allowances for carryover cooking after the food is removed from the oven.

• Put a glass of water in the oven with the food to absorb some of the microwaves.

• Set the food in the center of the oven or in that part of the oven that has the least microwave energy. (See 4-38MW, "Oven hot spots.")

4-50MW. To determine cooking time. If you don't have a specific recipe or cooking instructions, weigh the food. One pound of the following ready-to-cook food, cooked at High power, will take the following time:

• Vegetables and most mixtures—6 to 7 minutes.

• Meat cooked rare—6 to 7 minutes.

• Meat cooked medium—7 to 8 minutes.

• Meat cooked well done—8 to 9 minutes.

4-51MW. To prevent food from "exploding." Some foods, such as egg yolks, potatoes, sweet potatoes, whole tomatoes, whole squash, sausage and poultry livers, are covered with a skin or membrane. Moisture inside the food heats rapidly in a microwave oven, causing the skin to burst or explode.

To prevent bursting, pierce the skin or membrane in several places.

Pierce plastic pags of food before microwaving, or tie them closed loosely. Place the plastic bag in a dish to catch any liquid that might flow out.

Stir liquids to break up surface tension. Otherwise they may erupt.

4-52MW. Keep hot pads handy. Microwaves will not normally heat pans or dishes. But don't assume the container will be cool to the touch. Hot food may heat the container, especially if the food must cook more than a few minutes.

Before handling a container of food that has been microwaving, touch it lightly to see if it can be grasped with the bare hand.

4-53MW. Condensation. High-moisture foods will create condensation on the oven walls. At the end of the cooking time, wipe the condensation off the walls with a dry paper towel. Leave the oven door slightly open for a few minutes when rotating or stirring food and again at the end of the cooking time.

Condensation or small puddles of liquid may also appear on food, such as on the surface of cakes. At the end of the carry-over cooking time, carefully soak up the moisture with a dry paper towel.

4-54MW. Never operate an empty oven. Some ovens can be damaged if turned on when they are empty. If there's a possibility that the oven may be turned on accidentally, keep a glass of water in the oven when you're not cooking. Or unplug the oven when you're not using it.

4-55MW. Covering food. Don't cover food unless you are directed to do so in the recipe.

If too much liquid remains in a covered casserole, uncover during the last half of the cooking time.

Place paper toweling over certain foods that spatter heavily, such as bacon. Replace the toweling as it becomes soaked with fat.

4-56MW. Use of newspapers in the microwave oven. Never use newspapers in the microwave oven. Some printing inks contain compounds that attract microwaves. The newspaper could burst into flames.

4-57MW. High-altitude adjustments. As a rule, make the same recipe adjustments for microwave cooking at high altitudes as you would for conventional cooking. (See 5-3, "Cooking at high altitudes.")

Cooking times may have to be increased slightly. Begin by cooking and holding the food for the time recommended in the recipe. Increase microwave time, if necessary.

4-58MW. Salt. Don't salt the surface of solid foods. If the surface is salted, the salt draws moisture from the food and may toughen it. Salt interferes with the pattern of the microwaves and causes uneven cooking. It also leaves brown specks on the surface of the food.

Salt solid food after it has cooked.

Salt may be mixed into mixtures or dissolved in liquid.

4-59MW. To brown food. Place the food under a conventional broiler, but be sure the pan can withstand the high heat.

You can also buy browning sauces made especially for adding color to microwaved foods.

4-60MW. Processing home-canned food. Don't process home-canned food in the microwave oven. Because of uneven heating, you cannot be sure all of the food has reached the temperature necessary to kill harmful microorganisms. In addition, the jars may burst.

4-61MW. Deep-fat frying. Don't deep-fat fry in the microwave oven. The fat can overheat quickly and cause a serious accident or burn.

4-62MW. Drying in the microwave oven. If you're drying food or flowers in the microwave oven, follow the instructions carefully. Never leave the oven unattended. Food and other items can overdry quickly and catch fire.

4-63MW. Safety hints. Here are some safety tips for using microwave ovens.

• Read the operating instructions and safety precautions given in your owner's manual.

• Don't operate the oven if the door does not close firmly or is bent, warped or damaged in any way.

• Never insert objects through the door grill or around the door seal.

• Do not lift the oven by the door handle.

• Never lean on the door or put pressure on it. It may get out of line and not seal properly.

• If you suspect your oven is leaking microwaves, have it tested by a qualified service. Don't use do-it-yourself testing methods—they're unreliable.

• Keep the oven clean, following instructions in your owner's manual. Remove spatters with a paper towel or a damp cloth right after cooking. Never use a commercial oven cleaner.

• The door seal must be tight to keep harmful radiation from escaping. Keep the metal and plastic parts on the door clean to assure a tight seal. Clean door parts with a damp cloth. Never use abrasives such as cleansing powder or scouring pads. They mar the surface, preventing a tight seal.

• Never use the microwave oven for non-food items, such as drying clothes. They could explode or catch fire.

• Never heat sealed jars, cans, etc.—they may explode. Place the food into another container for heating.

• Use cooking thermometers made especially for microwave ovens. Don't use conventional cooking thermometers—they contain mercury, which is not compatible with microwaves.

• Don't attach magnets to microwave ovens. Magnets do not affect microwave energy but they can affect the solid circuitry. Avoid putting magnets on touch control ovens.

4-64MW. Adapting conventional recipes. The easiest method is to find a similar microwave recipe and compare it with yours.

It's impossible to give a fixed set of rules for converting recipes from conventional cooking to microwave cooking. Power settings and cooking times vary too greatly. You may find these general guidelines helpful but you will probably have to experiment with them a number of times to achieve satisfactory results.

On the average, a microwave recipe needs about one-fourth of the cooking time as the same recipe cooked in a conventional oven. A recipe that takes 1 hour to cook conventionally will microwave in about 15 minutes. However, stews, soups and steamed and poached foods usually take longer—from one-third to one-half of conventional cooking time.

Because moisture does not evaporate as quickly in the microwave oven as in the conventional oven, use only about 75% of the liquid called for. If the recipe specifies 1 cup of milk, use ¾ cup for microwaving.

Reduce seasonings slightly. Add more at the end of the cooking time, if necessary.

Use a large container to allow for boil-up.

Precook vegetables—such as chopped onion, celery and green pepper—before adding them to recipes. If used raw, they will not cook thoroughly in the mixture.

Determine approximate timing by the kind and amount of food in the recipe. Your owner's manual will give you the cooking time for certain foods, such as vegetables and grains. Example: If the recipe contains 3 raw potatoes, they will need 8 to 9 minutes to cook. Add to that the time needed for the other ingredients in the recipe.

Turn or stir halfway during cooking. Start checking doneness shortly after the food has been turned or stirred, in case you overestimated the time. Undercook the food to begin with, allow for carryover cooking, and then add extra microwave time if necessary.

If you use uncooked rice or pasta, allow enough time for it to absorb liquid. (See 9-10MW, "Microwaving rice"; 9-11MW, "Microwaving pasta"; and 9-12MW, "Microwaving other grains.") Be sure the recipe has enough liquid for absorption.

Using a recipe

5-1. Evaluating a recipe. Just because a recipe appears in print doesn't mean it will work out successfully. The recipe may not have been properly tested to begin with or it may have some printers' errors.

Before you decide to try it, read the recipe carefully. Evaluate it, keeping in mind that if it doesn't work, you'll waste money, food and time. A good recipe should give you the following information:

• Exact amounts of ingredients.

• Specific information regarding the kinds of ingredients.

• Ingredients listed in the order in which they are used to prepare the recipe. This makes the recipe easier to follow so you'll be less likely to omit an ingredient or step.

• Step-by-step instructions for preparing the recipe. Check the instructions with the list of ingredients. If ingredients are missing, or if the instructions are difficult to understand, look for another recipe.

• Kind and size of pan. A recipe is usually developed to fit a certain size pan. If you don't have the size specified, see 5-15, "Pan substitutions."

• Temperatures for cooking the food or other cooking instructions such as "simmer" or "chill."

• Cooking time.

• Yield or average number of servings.

5-2. To increase or decrease a recipe. Whether or not a recipe can be increased or decreased depends on the type of food:

• *Baked products—cookies, cakes and breads.* These foods depend on exact amounts of ingredients in specific relation to each other. If the ingredients can be cut in half or in thirds EXACTLY, you can probably make a smaller amount successfully. But if the ingredients cannot be divided evenly, you may have a failure. Recipes for most baked products can be doubled successfully.

• *Mixtures—casseroles, stews, salads, desserts.* Generally, these recipes can be increased or decreased successfully, although there may be some exceptions. Divide or increase the recipe to get the number of servings you need. For instance, if a recipe gives six servings and you want only two, use one-third of the amount given for each ingredient. Or double the amount to get 12 servings.

• *Roast meat.* A roast small enough for two generally doesn't give very satisfactory results. It overcooks easily and dries out. A better solution would be to buy a larger roast and use the leftovers for future meals.

• *Roast poultry.* If you want only one or two servings, buy poultry parts instead of whole poultry. Roast the parts as you would whole poultry but for a shorter time. If you enjoy stuffing, bake it in a separate dish along with the poultry.

If you decrease the recipe, cook it in a smaller pan. The food will cook in less time than specified in the recipe. If you double the recipe, you'll get better results if you cook it in two smaller pans instead of one larger one. A doubled recipe cooked in one large pan will take longer to cook than the original recipe.

5-3. Cooking at high altitudes. Since most of the populated areas in the United States are located at altitudes below 3,000 feet, recipes are generally developed for use below this altitude.

Atmospheric pressure is lower at high altitudes than it is at sea level. Because the lower atmospheric pressures affect cooking, recipes often must be adjusted for use at higher altitudes.

Following are some of the adjustments needed for high-altitude cooking. You may have to experiment a few times to achieve satisfactory results.

• At higher altitudes, water and other liquids boil at lower temperatures and evaporate faster. Therefore foods cooked in water and other liquids take longer to cook. Even though they are boiling, they are not cooking at as high a temperature as they would be at a lower altitude. Increase the cooking time rather than the heat. If you increase the heat, mixtures containing milk may scorch, curdle or boil over.

• Baked products rise faster because the gases from the leavening expand quickly. The result can be a coarse product. Generally, for products leavened with baking powder or soda, the following adjustments must be made in the amounts of sugar, baking powder and liquid:

3,000 feet
Baking powder: for each teaspoon, decrease ⅛ teaspoon.
Sugar: for each cup, decrease 0 to 1 Tablespoon.
Liquid: for each cup, add 1 to 2 Tablespoons.
5,000 Feet
Baking powder: for each teaspoon, decrease ⅛ to ¼ teaspoon.
Sugar: for each cup, decrease 0 to 2 Tablespoons.
Liquid: for each cup, add 2 to 4 Tablespoons.
7,000 Feet
Baking powder: for each teaspoon, decrease ¼ teaspoon.
Sugar: for each cup, decrease 1 to 3 Tablespoons.
Liquid: for each cup, add 3 to 4 Tablespoons.

• Yeast breads. Since gases from the leavening expand faster, the dough will rise faster. Some food experts believe the faster rising keeps the flavor from developing. You may want to experiment with the flavor. Punch the dough down after the first rising and let it rise again before you shape it. Compare the flavor with dough that has been allowed to rise just once. Because higher altitudes are usually dry, flour may be drier and may therefore absorb more liquid. You may need less flour than the recipe calls for.

• Deep-fat-fried foods brown more quickly at higher altitudes. Fried foods can easily overbrown on the outside and still be undercooked on the inside. As a general rule, lower the temperature of the fat about 3°F for each 1,000 feet above sea level.

• At altitudes above 5,000 feet, cornstarch mixtures must be cooked over direct heat rather than in a double boiler. The lower boiling temperature of the water will not give enough heat for the cornstarch to thicken.

5-4. Organize your work. Organization can help you do the most in the least amount of time with a minimum of cleanup. Here are some basic hints:

• Read the recipe beforehand. There may be steps that must be done the day before, such as soaking beans or marinating meat overnight.

• Keep a record of any changes or substitutions you make in a recipe for future reference.

• Gather all the equipment and ingredients you'll need at the work area. Then you won't have to interrupt the cooking process to look for something. A tray or cart is helpful for gathering food and small equipment.

• Do as much pre-preparation as you can. Pre-preparation means processes that have to be done before you can actually start putting the recipe together. For example, wash all fruits and vegetables. Peel, if necessary, and cut or prepare as directed. Cut or chop other foods such as bread, nuts or meat. Cook foods such as pasta. Brown meat. Measure as many ingredients as you can. Pour measured dry ingredients onto pieces of waxed paper. Grease baking pans. Once the pre-preparation is taken care of, putting the recipe together is a relatively simple process.

• Simplify your work. For instance, measure all dry ingredients first, such as flour and sugar. Then measure shortening. You won't have to wash the measuring cup until you're through measuring. Scrape bowls, pans, beaters and spoons with a rubber scraper—you save food and cut down on cleaning. Always cut on a cutting board, never on a table or counter. A cutting board is much easier and cheaper to replace than a marred table or counter surface.

• Clean up as you work. Keep hot sudsy water in the sink. As you use equipment, rinse it and put it in the hot suds. Whenever you have a break in your food preparation, wash the equipment, and rinse and dry thoroughly. You'll always have clean equipment to continue your work.

5-5. Equivalents, weights and measures.

Units of weight
1 ounce = 28.35 grams
1 pound = 16 ounces
          = 453.59 grams
1 gram = 0.035 ounces
1 kilogram = 1000 grams
            = 2.21 pounds

Units of volume
1 bushel = 4 pecks
1 peck = 8 quarts
        = 2 gallons
1 gallon = 4 quarts

1 quart = 2 pints
     = 4 cups
     = 32 fluid ounces
     = 946.4 milliliters
1 pint = 2 cups
     = 16 fluid ounces
     = 473.2 milliliters
1 cup = 16 Tablespoons
     = 8 fluid ounces
     = 236.6 milliliters
¾ cup = 12 Tablespoons
     = 6 fluid ounces
     = 177.5 milliliters
½ cup = 8 Tablespoons
     = 4 fluid ounces
     = 118.3 milliliters
⅓ cup = 5 Tablespoons plus 1 teaspoon
     = 2.7 fluid ounces
     = 78.8 milliliters
¼ cup = 4 Tablespoons
     = 2 fluid ounces
     = 59.2 milliliters
⅛ cup = 2 Tablespoons
     = 1 fluid ounce
     = 29.6 milliliters
1 Tablespoon = 3 teaspoons
     = ½ fluid ounce
     = 14.8 milliliters
1 teaspoon = 4.9 milliliters
1 jigger = 1½ ounces
     = 3 Tablespoons
     = 44.4 milliliters
a pinch = a little less than ¼ teaspoon
a dash = a few drops
1 liter = 1000 milliliters
     = 1.06 quarts

Temperatures
Very slow oven = 250°F to 275°F
Slow oven = 300°F to 325°F
Moderate oven = 350°F to 375°F
Hot oven = 400°F to 425°F
Very hot oven = 450°F to 475°F
Extremely hot oven = 500°F to 525°F

5-6. Substitutions of food. No matter how well you plan, you may find you're lacking an ingredient for a recipe at a time when it's inconvenient to run out and buy it. The following chart gives substitutes for basic ingredients. While the results may not equal the original recipe, they will usually be satisfactory.

INGREDIENT	SUBSTITUTE
1 teaspoon baking powder	= ¼ teaspoon baking soda plus ½ teaspoon cream of tartar
1 ounce unsweetened chocolate	= 3 Tablespoons unsweetened cocoa plus 1 Tablespoon butter
1 Tablespoon cornstarch	= 2 Tablespoons all-purpose flour (for thickening)
¾ cup cracker crumbs	= 1 cup dry bread crumbs
1 cup light cream	= ⅞ cup milk plus 3 Tablespoons butter
	= 1 cup undiluted evaporated milk
1 cup heavy cream	= ¾ cup milk plus ⅓ cup butter (for cooking, not for whipping)
1 cup sour cream	= 1 cup plain yogurt
	= 1 Tablespoon lemon juice plus evaporated milk to make 1 cup
	= 6 ounces cream cheese plus 3 Tablespoons milk
1 whole egg	= 2 egg yolks
	= 3 Tablespoons slightly beaten egg
1 egg white	= 2 Tablespoons frozen egg white
1 cup all-purpose flour	= 1 cup plus 2 Tablespoons sifted cake flour
1 cup sifted cake flour	= ⅞ cup sifted all-purpose flour (1 cup less 2 Tablespoons)
1 Tablespoon flour (for thickening)	= ½ Tablespoon cornstarch
	= 2 teaspoons quick-cooking tapioca
	= 1 whole egg
	= 2 egg whites
	= 2 egg yolks
1 cup granulated sugar	= 1 cup packed brown sugar
	= 2 cups sifted powdered sugar
1 cup sour milk	= 1 Tablespoon lemon juice or vinegar plus enough milk to make 1 cup

1 cup whole milk = ½ cup evaporated milk plus ½ cup water
= 1 cup skim milk plus 2 Tablespoons butter
1 pound fresh mushrooms = 3 ounces dried mushrooms
= 1 6-ounce or 8-ounce can
1 teaspoon dry mustard = 1 Tablespoon prepared mustard
1 Tablespoon snipped fresh herbs = 1 teaspoon dried herbs, crushed
= ½ teaspoon ground herbs
1 small onion = 1 Tablespoon minced dried onion
= 1 teaspoon onion powder
1 clove garlic = ⅛ teaspoon minced dried garlic
= ⅛ teaspoon garlic powder
1 8-ounce package stuffing mix = 4 cups croutons
= 4 cups toasted bread cubes
1 cup tomato juice = ½ cup tomato sauce plus ½ cup water
1 pound fresh tomatoes = 2 cups canned
1 10-ounce package frozen vegetables = 1¼ cups cut-up fresh vegetables
= 1¼ cups loose-pack frozen vegetables
1 16-ounce can vegetables, drained = 2 cups cut-up fresh vegetables, cooked and drained
= 2 cups frozen loose-pack vegetables, cooked and drained
1 10-ounce package frozen fruits, drained = 1¼ cups cut-up fresh fruit
= 1¼ cups frozen loose pack fruits, drained
1 16-ounce can fruit, drained = 1½ cups cut-up fresh fruit
= 1½ cups frozen loose-pack fruit, drained
For seafood substitutions, see 19-15, "Substitutions."

5-7. Food equivalents. Recipes often call for foods that have been prepared, such as cooked or chopped. Following is a chart of the amount of raw ingredient to start out with to get the amount of prepared food called for in the recipe.

WHEN YOU START WITH = YOU GET:
1 8-ounce package fine noodles = 5½ cups cooked
1 cup raw pasta = about 2 cups cooked

1 cup raw regular rice = 3 cups cooked
1 cup raw bulgur = about 3 cups cooked
1 cup quick-cooking oats = 1¾ cups cooked
1 cup cornmeal = 4 cups cooked
11 to 12 finely rolled graham crackers = 1 cup crumbs
2 slices fresh bread = 1 cup soft bread crumbs
1 slice dry bread = ⅓ cup dry bread crumbs
8-ounce piece Swiss or Cheddar cheese = 2 cups shredded
6 or 7 large eggs = 1 cup egg whites
11 or 12 large eggs = 1 cup egg yolks
1 medium-size potato = 1 cup sliced raw potato
1 pound potatoes (4 medium) = 2 cups cooked mashed
1 pound raw carrots = 2½ cups sliced carrots
1 small cabbage (1 pound) = 4 cups shredded cabbage
1 medium-size lemon = 2 Tablespoons juice
                            = 1 teaspoon grated rind
1 medium-size orange = ½ cup juice
                            = 4 teaspoons grated rind
1 medium-size apple = 1 cup sliced apples
1 pound dried fruit = 4 to 4½ cups cooked
1 cup dried lima beans = 2½ cups cooked
1 cup dried red beans = 2 cups cooked
1 cup white beans = 3 cups cooked
½ pound shelled walnuts or pecans = 2 cups chopped
1 pound walnuts in shell = 2½ cups shelled

5-8. Measuring ingredients. Modern recipes are developed
and tested with standard measuring cups and spoons. Using
anything other than standard measuring tools and the proper
techniques can lead to failure. For instance, a coffee cup is not
the equivalent of a standard measuring cup. Coffee cups vary
in size from about 6 to 10 fluid ounces while a standard measuring cup holds 8 fluid ounces.

For accurate measurements, use "dry" measuring cups
for dry ingredients, glass or clear plastic liquid measuring
cups for liquids and standard measuring spoons for smaller
amounts. (See 5-9, "Dry measuring cups"; 5-11, "Liquid measuring cup"; and 5-12, "Measuring spoons.")

5-9. Dry measuring cups. Dry measuring cups usually
come in a set of four cups, each a different size: 1 cup, ½ cup,
⅓ cup and ¼ cup. They are made of metal or plastic. Use these
cups to measure dry or solid ingredients such as flour and

shortening in any amount from several cups to fractions such as ½ or ¾ cup.

Don't use these cups to measure liquids. Because they don't have a head space, you can easily spill some of the liquid, resulting in an inaccurate measure.

If you're measuring a granular food such as flour or sugar, hold the cup over wax paper or the container to catch the spillover. Don't hold it over the bowl in which you're mixing. The spillover can add enough extra amount of the ingredient to ruin your recipe.

Spoon a dry ingredient, such as flour or sugar, into the measuring cup lightly. Don't scoop it up with the cup, pack it down with a spoon or shake the cup—you'll increase the measurement considerably.

Fill the cup to the top and slightly overflowing. Using a straight edge, such as a spatula or knife, level off the top of the cup. This gives you an accurate measurement. Use the wax paper as a funnel to pour the spillover back into the food container.

5-10. Level vs heaping measurements. Dry or solid ingredients can be measured in two different ways—level or heaping. "Level" means the ingredient has been leveled off even with the top of the cup or spoon with a straight edge, such as a spatula. "Heaping" means the food has been spooned into the cup or spoon to slightly overflowing, with the top slightly rounded.

Unless the recipe states otherwise, a measurement should always be level.

5-11. Liquid measuring cup. A liquid measuring cup is made of clear plastic or glass with a handle and a pouring spout. It also has a head space of about half an inch so you can carry the cup without spilling any liquid.

One side of the cup shows customary measures in both fractions of a cup and ounces. The other side may show metric measures in milliliters.

When you measure liquids, place the cup on a flat surface, such as a table, counter or windowsill. Never hold the cup in your hand to measure. You may tilt it and get an inaccurate measure.

Pour the liquid into the cup. When you look at the amount of liquid indicated on the side of the cup, look at it at eye level. If you look down on the cup, you won't get an accurate reading.

If necessary, stoop down so your eyes are at the same level as the top of the liquid in the cup. Then you can see the exact measure and add or pour off as necessary to get the amount you need.

5-12. Measuring spoons. Measuring spoons come in a set of four spoons—1 Tablespoon, 1 teaspoon, ½ teaspoon and ¼ teaspoon. Use them for dry, solid or liquid ingredients. Don't use ordinary tablespoons, soup spoons or teaspoons—they vary in size.

Level off dry ingredients with a straight edge, such as a spatula. When measuring liquids, pour carefully so you don't spill liquid. Never measure over the bowl in which you're mixing. A little extra baking powder or flavoring can ruin the best recipe.

5-13. Metric system. (Also see 5-5, "Equivalents.") You may find many international recipes written in the metric system. Conversion from metric to your standard measuring equipment is fairly simple.

If the recipes are Canadian or written in the United States, they will specify metric measuring equipment, cups and spoons, which have been standardized in both countries. A metric measuring cup contains 250 milliliters (mL). A standard measuring cup contains 240 milliliters (236.6 milliliters rounded to the nearest zero) or 8 fluid ounces.

If you don't have a metric measuring cup, you can still measure metric quantities. A teaspoon contains 5 milliliters. To get 250 milliliters, measure the ingredients in a standard measuring cup, which gives you 240 milliliters. Add two teaspoons for an additional 10 milliliters, or a total of 250 milliliters.

Recipes from other countries are usually written in metric units rather than in measuring cups and spoons. Perhaps this brief description of the metric system will encourage you to use metric recipes.

The metric system is a decimal system based on multiples and divisibles of 10. Units in the metric system are interrelated and easy and fast to use. The most familiar comparison is the United States monetary system, which is also a decimal system. While the American monetary system uses just two decimal points, the metric system can go far beyond that. However, the concept is still the same. The dollar bill, or the common unit, is divided into smaller units of 10 or 100.

The metric system works the same way, and it's much easier to use than the current standard system of dividing units into unwieldy fractions.

For cooking purposes, four common metric units are involved:

- **meter** measures length or distance
- **gram** measures mass or weight
- **liter** measures volume
- **Celsius** measures temperature

Prefixes precede the common unit and indicate the amount of the common unit. Here, too, although there are many kinds of prefixes, only a few are needed for cooking. These are:

deci or 1/10 or .1
centi or 1/100 or .01
milli or 1/1000 or .001
kilo or 1000

Deci, centi and milli make the unit smaller. Kilo makes it larger.

Symbols are used for the units and prefixes.

Common units	Prefixes
meter = m	deci = d
gram = g	centi = c
liter = L	milli = m
Celsius = C	kilo = k

Here are examples of metric symbols when a prefix and a common unit are combined:

kilogram = kg
centimeter = cm
deciliter = dL
milligram = mg

To understand the working of the metric system, compare it to a dollar bill:

Dollar bill	Common metric unit
dime = 1/10 of a dollar	deci = 1/10 of a unit
cent = 1/100 of a dollar	centi = 1/100 of a unit

To multiply or divide a dollar bill, you simply move the decimal point. The same applies to the metric system. For instance:

Dollar bill	Liter
$1.00	1 liter
$.10 or 1/10 of a dollar	0.1 liter or 1/10 of a liter
$.01 or 1/100 of a dollar	0.01 liter or 1/100 of a liter

To carry the example a little further:
- 1/10 of a dollar or $.10 is also called 1 dime . . . .
. . . . . .1/10 of a liter or 0.1 liter is also called 1 deciliter.
- 1/100 of a dollar or $.01 is also called 1 cent . . . .
. . 1/100 of a liter or 0.01 liter is also called 1 centiliter.

If you want to use an international metric recipe, the following will help you to convert it to your standard measuring equipment. A small pocket calculator will simplify the job. Note that the following conversions are for standard measuring equipment based on an 8-fluid-ounce cup. They are not to be used with the 250mL metric measure.

Meter
The meter is used primarily for pan sizes.
2.54 centimeters or .254 decimeters = 1 inch.

To convert the metric measurement into inches: If the measurement is given in decimeters, divide it by .254 to get inches. If it is given in centimeters, divide it by 2.54 to get inches. Round off the final number to eliminate fractions. For instance, a 22cm pan divided by 2.54 equals 8.66 inches or 9 inches rounded off.

Liter
Liter measures volume and equals gallons, quarts, pints, fluid ounces and measuring cups. One liter is slightly larger than a quart.

A liter = 4.24 standard 8-ounce measuring cups. It also equals 2.1 pints, 1.06 quarts and 0.26 gallon.
1 milliliter = .03 fluid ounce
30 milliliters = 1 fluid ounce
.024 liter or 240 milliliters = 1 standard 8-ounce cup.

Gram
Gram measures weight and equals ounces and pounds.
1 gram = 1/28 of an ounce or .035 ounce
28 grams = 1 ounce
1 kilogram = 2.2 pounds

If a recipe calls for 500 grams of ground meat, divide 500 by 28 grams, which gives 17.85 ounces, rounded off to 18 ounces or 1⅛ pounds.

Celsius
Temperatures are read on the Celsius scale, which was once known as Centigrade. The Centigrade scale was renamed Celsius after the man who invented it.

On the Celsius scale, water freezes at 0°C and boils at 100°C.

Although many formulas exist for converting Celsius to Fahrenheit, they are most impractical since they result in temperatures which are impossible to select on an average thermostat, such as 382°F or 407°F.

The following chart gives a range of temperature conversions, the most practical and easiest approach:

120°C to 135°C = 250°F to 275°F
150°C to 165°C = 300°F to 325°F
175°C to 190°C = 350°F to 375°F
205°C to 220°C = 400°F to 425°F
230°C to 245°C = 450°F to 475°F
260°C to 275°C = 500°F to 525°F

Begin to check the food near the end of the baking or cooking time to determine doneness. You may have to experiment with several temperature settings to find the most appropriate one for the recipe.

5-14. Measuring hints.

• *Brown sugar.* If brown sugar is lumpy, roll out the lumps with a rolling pin. If the recipe calls for "packed brown sugar," pack it down firmly into the cup with the back of the spoon so it holds its shape when turned out. If the recipe does not specify "packed," spoon the sugar into the cup without packing.

• *Granulated or confectioner's sugar.* If the sugar is lumpy, sift it first, then spoon it into a dry measuring cup.

• *White flour.* Follow recipe directions for sifting white flour before measuring. If the recipe specifies "sifted flour," sift before measuring. If it just calls for "flour," do not sift.

• *Whole grain flour.* Never sift whole grain flours such as whole wheat or rye—the coarse particles will not go through the strainer. Before measuring, stir the flour with a spoon so it will be easier to pour into the measuring cup.

• *Butter or margarine.* If you buy butter or margarine in stick form, it's already premeasured. Each ¼-pound stick equals ½ cup or 8 Tablespoons. Half of a ¼-pound stick equals ¼ cup or 4 Tablespoons. To measure 2 Tablespoons, cut off one-fourth of a ¼-pound stick.

• *Shortening or other solid fat.* Pack well into the dry measuring cup or measuring spoon. Work out air bubbles as you pack and level off the top. Or use the water displacement method: Subtract the amount of shortening needed from 1 cup and fill a liquid measuring cup with that amount of water. Spoon fat into the cup, pushing it below the surface of the water. When the water level reaches 1 cup, you will have measured the amount of fat you need. Example: If you need ¼ cup of shortening, subtract ¼ from 1 cup, which leaves ¾ cup. Fill the liquid measuring cup with ¾ cup of water and add fat until the liquid measures 1 cup. The fat will measure ¼ cup.

• *Melted fat.* Fat can be measured before or after melting—the amount will be the same.

5-15. Pan substitutions. Recipes usually specify a certain type and size of pan. If you don't have that particular pan, you can usually substitute another one, but the substitution may affect the cooking time. For instance, if you use a square pan instead of a loaf pan, the food may cook in less time because the square pan is more shallow. If you use a loaf pan instead of the square pan, the food may take a little longer to cook because the pan is deeper.

Don't use a pan that is greatly smaller or larger than the size recommended. If it's too small, the food will run over. If it's too large, the food may dry out or overcook.

Following is a list of common pan sizes and the number of cups each holds:

4 cups
1-quart baking dish or casserole
9-inch pie pan
8x1¾-inch round layer cake pan
7⅜x3⅝x2¼-inch loaf pan
8½x2¼-inch ring mold
6 cups
1½-quart baking dish or casserole
8x1½-inch round layer cake pan
9x1½-inch round layer cake pan
10-inch pie pan
8½x3⅝x2⅝-inch loaf pan
7½x3-inch "Bundt" fancy tube pan
7x5½x4-inch melon mold
8 cups
2-quart baking dish or casserole
8x8x2-inch square pan
11x7x1½-inch baking pan
9x5x3-inch loaf pan
9¼x2¾-inch ring mold
9 cups
9x3½-inch fancy tube pan

10 cups
2½-quart baking dish or casserole
9x9x2-inch square pan
11¾x7½x1¾-inch baking pan
15x10x1-inch jelly-roll pan
12 cups
3-quart baking dish or casserole
13½x8½-inch glass baking dish
9x3½-inch angel cake pan
10x3¾-inch fancy tube pan
9x3½-inch fancy tube mold
8x3-inch spring-form pan
15 cups
13x9x2-inch baking pan
16 cups
10x4-inch fancy tube mold
9x3-inch spring-form pan
18 cups
10x4-inch angel cake pan
19 cups
14x10½x1½-inch roasting pan

Milk, cream, yogurt

BUYING

6-1. Kinds of milk. Milk varies in milkfat content. Homogenized whole milk has at least 3.25% milkfat. Skim and lowfat milk has anywhere from less than 0.5% to 2.5% milkfat. If you're watching calories, buy milk with the lowest milkfat content.

Different kinds of milk are available:

• *Buttermilk* varies in milkfat, depending on the kind of milk used. Lactic acid added to milk produces the smooth, thick texture and tangy flavor so characteristic of buttermilk.

• *Acidophilus milk* is either a lowfat or skim milk with lactobacillus acidophilus bacteria culture added to it. These bacteria are among many normally found in the human intestinal system, but conditions such as illness or antibiotic treatments may upset the bacterial balance in the intestines. Although research is still needed, some health experts believe that eating food containing lactobacillus acidophilus bacteria will help to maintain bacterial balance in the intestines and minimize gastrointestinal disturbances.

• *Chocolate milk* is made by flavoring whole, lowfat, or skim milk with chocolate syrup, cocoa or a chocolate powder. Usually, a sweetener is added. Chocolate milk varies in calories, depending on the type of milk used and the amount of sweetener and cocoa or chocolate added.

• *Evaporated milk,* available whole or skim, has had half of the water removed. Use it full strength in place of cream. To use as milk, add water according to instructions on the container.

• *Sweetened condensed milk* is concentrated milk with at

119

least 40% sugar added. Because of its high sugar content, it is used mainly in candy and dessert recipes.

• *Goat's milk* is used by people who are allergic to cow's milk or who are on special diets. It is sold fresh or canned.

• *Nonfat dry milk* is a powdered form of milk from which water and fat have been removed.

6-2. Kinds of cream. Cream is the fatty part of milk and varies in the amount of milkfat it contains. To whip satisfactorily, cream must contain at least 30% or more milkfat.

• *Half-and-half* is a mixture of milk and cream. It has between 10.5% and 18% milkfat.

• *Light cream,* also known as coffee or table cream, contains between 18% and 30% milkfat.

• *Light whipping cream* contains between 30% and 36% milkfat.

• *Heavy whipping cream* has more than 36% milkfat.

• *Plain sour cream* has at least 18% milkfat.

6-3. Yogurt. Yogurt is made by fermenting either whole, lowfat or skim milk.

The calories in the yogurt depend on the type of milk used and on the flavorings and sweetened fruit added to it. Calories in 1 cup of yogurt vary from 125 for plain nonfat to 250 for sweetened and flavored.

Because of its cream-like quality, plain yogurt makes a low-calorie substitute for sour cream. However, it adds a tangier flavor to food.

STORING

6-4. Storing fluid milk and cream. These products are highly perishable. If containers sit at room termperature for even a short time, harmful bacteria will begin to grow.

Refrigerate milk in its original container, which was sterilized before the milk was put into it. Don't transfer milk to another container for storage, such as a pitcher. Milk is a delicate product and can spoil easily if contaminated. If a strong food was previously stored in the container, the milk may pick up the flavor.

Milk and cream are sensitive to odors. Keep containers closed so odors from other foods in the refrigerator are not absorbed. If milk or cream has an off flavor, it means one of two things—it has either picked up odors or it is starting to spoil.

Keep milk away from light. Milk is a good source of ribo-flavin but light destroys this vitamin. Use milk and cream within 3 to 5 days.

6-5. Freezing milk. Don't freeze milk—freezing affects the flavor and appearance. If milk has accidentally frozen, it can still be used. However, if the container has popped open from the pressure of the frozen milk, don't used the milk—it's been exposed to bacteria and may be contaminated

6-6. Storing canned and nonfat dry milk. Store un-opened cans of evaporated and condensed milk in dry, cool storage areas. Once the cans are opened, refrigerate them.

Store unopened packages of nonfat dry milk in dry, cool storage areas. Moisture in the air may cake dry milk. Reseal opened packages carefully and store in a cool, dry area. If packages cannot be resealed, transfer the dry milk to a container with a tight-fitting lid. Once the nonfat dry milk is reliquified, refrigerate it.

6-7. Storing yogurt. Keep yogurt refrigerated and use within about 10 days. If yogurt separates, stir the liquid back in.

CONVENTIONAL COOKING

6-8. Cooking milk—general information. Because milk is a protein food, it requires low temperatures and slow cook-ing. Cook milk slowly at temperatures below 140°F.

Modern ranges have controls which can keep temperatures low enough to cook milk in a saucepan on top of the range without scorching. Because older ranges may give too much heat even at lowest settings, a double boiler may be necessary to cook milk without scorching.

6-9. Scorched milk. As milk is heated, the milk solids settle on the bottom and stick to the pan in the form of a white coating. The solids include proteins and lactose or milk sugar. As the milk overheats, the lactose caramelizes or browns, and the solids scorch rapidly, giving the milk an off flavor.

Scorched milk can be used in cooked mixtures if combined with stronger flavors, such as seasonings, chocolate, strong-flavored vegetables, or fish.

6-10. Scalded milk. A recipe may call for scalded milk.

This means the milk is heated to just below boiling. To scald milk, use low heat and cook the milk only until bubbles appear around the sides of the pan.

6-11. Scum or skin. As milk heats, the surface liquid evaporates, causing a scum or skin to form. The scum is made up of milk solids, especially protein and fat. Most people don't like it because it's tough and rubbery. Scum can also prevent steam from escaping, causing boil-overs.

To keep scum from forming, stir the milk constantly as it cooks or cover the pan.

If scum forms, beat it into the milk. You can discard it if you wish, but you'll be throwing out valuable nutrients.

6-12. Curdled milk. Milk curdles for several reasons.

• The temperature is too high or the mixture cooks too long. Remember, milk is a protein food and susceptible to high heat. Cook milk according to directions given in 6-8, "Cooking milk —general information."

Creamed mixtures such as scalloped potatoes often curdle because the mixture must be cooked long enough to cook the potatoes. Precook the potatoes to help prevent curdling.

• Cold milk is added directly to hot food. To prevent curdling, warm the milk before adding it to a hot mixture: either heat it slightly or pour some of the hot mixture into the cold milk, stirring constantly. Then stir the warmed milk into the hot mixture.

• The mixture has too much salt. Creamed mixtures containing cured meats such as ham will often curdle because of the curing salts used in the meat. To prevent curdling, eliminate the salt called for in the recipe. If the cured meats are heavily salted, the mixture may still curdle.

• Milk is mixed with an acidic food. If milk and any acidic food, such as lemon juice, vinegar, or tomato, are mixed, the milk curdles. To avoid curdling, begin by adding a small amount of the acidic food gradually to the milk, stirring constantly, to slightly acidify the milk. Then pour the acidified milk slowly into the remaining acidic food, stirring constantly.

If the milk mixture has curdled, you may still be able to use it:

• Try beating it vigorously to break up the curdling and make the mixture smooth.

• Strain the mixture to remove the curdles. You may have to add a little more milk to make up for the amount removed.

6-13. Boil-overs. Milk generally boils over because scum forms over the top, preventing steam from escaping. (See 6-11, "Scum or skin.") The steam forces the milk to rise to the top and over the sides of the pan.

To prevent boil-overs when cooking milk, stir to prevent scum from forming. Cook at low temperatures for as short a time as possible.

6-14. To sour milk. Raw milk will eventually turn sour because of the microorganisms it contains. But during pasteurization, heat destroys the microorganisms. Instead of turning sour, pasteurized milk spoils and develops an unpleasant flavor.

Recipes occasionally call for sour milk. An acidic food, such as lemon juice or vinegar, can be used to sour pasteurized milk. Pour 1 Tablespoon vinegar or lemon juice into a cup and fill to the 1-cup line with milk. Stir and allow to stand at room temperature for a few minutes.

6-15. Cooking cream. Because cream has a high fat content, it reacts to heat and acidic foods more quickly than milk does. When cooking with cream, take even greater care than you do when cooking with milk.

Mixtures containing cream should be cooked at lower temperatures and more slowly than those made with milk. If the mixture contains an acidic food, such as lemon juice, cook it in a double boiler.

6-16. To whip cream. To whip, cream must have at least 30% milkfat. The fat gives body to the whipped cream. The cream must be cold so the fat is firm. If the cream is at room temperature, the fat may begin to soften and the cream won't whip. The bowl and beater should also be cold. If the room is warm, set the bowl in a larger bowl of ice water.

Whip the cream slowly. Stop beating as soon as the cream piles into a soft mound. If beaten too long, whipped cream will quickly turn into butter. Even a few extra seconds of beating can turn perfect whipped cream into globs of butter.

6-17. To use instant nonfat dry milk. Instant nonfat dry milk can add extra nutrients to recipes. It's also a good way to get your daily allotment of milk. Here are a few suggestions for adding instant nonfat dry milk to some of your favorite recipes:

• Ground meat, fish, or chicken: add ½ to ¾ cup instant

nonfat dry milk to each pound of ground meat. Mix the dry milk with the meat, liquid, or crumbs.

• Mashed vegetables, such as potatoes, squash, sweet potatoes, rutabagas, and turnips: add ⅓ cup instant nonfat dry milk to each 2 cups of mashed vegetable. Use a little cooking water to give the mixture the right consistency. Season as desired.

• Sauces, gravies, soups, custards: Add ¼ cup instant nonfat dry milk to each cup of fluid milk. OR add ½ cup instant nonfat dry milk to each cup of water or broth in a recipe.

• Cooked cereals: Mix equal amounds of instant nonfat dry milk and cereal before cooking. Then follow the directions on the package for cooking the cereal.

MICROWAVE COOKING

6-18MW. Scorching. Milk mixtures generally will not scorch in a microwave oven unless they are cooked for an unusually long time.

6-19MW. Boil-overs. Milk boils over easily in a microwave oven. Don't cook it on High power and be sure the pan is large enough to allow for foaming. Turn the power off immediately if the milk shows signs of foaming.

6-20MW. Nonfat dry milk as an ingredient. Reconstitute nonfat dry milk before using it as an ingredient in a recipe that must thicken, such as pudding or sauce. If you add the dry milk powder directly to the mixture, the mixture may not set or thicken.

Cheese

BUYING

7-1. Fresh cheese. Fresh cheese includes cottage cheese, ricotta, pot or farmer's cheese, cream cheese, Neufchatel and mozzarella. It is usually mild in flavor with a relatively soft or spongy texture.

Because fresh cheese is highly perishable, it retains its freshness and flavor for a relatively short time, even when properly refrigerated. Buy only what you can use in a few days.

7-2. Ripened cheese. Ripened cheese has been allowed to age, giving it a characteristic flavor described as "mild," "mellow," or "sharp." Depending on the manufacturing process, it can be classified as soft, semisoft, firm, hard, and blue-vein mold.

• *Soft ripened cheeses* included Brie, Camembert and Limburger.

• *Semisoft ripened cheeses* include brick, Muenster, Monterey Jack and Port du Salut.

• *Firm ripened cheeses* include Swiss, Cheddar, Colby, Edam, Gouda and provolone.

• *Hard ripened cheeses* include Parmesan and Romano. These are generally grated.

• *Blue-vein mold cheeses* include blue cheese, Gorgonzola, Roquefort and Stilton. If blue cheese is imported, the name may be spelled "bleu."

For cooking, the melting ability of the cheese is important. As a rule, firm cheeses with a high fat content have the best melting quality.

125

Sharper cheeses give a more pronounced cheese flavor to cooked mixtures.

One pound firm cheese = 4 cups grated.

7-3. Processed cheese. Several types of processed cheese are available, each with its own characteristics:

• *Pasteurized process cheese* is a pasteurized blend of fresh and aged natural cheeses. It melts easily when heated.

• *Pasteurized process cheese food* contains ingredients other than cheese, such as nonfat dry milk, whey solids, water and sometimes other food such as pimientos or olives. It has a high moisture content and a mild flavor. It is easy to spread.

• *Pasteurized process spread* is similar to process cheese food but it has more moisture and less milkfat.

• *Coldpack cheese or club cheese* is a blend of fresh and aged natural cheeses, made into a uniform product without heating. It spreads more easily than natural cheese.

• *Coldpack cheese food* is similar to coldpack cheese but includes other dairy ingredients such as nonfat dry milk or whey solids.

7-4. Read the label carefully. Many cheeses look alike and are sold in similar-looking packages. It's easy to be confused and buy the wrong one.

Labels for natural cheeses will give you the variety name, such as "Cheddar," "Swiss" or "blue." They may also indicate the sharpness of the flavor, such as "mild," "mellow" or "sharp."

If the cheese is processed, the label will give this information along with a list of the ingredients added to the cheese.

Some labels may show grades of cheese and some may have a "Quality Approved" inspection shield by the U.S. Department of Agriculture.

Before you shop, decide on the type of cheese you need so you will know what to look for. Also take time to become acquainted with the many varieties available. You may want to experiment with different ones for both serving and cooking.

STORING

7-5. Storing fresh and ripened cheese.

• *Fresh cheese.* Refrigerate in original wrapper or carton. Use within a few days.

• *Ripened cheese.* Refrigerate in the original wrapper or in plastic wrap or aluminum foil. Be sure it is tightly wrapped to keep it from drying out and to keep the aroma from circulating throughout the refrigerator. Ripened cheese can usually be kept for several weeks. If mold forms, scrape it off before using. However, mold may give some cheeses a strong or unpleasant flavor. If the cheese dries out, grate it and use as a topping or as an ingredient in recipes. Ripened cheese may be frozen but expect a change in flavor and texture. Before freezing cheese, cut it into portions of usable size.

CONVENTIONAL COOKING

7-6. Serving fresh and ripened cheese.
• *Fresh cheese.* Serve fresh cheese chilled. Most fresh cheeses can be served as snacks, in salads or with fruit for dessert.
• *Ripened cheese.* Serve ripened cheese at room temperature to bring out its flavor and texture. If it is served cold, it will have a hard texture and lack flavor. Remove ripened cheese from the refrigerator about an hour before serving to bring it to room temperature.

7-7. Cooking cheese. Cheese is a protein food, which means it must be cooked at low temperatures for a short period of time.

When overcooked, cheese becomes tough and rubbery and the fat separates into small drops of grease. Cheese also gets stringy when it is overcooked. However, some varieties of cheese, such as mozzarella, get stringy even when they are cooked properly.

To hasten melting without overcooking, use one of these methods:
• The smaller or thinner the piece of cheese, the faster it will melt. Cut the cheese into small pieces or very thin slices or grate or shred it. Don't cut it into large chunks.
• If possible, add the cheese during the last few minutes of cooking. Cook just long enough to melt it.
• If the cheese is to cook for any length of time, such as in a casserole, sprinkle a layer of buttered crumbs over the top of the casserole to keep the cheese from overcooking.

MICROWAVE COOKING

7-8MW. Microwaving cheese. Cheese overcooks easily in a microwave oven. When overcooked, it's stringy and tough and may also develop a grainy texture and separate into puddles of grease.

To avoid overcooking cheese, cook it on a lower power, usually no higher than 80%. If your oven has only High power, divide the cooking time into several shorter periods with carryover cooking in between. Check the food frequently for doneness.

If you're using cheese as a topping, put it on just before the rest of the food is done so it will cook only a short time. The heat from the cooked food will help to melt it.

8 Eggs

BUYING

8-1. Egg sizes and grades. Eggs are sold by size and grade. Both size and grade appear on the egg carton or on the tape sealing the carton.

Standards for egg sizes are set up by the U.S. Department of Agriculture. The size of the egg has no relation to quality. The most common egg sizes are:

Size	Minimum Weight Per Dozen
Extra large	27 oz. (765 g)
Large	24 oz. (680 g)
Medium	21 oz. (595 g)

Other sizes sometimes available are: Jumbo (30 oz. or 852 g); Small (18 oz. or 510 g); Peewee (15 oz. or 425 g).

Which size is the best buy? Today's prices change so rapidly that the best method is to figure out the price per pound for different sizes of the same grade. Prices are generally determined by the supply of eggs, not the size. Large sizes can often be a better buy than the smaller ones.

Eggs are graded by the U.S. Department of Agriculture as AA (or Fresh Fancy), A, B, and C. All grades have the same nutrients. However, the higher grades have a better appearance when broken out. Generally, stores carry Grades AA and A, occasionally B.

If appearance is important, such as in fried whole eggs or poached eggs, buy Grade AA. The egg is thick and firm and won't spread out as much as the lower grades. The yolk won't break as easily when the egg is cracked open. For other uses, buy Grade A.

8-2. Hints for buying eggs. Most recipes are developed for Large eggs.

Two or three eggs are considered an average serving for one person.

Buy eggs only from refrigerated cases. Eggs are highly perishable and lose quality quickly if they are kept at room temperature.

When selecting eggs, open the egg carton, if possible, to make sure the eggs are clean and whole. Dirty or cracked eggs could be contaminated and cause food-borne illness. If any eggs crack while bringing them home, use them as soon as possible in a fully cooked dish such as custard or meat loaf.

There's no difference in the nutritional value or quality of brown and white eggs. Certain breeds of hens lay brown eggs instead of white ones. The same applies to fertilized eggs— they are no more nutritious than unfertilized ones.

STORING

8-3. Keep eggs refrigerated. Store eggs in the refrigerator in the original container. Don't store them in the egg holder on the refrigerator door. Eggs absorb aromas and must be kept covered.

Don't wash eggs before storing them. Washing removes the protective coating which prevents bacteria from getting inside the shell and keeps the egg from drying out.

Raw eggs will keep in the refrigerator up to 5 weeks, depending on how fresh they were when you bought them.

If eggs are stuck in the cardboard container, don't try to force them out—you'll only crack them. Instead, wet the inside of the carton and the eggs will loosen. Transfer the eggs to another covered container for storage.

Refrigerate leftover cooked eggs and egg mixtures immediately. Use hard-cooked eggs within a week.

8-4. Freezing eggs. If you have leftover egg yolks or whites, you can freeze them for future use.

Freeze each white in a separate compartment in an ice cube tray, then store in a plastic container or clean jar with a tight-fitting lid.

Store yolks in a separate container. Add either ⅛ teaspoon salt or 1½ teaspoons sugar for every 4 yolks to keep them from thickening. Mark the container. Use yolks with sugar only for desserts.

To substitute whites or yolks for whole eggs, see 5-7, "Food equivalents."

Don't freeze cooked egg whites—they get tough and rubbery.

CONVENTIONAL COOKING

8-5. Eggs are a protein food. Because eggs are a protein food, they are sensitive to heat and must be cooked at low temperatures only until done. If cooked at high temperatures or too long, eggs become tough and rubbery.

8-6. Cooking eggs in the shell. Whole eggs crack as they cook because the air inside the eggs begins to expand as it heats. They are more apt to crack if you start them in warm or hot water. If eggs crack whenever you cook them, try one of the following:

• Before cooking the eggs, prick the large end of the egg with a pin or thumbtack. Most of the air is concentrated in the large end. The small hole gives the expanding air a means of escape so the shell remains intact.

• Add several tablespoons of vinegar to the cooking water. If the shell cracks, the acid in the vinegar coagulates the white so it does not run out of the crack.

• Start eggs in cold water.

To cook eggs, place them in a saucepan and cover with cold water. Cover the pan and bring the water to a boil. Remove the pan from the heat. For soft-cooked eggs, let the eggs stand in the hot water for 1 to 4 minutes, depending on how you like them. For hard-cooked eggs, let the eggs stand in the hot water for 12-15 minutes, depending on the size of the egg.

8-7. Discolored yolks in hard-cooked eggs. Yolks discolor because the eggs are overcooked. When eggs overcook, a chemical reaction takes place between the iron in the yolk and the hydrogen sulfide in the white. They combine to create another chemical, ferrous sulfide or iron sulfide, which forms a dark gray-green deposit around the yolk. Although harmless, the discoloration detracts from the appearance of the egg.

To keep hard-cooked eggs from discoloring, plunge them into cold water as soon as their cooking time is up. Let them stand in the cold water until thoroughly cooled. If the yolks are still discolored, it means the eggs stood too long in hot water.

If you're hard-cooking more than 3 or 4 eggs, use ice water to chill them after they are cooked. Stir occasionally and add more ice if necessary.

8-8. Peeling hard-cooked eggs. To peel hard-cooked eggs easily, cool them. Hot eggs are more difficult to peel. First crackle the shell by tapping it gently all over. Then roll the egg between the palms of your hands to loosen the shell. Peel, starting at the large end. Dip the egg into cold water to help ease off the shell.

If parts of the shell stick to the egg and are difficult to remove, it means the egg was very fresh.

8-9. To break a raw egg easily. Tap the egg firmly but gently in the center with the edge of a fork, knife or spatula so it cracks. If you tap the egg too hard, you might break the yolk. Don't crack an egg on the edge of the bowl—you might crush the shell, scattering pieces of the egg shell into the mixture.

If pieces of the shell fall into the mixture, remove them with a large piece of shell or with a clean spoon.

8-10. Poaching eggs. (See 4-4, "Poaching.") Poached eggs are cooked whole without the shell in hot water, milk, broth or other liquid. Use a shallow, lightly greased skillet filled with about 2 inches of liquid. Greasing the skillet keeps the eggs from sticking. Heat to boiling, then reduce the heat to simmering. (See 4-2, "Boiling" and 4-3, "Simmering.") To make whites thicken quickly and hold their shape, add ¼ cup of an acidic food, such as lemon juice or vinegar, to the water.

Break eggs, one at a time, into a small dish. Slide each egg into the simmering liquid, holding the dish as close to the water's surface as possible.

Cover the pan. Simmer until firm, usually 3 to 5 minutes.

Lift each poached egg out of the water with a slotted spoon, and rest the spoon on a paper towel briefly to drain the egg. Serve immediately.

8-11. Frying whole eggs. The challenge in frying whole eggs is to keep the yolk whole as you break the egg into the skillet. The simplest way to do this is to break the egg into a small dish first and then gently slide it from the dish into the skillet. Yolks seem to break more easily if the eggs are broken directly into the skillet.

When frying eggs, use a small amount, 1 or 2 Tablespoons, of butter or oil. Have the fat just hot enough so a drop of water sizzles.

Slip the eggs from the dish into the skillet. Reduce the heat immediately and cook slowly to the desired firmness. If the pan is too hot or the heat too high, the eggs develop a brown crust.

The part of the egg touching the pan will cook more quickly than the rest of the egg. If you wait for the top to cook, the bottom will be overcooked. To cook the tops of the eggs, you can spoon some of the hot butter over them or turn the eggs over with a pancake turner. Or add about a teaspoon of water to help create steam and put a lid on the skillet—the tops will cook quickly.

8-12. Scrambling eggs. When scrambling eggs, add a Tablespoon of liquid, such as water or milk, for every egg. The eggs scramble lighter and fluffier. If you want an all-yellow mixture, mix the eggs thoroughly. If you want streaks of yellow and white, mix them just slightly.

Use medium heat and a Tablespoon or two of butter. Pour the eggs into the skillet as soon as the butter melts and bubbles slightly. Don't stir the mixture in the skillet. Stirring makes the eggs mushy instead of fluffy.

As the egg mixture begins to set, gently draw a pancake turner completely across the bottom of the pan, forming large, soft curds. Repeat as needed until the eggs are thickened.

Remove the eggs from the skillet when they are just a little underdone. The heat in the eggs completes the cooking.

To add other food to scrambled eggs, such as chopped mushrooms, onions or green pepper, saute them first in a small amount of butter until tender. Then pour in the beaten eggs, stir just enough to mix and cook only until the eggs are done, following the procedure described above. If you use raw vegetables, they won't cook in the brief time it takes to cook the eggs. If you cook the mixture until the vegetables are tender, the eggs overcook.

8-13. Omelets. An omelet is a thick but light "pancake" made from beaten eggs, water and seasoning. Cooking an omelet takes patience, skill and organization. Since an omelet cooks in only a few minutes, all ingredients should be on hand and ready to use, including the filling.

Use a shallow pan with rounded sides. The sloping sides make it easier to use a pancake turner and to slide out the finished omelet.

Use medium heat. Pour the scrambled egg mixture into the pan when the butter has melted. If the butter is too hot or the heat too high, the egg mixture will stick to the pan.

Never stir or mix the egg mixture as it cooks. Instead, lift the cooked bottom occasionally with a pancake turner to allow the uncooked egg to flow under. Tilt the pan, move the cooked portion as needed and check to see that the omelet is not sticking to the pan.

When the omelet is still moist and creamy-looking, sprinkle a filling such as grated cheese or a spicy sauce over the top. With a pancake turner, fold the omelet in half and slide it out of the pan onto a plate.

8-14. To separate an egg. When separating eggs, don't separate them into the bowl you'll use for mixing. Instead, first let the white fall into a small dish or cup and then pour it into the mixing bowl. This is a safeguard in case the yolk breaks as you're separating the egg.

Egg yolk contains fat, which prevents the egg white from beating to a fluffy consistency. If the yolk breaks, don't try to use the white. Even a drop of egg yolk has enough fat to keep the white from beating up to a high volume. Instead, refrigerate the egg and use it in cooking or baking.

Eggs separate most easily when cold, so keep them refrigerated until you are ready to use them.

To separate an egg, use clean, fresh eggs. Crack an egg in the center. Hold the cracked egg in both hands over a cup or small bowl or dish, with one end pointed up. Remove the upper half of the shell. The yolk will remain in the bottom half as the white pours out. Gently move the yolk to the other shell half to allow the white in the bottom half to pour out. Do this several times. Be careful not to break the yolk. Place the yolk in a separate bowl. Pour the white out of the small bowl into the mixing bowl. Repeat the process with each egg.

8-15. Beating egg whites. Egg whites beat to their fullest volume when at room temperature. After separating cold eggs, let them stand at room temperature for about 30 minutes before beating.

Use a clean bowl and utensils. If the bowl or utensils have any fat residue, the egg white will not beat to a fluffy consistency. Avoid using a plastic bowl for beating egg whites— grease tends to stick to plastic and is difficult to wash off. Even the slightest amount of grease clinging to the plastic will keep the eggs from beating to full volume.

If you use an aluminum bowl, the action of the beater

against the aluminum may turn the egg whites a gray color. As whites are beaten, they change in color and texture— they become fluffy, white and, shiny. Egg whites can be beaten to any consistency called for in a recipe, such as foamy, soft peaks or stiff peaks.

• *Foamy whites.* At this stage, the air is beginning to mix with the whites. Bubbles and foam form on top but the whites are still transparent.

• *Soft peaks.* The mixture is white, shiny and at full volume. The whites stand up in peaks that bend over.

• *Stiff peaks.* The mixture is white, shiny and still at full volume but the peaks stand up straight.

Don't beat egg whites past the stiff-peak stage. Even a few extra seconds of beating can be too much. Overbeaten whites are dry and break up into pieces, allowing air to escape. They are difficult to blend with other ingredients. Overbeaten whites will not expand properly when heated. (See 20-8, "Air as a leavening.") If you use them in a mixture, it will have a dry texture, it won't rise to full volume and it may even collapse.

An acidic food such as cream of tartar helps to stabilize the beaten whites or foam. Some recipes call for vinegar or lemon juice, which also stabilizes the whites. If eggs are beaten in a copper bowl, the copper reacts with the whites the same as cream of tartar—it stabilizes the foam. A stainless steel or glass bowl with cream of tartar works just as well.

Salt decreases the stability of the foam, so don't add it directly to the whites. Add it to other recipe ingredients.

To combine beaten whites with other ingredients, pour the heavier mixture onto the beaten whites and blend with a folding motion. This means cutting into the mixture with the edge of a mixing spoon or rubber scraper. Cut down through the mixture, across, up and then across through the top of the mixture. Give the bowl a quarter turn about every 3 strokes as you fold. Don't lift the spoon out of the mixture—every time you do, you'll lose air and volume. Repeat the folding motion only until the mixture is well blended.

Unless specified otherwise in a recipe, never beat or stir beaten whites into a mixture. You'll beat out the air trapped in the foam and the product will not rise properly.

8-16. Meringues. A meringue is made by beating sugar and flavoring into egg whites. There are two types of meringues—soft and hard.

• *Soft meringue.* Soft meringue is most commonly used as a topping for baked desserts such as lemon cream pie. The usual ratio is 2 Tablespoons sugar to 1 egg white. A 3-egg-white meringue will cover a 9-inch pie. A soft meringue is beaten with the sugar just until soft peaks form. When spreading meringue on a pie, be sure it covers the edge of the pastry. This will seal and hold the meringue in place so it doesn't shrink as it bakes. Spread the meringue on hot filling. If spread on even slightly cool filling, the meringue may weep—a layer of liquid will form between the meringue and pie filling. Bake in a preheated oven at 350°F for 12 to 15 minutes or until the peaks are lightly browned. If overbaked either at too high a temperature or too long, the meringue will develop a tough, chewy skin.

• *Hard meringue.* Hard meringue is used in cookies or for dessert shells. The usual ratio is 4 Tablespoons sugar to 1 egg white. If you use too much sugar, the shells will be sticky. Beat the egg whites and sugar until stiff peaks form. To make meringue shells, shape on a cookie sheet or in a baking pan. Bake in a preheated oven at 225°F for 1½ hours. Turn off the oven and allow the shells to dry out in the oven for at least 1 hour. Cool. Fill them just as you would a pastry shell. If the weather is humid, you may find it difficult to dry the meringue —the shells may be sticky to the touch.

MICROWAVE COOKING

8-17MW. Whites and yolks cook at different rates. Because of fat content, yolks attract more microwaves and therefore cook faster than whites.

8-18MW. Egg in shell. Never cook eggs in the shell in the microwave oven. Heat and steam build up inside the egg, but the shell keeps them from escaping. As the pressure increases, the eggs explode.

8-19MW. Cooking power. Eggs are delicate and overcook easily, so they are best cooked at lower powers. If your oven has only High power, place a cup of water in the oven along with the eggs. Water absorbs some of the cooking power, but it will also increase the cooking time.

8-20MW. Cook eggs covered. Always cook eggs covered unless the recipe specifies otherwise. The cover helps to distribute the heat more evenly.

8-21MW. Pierce egg yolk before cooking. With a wooden pick or the tip of a sharp knife, always break the membrane of the egg yolk before cooking a whole egg. This allows heat and steam to escape. Otherwise, the yolk will explode as heat and steam build up quickly.

8-22MW. Scrambling eggs. When scrambling eggs, mix them very lightly with a fork. If you beat too much air into them, they'll be tough. To test scrambled eggs for doneness· they should still be moist on the bottom or look slightly underdone. Carryover cooking will complete the cooking.

8-23MW. Poaching eggs. Use only enough water to cover the eggs. Be sure to pierce each yolk to keep the egg from bursting. Sometimes eggs may jump out of the dish while being poached. The high fat content of the yolk attracts more microwave energy, creating more friction in the yolk than in the white. The friction makes the yolk "restless," and the egg "jumps around."

8-24MW. Reheating cooked eggs. Never reheat any cooked egg unless it is finely chopped. If you reheat a whole cooked egg, whether cooked in liquid, fried or poached, the yolk attracts more energy. Moisture and heat build up pressure quickly. If the egg doesn't explode in the oven, it may burst when you cut or bite into it.

9 Grains

BUYING

9-1. Kinds of rice. Several types of rice are sold:

• *Long grain rice* cooks dry and fluffy. It is used as an accompaniment to other foods.

• *Medium and short grain rice* cook firm and sticky. Because the grains tend to stick to each other, medium and short grain rice are most commonly used for croquettes, puddings and rice rings.

Rice is sold in several different forms:

• *Regular milled white rice* is the most popular and least expensive. During the milling process, the hull and bran are removed from the grain and the remaining rice kernel is polished. Because milling removes nutrients, white rice is enriched to add nutrients.

• *Brown rice* has only a small amount of bran removed. The remaining bran gives it a nutty flavor and chewy texture. Because less of the bran is removed, brown rice has more nutrients than white rice, but it does not keep as well. Brown rice takes a little longer to cook than white rice.

• *Parboiled or converted rice* is steamed before it is milled. The nutrients from the hull and bran are absorbed by the kernel and are not lost during milling. Parboiled rice is also enriched. It takes longer to cook than regular white rice.

• *Precooked rice* is cooked and dehydrated before packaging. It cooks quickly but costs more than regular white rice.

• *Wild rice,* technically, is not a rice but a wild grass. The dark brown grain has crisp texture and nut-like flavor. It grows wild in the Great Lakes region but is also being grown experimentally in other areas. Wild rice is extremely expensive because of the limited supply.

9-2. Buying rice. Decide which kind of rice you need. Read the label carefully to be sure you are buying the type best suited for your purpose.

Rice is sold in either plastic bags or packages with clear windows so you can examine the contents. Buy packages that contain whole grains. Rice broken into tiny particles will have lost nutrients and quality.

Be sure milled rice is enriched.

9-3. Kinds of pasta. Pasta includes all macaroni and noodle products. It is made from durum wheat, which is milled into semolina flour, a special flour that gives pasta its characteristic yellow color and nutty flavor. (See 20-2, "Kinds of flour.") Durum wheat also makes a harder product which holds its shape and firm texture when cooked. Macaroni products are made from durum wheat flour and water. Noodles have egg solids added for tenderness.

Pasta comes in about 200 different shapes, but these can be divided into four basic categories:

• *Hollow pasta* varies in length and is hollow on the inside. Some types are flat and curved to form a hollow. It includes long, thin macaroni, elbow macaroni and manicotti.

• *Long, thin pasta* is solid, not hollow. It includes vermicelli and spaghetti.

• *Flat pasta* is ribbon-like and comes in different widths and lengths. It includes noodles, lasagne and linguini.

• *Decorative pasta* comes in a variety of shapes such as shells, alphabets, wheels and twists. Some of the large shells can be stuffed.

Many of the different shapes can be used interchangeably to add interest to standard recipes.

9-4. Buying pasta. See 2-10, "Buying packaged food."

Read the label to be sure the pasta is enriched.

Look for packages with windows so you can examine the product.

If the shape is important, such as lasagne or manicotti, choose whole, unbroken pasta. Avoid crushed or damaged packages.

9-5. Buying other grains. Besides rice and pasta, the following grain products are also available:

• *Cornmeal* is ground milled corn, either white or yellow. Yellow cornmeal has more nutrients than the white.

• *Grits* are made from ground milled white corn, but they have a coarser texture than cornmeal. They are available in regular and instant form.

• *Bulgur* is precooked, dried, cracked wheat. A traditional food in the Middle East, bulgur has a nutty flavor and chewy texture. It can be used in place of rice.

• *Barley* is most commonly sold as pearl barley, which has the hull and bran removed. It has a mild flavor and a chewy texture. Barley is used mainly in soup but can also be cooked and served as a side dish.

• *Kasha (buckwheat groats)* is available either whole or coarsely ground. Kasha has a nutlike flavor with coarse texture. Traditional in eastern European cooking, it can be used as a side dish and a substitute for wild rice.

• *Triticale* is a hybrid cross of wheat and rye recently introduced in the United States. It is available as flour, flakes and berries. Triticale has a mild rye-wheat flavor.

• *Oats* are available in regular, quick-cooking and instant forms. While oats are considered a breakfast cereal they can also be used in cooking.

• *Wheat germ* is the embryo of the wheat kernel removed during the milling process. It is highly nutritious and flavorful and can be sprinkled on ready-to-eat foods or used in cooking.

• *Wheat bran* is the bran or outer husk of the wheat kernel removed during milling. It has a high fiber content. Although it is considered a breakfast cereal, it can also be sprinkled on ready-to-eat foods and used in cooking.

STORING

9-6. Storing grains.

• *Unopened packages.* Store unopened packages in a cool, dry storage area.

• *Opened packages.* Store the unused portion in a tightly sealed package. If the original package will not seal properly, transfer the contents to a plastic bag or container with a tight-fitting lid. Close securely to protect the contents from dirt and pests.

• *Whole grain products.* Whole grain products should be refrigerated if you plan to keep them for any length of time. They contain natural oils which can become rancid if kept too long in dry storage.

CONVENTIONAL COOKING

9-7. Cooking rice. Different types of rice require different cooking times and methods. Follow the directions on the package.

If overcooked, most rice is soft and sticky. When undercooked, it is hard and gritty and tough to chew.

Here are some hints for cooking rice:

• Don't rinse rice before or after cooking. You'll wash away valuable nutrients.

• Stir rice as little as possible. Stirring scrapes the starch off the grains, making the rice sticky.

• If you live in a very hard-water area, the minerals in the water may give cooked rice a yellowish tinge. You can overcome this by adding a little lemon juice to the cooking water.

• You can flavor rice by cooking it in milk, broth or juice instead of water.

• To keep rice warm or to reheat it, place it in a colander and cover. Set the colander over a pan of simmering water. The steam warms the rice without making it sticky.

• If you're cooking rice to use in a recipe that will be cooked, undercook the rice slightly so it won't get mushy with additional cooking.

9-8. Cooking pasta. To cook pasta, use 2 quarts of water for every half pound (8 ounces) of pasta. Add about a teaspoon of cooking oil to keep the water from foaming. It also helps to keep the pasta from sticking together.

Bring the water to a boil in a large kettle. Be sure the kettle is large enough to allow the pasta to move around freely. Otherwise, it may stick together as it cooks.

Add the pasta slowly so the boiling does not stop. If the boiling stops, the pasta will stick together. Stir occasionally to keep from sticking.

If pasta is to be served immediately, cook it only until tender. It should be firm in the center.

If the pasta is to be used in a recipe that will be cooked, shorten the boiling time just a little. The cooking will be completed as part of the recipe.

Drain pasta immediately and thoroughly in a strainer, wire basket or colander. Don't rinse with cold water—you'll wash away valuable nutrients.

You can reheat pasta or keep it hot by putting it in a strainer or colander. Cover and set it over simmering water. The steam will heat it and reduce sticking.

9-9. Cooking other grains. Except for ready-to-eat breakfast cereals, grains must be cooked. Since all require different cooking times and methods, follow package directions.

Here are some hints for cooking grains:

• When undercooked, most grains are chewy. If overcooked, they become sticky.

• Stir grains as they cook to keep them from lumping, sticking to the bottom of the pan, or scorching. However, stir them as little as possible once they begin to boil. If overstirred, they turn gummy and pasty.

• Since most grains are delicately flavored, be cautious when adding seasonings.

MICROWAVE COOKING

9-10MW. Microwaving rice. Generally, it takes about the same amount of time to cook rice in a microwave oven as it does the conventional way. Rice must absorb moisture in order to soften, and this process just can't be speeded up, no matter how fast the microwaves cook.

To cook long-grain rice in the microwave oven, combine 1 cup of rice with 2 cups of water. Cook for 8 minutes on High and let stand for carryover cooking. Stir halfway through the cooking time. Use a large enough container since rice has a tendency to boil over.

Stir the rice only once since it tends to get mushy if stirred too much.

To reheat, cook on High power in a covered casserole until it is steaming hot. Stir once about halfway through the heating time.

9-11MW. Microwaving pasta. Like rice, pasta needs time to absorb liquid in order to soften. As a rule, it takes just as long to microwave pasta as it does to cook it the conventional way.

If you prefer to cook pasta in the microwave oven, here are some guidelines:

• Because pasta sticks together easily as it cooks, stir it frequently during cooking.

• Pasta boils over easily. Use a large enough container and rub oil around the rim to keep it from boiling over.

• If you're adapting a conventional recipe to the microwave, precook the pasta. If you use uncooked pasta in a recipe, allow enough time for the pasta to absorb liquid and soften.

• To reheat pasta, cook it on High power for 1 to 2 minutes for every cup of cooked pasta.

• You can cook pasta for future use and freeze it. Drain the cooked pasta and stir in 1 or 2 Tablespoons butter to keep it from sticking. Freeze. Defrost first and then reheat.

9-12MW. Microwaving other grains. Grains, such as breakfast cereals, tend to boil over when cooked, so use a large enough pan or dish. Stir several times during cooking to prevent boil-overs and to distribute heat evenly.

Cover the pan during carryover cooking.

143

10 🍴 *Thickeners*

10-1. Using thickeners. Thickeners have two main purposes. They thicken liquids so they can be eaten, such as sauces, puddings and pies. In addition, thickeners are used to keep fat-liquid mixtures such as salad dressings and sauces from separating.

Many different foods can be used as thickeners but the most common ones for home cooking are flour, cornstarch, tapioca, eggs, gelatin, vegetables, arrowroot, potato starch, rice flour and rice starch.

Here are basic guidelines for using thickeners:

You cannot add a thickener by itself to a hot liquid—it will cook into lumps. Before it can be added to hot food, a thickener must be dispersed—it must be mixed with a small amount of another food such as sugar or a cold liquid. This separates the thickener granules. When they're added to hot liquid they won't clump together.

Each thickener has its own characteristics and must be used in a specific way. For best results, carefully follow directions for using each type of thickener.

Don't overcook thickened mixtures. Most thickeners will lose their thickening power if they are overcooked.

Cook the mixtures over low heat. If you use high heat, the liquid will evaporate quickly. Loss of liquid could make the mixture unpleasantly thick.

After cooking, the surface of a thickened mixture may dry out as it stands, forming a skin. To keep the skin from forming, press a piece of wax paper or plastic wrap over the surface of the mixture until ready to serve. Don't cover the surface with wax paper or plastic wrap while cooking.

CONVENTIONAL COOKING

All-purpose flour

10-2. Characteristics of all-purpose flour. Foods look opaque and pasty when thickened with flour. The foods most commonly thickened with flour include white sauce, brown sauce, soups, stews, gravies and some pies.

The following is a general guideline for the amount of all-purpose flour needed to thicken one cup of liquid to the degree of thickness indicated:

Thin sauce—1 Tablespoon all-purpose flour to 1 cup liquid.

Medium sauce—2 Tablespoons all-purpose flour to 1 cup liquid.

Thick sauce—3 Tablespoons all-purpose flour to 1 cup liquid.

If you use other flours such as whole grain, the proportions will differ, depending on the flour.

The thickening power of all-purpose flour is reduced by the following:

• Browning the flour. (See 10-5, "Brown sauce.")
• An acidic food such as vinegar, lemon juice, wine or tomatoes.
• A large amount of sugar.
• Overcooking.

10-3. To thicken with all-purpose flour. First measure the flour into a small bowl. Don't add it directly to the liquid—it will form lumps.

Gradually pour a small amount of cold liquid or water into the flour. Don't use hot liquid—it will cook the flour into a lump. Stir constantly to make a smooth paste. Use only enough liquid to make a thin mixture.

Very slowly pour the flour mixture into the liquid to be thickened, stirring constantly. Cook, stirring constantly, until the mixture thickens.

If all-purpose flour is used to thicken a fruit pie, it is generally mixed or sifted with the sugar and then combined with the fruit. If the pie filling is too thin, it has too little flour or the fruit may be too juicy or have a high acid content. If too thick, it has too much flour or the fruit is low in juices.

10-4. White sauce (also known as cream or bechamel sauce). To make a white sauce, use 1 Tablespoon butter for every Tablespoon of flour needed. (See 10-2, "Characteristics of all-purpose flour.") Melt the butter in a saucepan over medium

145

heat. Measure the flour and add to the melted butter, blending well. Cook and stir over low heat until the mixture bubbles. Be careful not to brown the flour as it will discolor the sauce and reduce the thickening power of the flour. If the flour is not cooked long enough, the sauce will have a pasty flavor. The cooked fat-flour mixture is call a "roux" and serves as the basis for many sauces and gravies.

Warm the milk or cream before adding it to the flour. If you add a cold liquid, it chills the fat-flour mixture and the sauce is more likely to lump. Begin by adding only a small amount of liquid to the flour mixture, stirring well to make a smooth paste. Continue adding the liquid gradually while stirring to keep the mixture smooth. Cook, stirring constantly, until the mixture thickens.

The white sauce is easy to vary:

• Use cream or part cream for a richer sauce. You can also add more butter.

• Add other foods such as grated cheese, prepared mustard, herbs, horseradish or sliced hard-cooked eggs.

• Instead of using milk for the liquid, use chicken, veal or beef stock.

10-5. Brown sauce. Use the same method outlined in 10-4, "White sauce." However, brown the flour well. Remember that browning reduces the thickening power of flour, so you'll need more flour in proportion to fat and liquid. How much more will depend on the degree of browning.

Browning the flour adds a distinctive flavor to sauces and other foods.

10-6. Beurre manie. Beurre manie is a kneaded mixture of butter and flour—another way of dispersing flour to add to hot mixtures. The advantage of this method is that you can make it up ahead of time and add it directly to hot liquids.

To make beurre manie, measure out equal amounts of butter and flour. Blend them together into a thick paste, using a fork, pastry blender or your fingers. Roll the paste into small balls. Or shape the mixture into a long roll or rectangle and cut off pieces as you need them. You can also pat the mixture out and cut it into squares. Use whatever method is most convenient for you. Refrigerate and use as needed. It will keep refrigerated for 2 to 3 weeks.

To use beurre manie, bring the liquid to be thickened to a simmer. Drop a small ball or square of beurre manie into the hot mixture. Begin with small amounts—you can always add more. Stir constantly as the mixture thickens, adding more beurre manie as needed. After the liquid has thickened to your liking, taste it. If it has a pasty or floury taste, let it simmer a little longer to cook the flour.

10-7. Problems. Some of these problems may occur when thickening food with flour:

• *Too thick.* Add more liquid, a little at a time, and stir constantly while cooking. Taste the mixture for flavor. You may have to add more seasoning.

• *Too thin.* Add more flour, using either the beurre manie method (see 10-6) or disperse the flour by stirring a small amount of cold liquid into it (see 10-3, "To thicken with all-purpose flour").

• *Lumps.* Beat the mixture briskly with a wire whip or a spoon. If that doesn't work, you may have to work it through a sieve to break up the lumps.

• *Floury flavor.* Simmer the mixture a little longer until the flour is cooked.

Cornstarch

10-8. Characteristics of cornstarch. Cornstarch is a fine, white, starchy flour made from corn. Liquid thickened with cornstarch does not turn opaque, but remains as clear as it was originally. Cornstarch is most commonly used in Oriental cooking and for thickening desserts such as fruit pies.

Cornstarch has twice the thickening power of flour. That means you need only half as much cornstarch as flour to thicken the same amount of liquid. One Tablespoon of cornstarch = 2 Tablespoons of all-purpose flour.

The thickening power of cornstarch is reduced by the following:

• Overcooking.

• An acidic food such as lemon juice, vinegar, wine or tomatoes.

• A large amount of sugar.

When judging the thickness of a cornstarch mixture, keep in mind that it will thicken as it cools.

10-9. To thicken with cornstarch. Measure the cornstarch into a small bowl. Don't add it directly to liquid—it will form lumps that cannot be broken up. Gradually, add a small amount of the cold liquid to be thickened, stirring constantly to form a smooth mixture.

Very slowly, pour the cornstarch mixture into the liquid to be thickened, stirring constantly. Cook over medium heat, stirring constantly, until the mixture thickens and becomes clear. Be careful not to overcook.

10-10. Problems. Some of the following problems can occur when thickening with cornstarch:

• *Too thin.* Add a little more cornstarch. First add a little cold water to the cornstarch and then pour it into the mixture.

• *Too thick.* Thin down by gradually stirring in a small amount of the liquid used in the mixture. Heat the liquid first. If you pour in cold liquid, the additional heat required to make it hot may overcook the cornstarch.

Tapioca

10-11. Characteristics of tapioca. Tapioca is a starch made from the root of the cassava, a tropical plant. Tapioca can be purchased as pearl tapioca and quick-cooking tapioca. The pearl tapioca must be soaked several hours before using while the quick-cooking can be cooked immediately.

When tapioca cooks, part of it dissolves to thicken the liquid and part of each granule turns into a small, semi-clear, jelly-like bead. The beads can be seen throughout the mixture.

Tapioca is generally used to thicken puddings and fruit pies.

Mixtures thickened with tapioca can usually be frozen, depending on the other foods in the mixture.

Following are general guidelines for the amount of tapioca to use, depending on the degree of thickening desired:

• *Puddings*—use 1½ Tablespoons of tapioca for every cup of liquid.

• *Fruit pie fillings*—use 1½ to 3 Tablespoons of tapioca for an 8- or 9-inch pie. The amount will depend on the size of the pie and the juiciness of the fruit.

• *Liquids, such as soup*—use 1½ to 3 Tablespoons for every quart (4 cups) of liquid.

Tapioca thickens as it cools.

10-12. To thicken with tapioca. Add the tapioca to the mixture as directed in the recipe. Be sure to blend the ingredients thoroughly so the tapioca granules are distributed evenly throughout the mixture. Cook or bake according to recipe directions.

10-13. Problems. Here are some problems that may occur when using tapioca:

• Excess stirring makes the mixture thick and sticky. Stir tapioca during cooking only if specified in the recipe. Don't stir tapioca as it cools.

• Not much can be done to change the thickness of a tapioca mixture once it has set. Make a note on the recipe to either reduce or increase the amount of tapioca next time.

Eggs

10-14. Eggs as thickeners. When eggs are cooked, the protein coagulates or thickens. Because of this characteristic, eggs or egg yolks are often used as thickeners. Besides their thickening properties, eggs add nutrients, richness, color and flavor to mixtures.

Eggs are generally used to thicken custards, puddings, cream pie fillings and sauces.

Two egg yolks have about the same thickening power as a whole egg. As a rule, 1 large egg will thicken 1 cup of liquid, but that depends on the other foods in the mixture. Sometimes a recipe calls for other thickeners, such as flour or cornstarch, in addition to the eggs.

Eggs will curdle easily and lose their thickening power under the following conditions:

• Added to a hot liquid.

• Mixed with an acidic food such as lemon juice.

• Overcooked.

If you can catch the mixture just as it is beginning to curdle, you may be able to save it by beating vigorously. It may help to add a Tablespoon or two of ice water or one or two ice cubes to lower the temperature and help prevent further curdling.

Once the mixture has completely curdled, there isn't much you can do to save it. Depending on the mixture, you can try to remove the lumps by straining it through a sieve lined with several layers of fine cheesecloth. Then try to thicken the mixture again. But if the mixture is a sauce, it might be better to start over.

If certain mixtures curdle every time you prepare them, try using another thickener along with the eggs, such as a little flour or cornstarch. Flour or cornstarch can stabilize the mixture and help keep it from curdling.

10-15. To thicken with eggs. Break the eggs into a bowl

and beat them lightly. Carefully pour a small amount of the hot or acidic liquid into the beaten eggs, stirring constantly. Pour the diluted egg mixture a little at a time into the remaining liquid, stirring constantly.

Cook or bake the mixture as the recipe directs.

10-16. Custards. A stirred custard is soft and is stirred during cooking. A baked custard is more firm and is baked in the oven. Never stir a baked custard as it is baking—it turns into a soft custard and will not regain its firmness.

The usual ratio is 1 egg and 1 teaspoon sugar for 1 cup milk. However, for a richer custard, you can use up to 4 eggs and 4 Tablespoons sugar for 1 cup milk. Adding more sugar makes the custard less firm and increases the cooking time. Adding more eggs makes the custard more firm and shortens the cooking time.

Gelatin

10-17. Characteristics of gelatin. A liquid thickened with gelatin is transparent, firm and springy. Gelatin is generally used in molded desserts and salads.

Two forms of gelatin are available—flavored and unflavored. In flavored gelatin, the gelatin granules have been dispersed with a large amount of sugar. You need only add the flavored gelatin to hot liquid as directed on the package. Boxes of commercially flavored gelatin come in different sizes. Directions on the package will tell you how much liquid the gelatin will thicken.

Unflavored gelatin granules must first be dispersed before they can be added to hot liquid. This is usually done by soaking unflavored gelatin in cold liquid. Generally, 1 Tablespoon or 1 envelope of unflavored gelatin will thicken 2 cups of liquid, but that depends on the liquid and other foods in the mixture.

The following can keep gelatin from thickening:

• Adding an acidic food such as lemon juice or vinegar.
• Using a large amount of sugar in the mixture.
• Adding solid foods such as fruits, vegetables or nuts.
• Adding canned fruits or vegetables without first draining them thoroughly.
• Using certain fresh or frozen fruits and juices containing enzymes that keep gelatin from setting. These include fresh and frozen pineapple, figs, mangoes and papayas. Use these

fruits and juices only in canned or cooked forms.
• Gelatin granules are not completely dissolved. The gelatin must be heated and stirred until all the granules are dissolved.
• The gelatin mixture is not refrigerated long enough, for at least several hours. Liquid will thicken much faster than a mixture of liquid and solid food.

Never freeze gelatin mixtures unless they are mixed with high-fat foods such as whipped toppings or cream. They become tough and rubbery.

Don't put a gelatin mixture in the freezer for even a short time to speed up the gelling process. The mixture will get gummy and the surface may crack.

If gelatin refuses to set, review your recipe. Analyze every step you took. If the gelatin wasn't dissolved completely, you might try to dissolve the gelatin by reheating the mixture and then refrigerating it. Otherwise, all you can do is start anew.

10-18. To thicken with unflavored gelatin. Pour ¼ cup cold water into a small bowl. Sprinkle 1 Tablespoon or 1 envelope of unflavored gelatin over the water. Do not stir. Merely let the granules soak until they have absorbed all of the moisture. As soon as all the cold water has been absorbed, mix the gelatin with hot liquid.

If the liquid cannot be heated, such as whipping cream, soften the gelatin in ¼ cup cold water. Then heat the softened gelatin over hot water until it is completely dissolved. Mix the dissolved gelatin into the liquid, which should be at least at room temperature.

10-19. Solid food in gelatin mixtures. To keep solid food such as fruits and vegetables from floating or sinking in a gelatin mixture, let the gelatin thicken until it is syrupy. Then gently stir in the food.

10-20. Molded gelatin. (See 10-17 to 10-19 on using gelatin as a thickener.) Gelatin mixtures are often made in a decorative mold to give them an attractive shape.

When making a molded gelatin mixture, follow the recipe carefully. You must have exact amounts of liquid and other foods in relation to the amount of gelatin. Otherwise, the mixture may not thicken.

Pour the mixture into a lightly oiled mold. The oil helps the molded gelatin come out of the mold more easily. Chill until the mixture is firm.

To unmold, rinse a serving plate in cold water so it will be easier to slide the mold to the center of the plate. Do not dry the plate.

Dip the mold into warm (not hot) water just to the depth of the gelatin for about 5 seconds. Don't use hot water—it'll melt the gelatin. Lift the mold from the water and continue to hold it upright.

Carefully loosen the gelatin from the side of the mold with the tip of a sharp knife. Tilt or shake the mold gently to loosen the gelatin.

Place the serving plate upside down on top of the mold. Turn the plate and mold together so the plate is right side up and the mold with the gelatin is resting on the plate. Shake gently to loosen the gelatin. Lift the mold slightly and slide the gelatin into place in the center of the plate. Lift the mold off.

If the gelatin doesn't come out the first time, repeat the process.

Other thickeners

10-21. To thicken with vegetables. Some vegetables are high in starch and can be used to thicken soups, stews, gravies and sauces. These vegetables include cooked potatoes, peas, lima beans and legumes (dried beans, lentils and peas). This is a practical way to use leftover cooked starchy vegetables.

To thicken with cooked vegetables, puree or mash them, using a food mill, blender or a fine-screened strainer. Add them to the liquid to be thickened. Heat.

Vegetables vary in their thickening power, depending on the amount of starch they contain. You may have to experiment a few times to get the correct proportions.

10-22. Less common thickeners. Arrowroot, potato starch, rice starch and waxy rice flour are among many less commonly used thickeners. Each has its own characteristics and method of preparation, as follows:

• *Arrowroot has twice the thickening power of flour. 1 Table-*spoon arrowroot = 2 Tablespoons flour. Use it as you would flour. Arrowroot gives a very transparent mixture. It will thin if stirred too much.

• *Potato starch* has the same properties as arrowroot.

• *Rice starch* has the same properties as cornstarch.

• *Waxy rice flour* gives the same results as all-purpose flour but is less likely to lump. It gives more satisfactory results with sauces and gravies that are to be frozen—they are less likely to curdle and separate when thawed. It has less thickening power than flour. Use 4 or 5 Tablespoons of waxy rice flour for every 2 cups of liquid.

MICROWAVE COOKING

10-23MW. Containers. A 4-cup glass measuring cup is a convenient container for preparing sauces in the microwave oven. If the sauce contains milk, be sure the container is large enough to allow the sauce to foam up without boiling over. Use wax paper as a cover.

10-24MW. Flour-base sauces. Sauces thickened with flour are likely to lump, so be sure to stir the mixture frequently. If lumps form, work them against the sides of the container with a wooden spoon until they disappear.

10-25MW. Sauce thickened with flour or cornstarch. If the sauce contains flour or cornstarch, it must cook long enough to boil in order to thicken. A flour sauce must also cook long enough to eliminate the floury flavor.

10-26MW. Sauce thickened with egg yolk. If the sauce is thickened with egg yolk, don't boil it—it will curdle. Stir the sauce frequently to distribute the heat evenly. Otherwise, parts of the sauce may overcook and curdle.

10-27MW. Hollandaise sauce. Allow the melted butter to cool slightly before adding the remaining ingredients. If the butter is too hot, the sauce may curdle. Do not add lemon juice directly to the milk but add it to the mixture as the last ingredient.

10-28MW. Custards. Don't stir baked custard when cooking it in the microwave oven—it won't set. Instead, rotate the containers.

10-29MW. Dissolving unflavored gelatin. Soften 1 Tablespoon unflavored gelatin in ½ cup cold water. Be sure the gelatin is completely soaked. Microwave on High power for 45-60 seconds, stirring once about halfway during cooking.

STORING

10-30. Storing thickened foods. Refrigerate leftover thickened foods immediately.

If gelatin mixtures are allowed to set out at room temperature for any length of time, they begin to melt.

Mixtures thickened with flour may not freeze well. They may separate when thawed.

Seasonings

BUYING

11-1. Kinds of seasonings. Herbs are plants grown in temperate climates. Not all herbs are used for cooking. Aromatic herbs are prized for their fragrance, some herbs are poisonous and many are used purely for medicinal purposes.

Cooking herbs can be used either fresh or dried. Fresh herbs can be purchased in some stores or you can grow them in your garden. The easiest way to use herbs is to buy commercially dried herbs—whole leaves, ground or crushed.

Spices come from plants grown in the tropics. They are sold most commonly in a dried, ground form. Some, however, are sold whole, such as nutmeg, cloves, peppercorns and cinnamon bark. Whole spices can be easily ground with special little grinders or graters.

Chemicals are also used as seasoning. The most common one is sodium chloride, also known as salt. Sodium is a crystalline substance, abundantly available in nature. Most foods naturally contain sodium, although some have larger amounts than others.

Sauces are commercially prepared mixtures used to season food. *Worcestershire sauce* is a dark, spicy and somewhat vinegary sauce which not only adds a distinctive flavor to foods but also a darker color. *Hot pepper sauce,* made from hot red chili peppers and vinegar, is extremely hot and should be used carefully, drop by drop. *Bitters* is a clove-flavored sauce with a slightly pink color. *Soy sauce,* essential in Oriental cooking, is a fermented sauce made of soy beans.

Mustards are pungent seasonings made of ground mustard seeds combined with other ingredients. Many varieties are available: *American mustards* are usually mild and bright yellow. *French mustards,* such as Dijon, are a blend of ground mustard seed with spices and wine or grape juice; flavors vary from sharp to delicate. *English mustard* is a combination of ground mustard seeds with liquid but without spices or vinegar, resulting in a very hot, yellow mustard. *German mustards* vary considerably, from those with only flour and vinegar added to those combined with herbs and spices.

Vinegars are acidic liquids and add a distinctive sour flavor to foods. Vinegars are made from soured or fermented alcohol or wine, and vary in strength and color. *Distilled white vinegar* is generally the most mild, with about a 4% acid content. *Wine, cider* and *malt vinegars* have a slightly higher acid content—between 5% and 6%. *Herb vinegars* are made by adding herbs to any vinegar.

Aromatic fruits and vegetables with distinctive flavors can be used as seasonings. Some of the most popular include lemons, limes, oranges, garlic, onions, celery, parsley, chives, leeks, .shallots, green or red peppers and chili peppers.

11-2. Guidelines for buying seasonings.

Because seasonings are generally used in small amounts, buy small jars or bottles unless you plan to use them up quickly. Herbs and spices in particular lose their flavor and aroma quickly, especially if they are not stored properly.

Buy herbs and spices in metal containers rather than in glass jars. Exposure to light causes loss of color and flavor.

If you must buy herbs and spices in glass jars, check the contents carefully for color. Rotate the jar—if any of the herbs look faded, you'll know they've been exposed to light for a long time.

If you have a choice of brands of whole herbs and spices, buy the brand with larger pieces rather than small or broken ones.

STORING

11-3. Storing seasonings. As a rule, most seasonings can be stored in a dark, cool, dry area. However, check the label for storage instructions. Some seasonings, such as mustard, may contain perishable ingredients and must be refrigerated.

Be sure the containers are tightly closed.

Herbs and spices in clear glass jars may look attractive on open kitchen shelves, but light and heat cause loss of color and flavor. Herbs and spices in cans or dark glass jars may be stored on open shelves, away from heat.

11-4. Seasonings lose their flavor. Write the purchase date on containers so you'll know how long you've had the seasonings.

While shelf life varies depending on storage conditions, don't expect seasonings you bought 6 or 8 months ago to give the same flavor results as newly purchased ones. You may have to add a little more after you've tasted the food. If you're making a special recipe that depends on seasonings, it may be worthwhile to buy new ones.

11-5. Freezing dried herbs and spices. Keep jars of seldom-used herbs and spices in the freezer. The cold temperatures and darkness may increase their shelf life. Be sure the containers are tightly sealed.

FRESH HERBS

11-6. Availability of fresh herbs. You can often buy fresh herbs such as basil and dill in some supermarkets, specialty stores or farmers' markets. Or if you wish, you can grow them in your garden.

Basic gardening books and local garden supply stores give you information on growing herbs in your area.

Herb growing can turn into a profitable hobby—gourmet cooks and some restaurant owners may be willing to buy your surplus. Some enterprising herb growers have formed herb co-ops and provide a regular supply of fresh herbs to supermarkets, restaurants and gourmet cooks in the area.

11-7. Harvesting fresh herbs. Herb leaves have the most potent flavor and aroma just before the plant begins to bloom.

The day before harvesting, hose the plants down to wash off as much dirt and dust as possible. The next day, wait until the dew dries from the plants before picking them.

If necessary, rewash the plants gently under cold running water, being careful not to bruise the leaves. Let the herbs drain thoroughly and pat as dry as possible with paper toweling, but don't bruise the leaves. Bruising releases the oils, causing loss of flavor and aroma.

11-8. Drying fresh herbs. Air dry herbs in a warm, dry, well-ventilated area such as a breezeway, attic or room. If possible, avoid drying herbs in an oven—even the lowest temperatures are too high. The herbs can scorch and lose aromatic oils.

For air drying, use small brown paper bags to protect the herbs. Tie a small bunch of one kind of herb together at the stem with string. Cut a small hole in the bottom of a paper bag. Place the tied herbs in the bag, stems down, and push the tied stems through the hole. Turn the bag upside down, holding the herbs by the stems protruding from the hole. The bag will protect the herbs from dust. Use the string tied around the stems to hang the bunch of herbs for drying.

Drying time will depend on temperature and moisture in the air. Dry herbs should be brittle and yet retain a pleasing natural color. To find out if the herbs are dried, place several dried leaves in a tightly closed glass jar. If any mold, discoloration or condensation develops, continue drying.

11-9. Storing home-dried herbs. For longest shelf life, store home-dried herbs in lightproof containers, such as dark-colored glass containers, metal cans or pottery jars. Seal the containers tightly to keep out moisture. Write the date on the container.

11-10. Freezing fresh herbs. Fresh herbs are easy to freeze, either in individual packages or in bulk:

• *Individual packages.* Measure out recipe-size portions and wrap each in individual packets of freezer wrap or heavy-duty plastic. Label and freeze. For easy handling in the freezer, staple packets to a heavy sheet of paper or cardboard. Freeze. Pull off each packet as needed.

• *Bulk.* Spread the leaves out on a baking sheet and place in the freezer. Freeze 24 hours. Check regularly and loosen and turn the leaves so they won't freeze together in a solid mass. Transfer the loose frozen leaves into a large heavy-duty plastic bag and keep frozen. Use as needed.

Don't defrost frozen herbs before using—they become limp and difficult to handle. Frozen herbs cannot be used as garnishes but use them in cooking just as you would the fresh.

CONVENTIONAL COOKING

11-11. Cooking with fresh herbs. Fresh herbs do not have as strong a flavor as dried. As a general rule, you will need 2 Tablespoons of fresh herbs to replace ¼ teaspoon ground or ½ teaspoon crushed dried herbs. However, this will vary with the herb, since some fresh herbs have a stronger flavor than others.

Be safe—begin with a small amount, taste for flavor and add more if needed.

To "chop" fresh herbs, cut them with scissors.

11-12. Experiment with seasonings. Always begin your experiment by adding small amounts. Once you've overseasoned a food, there's very little you can do to change the flavor.

Keep in mind that heat brings out the flavor of food. When you add seasonings, let the food cook about 10 minutes before you taste it again. If more is needed, wait another 10 minutes before tasting after the second addition.

11-13. Increasing recipes. When you're increasing recipes, don't automatically increase the seasoning by the same amount as you increase the recipe. If a recipe calls for a Tablespoon of Worcestershire sauce and you double it and add 2 Tablespoons, you may find the flavor a little too strong. Use the amount of seasoning for a single batch of the recipe and increase it gradually, if necessary, only after tasting the mixture.

11-14. Don't overcook herbs and spices. As a general rule, herbs and spices should be added to a mixture during the last 30 to 45 minutes of cooking. If they cook longer, they can lose their original flavor and become bitter.

11-15. How to remove whole herbs and spices. You may want to remove whole herbs and spices, such as bay leaf or peppercorns, after the mixture has cooked. To do this easily, use a metal tea ball or tie the seasonings in a cloth bag. When the mixture has cooked, remove the bag or ball.

11-16. Crush herbs. When using dried herbs such as basil or thyme, crush them first to release the flavor. Hold them in the palm of one hand and crush them with the thumb of the other hand. Or, if you prefer, use a mortar and pestle.

11-17. Fines Herbes. Fines Herbes is usually a mixture of fresh parsley, tarragon, chives and chervil, added near the end of the cooking time. It is frequently used in soups, sauces and casseroles containing cheese and eggs. Some stores carry a commercially prepared dried Fines Herbes mixture.

159

11-18. Bouquet garni. Bouquet garni generally consists of a combination of aromatic vegetables and herbs such as a celery rib, leek, parsley, thyme, bay leaf, onion, garlic and clove. You can use whatever combination you like. The seasonings are tied together in a bundle or in a cloth bag or placed in a tea ball.

11-19. Aromatic vegetables. Aromatic vegetables such as carrots, parsley, celery, onions and garlic can be used to season foods such as soups and then removed when the food has cooked.

If you're adding aromatic vegetables to a mixture, such as meatloaf or a casserole, first chop them and saute in a small amount of butter. Add the flavored butter to the mixture along with the sauteed vegetables. Sauteing not only releases their flavor but also softens them. You can also steam them. If they are not cooked first, they may not cook completely in the mixture and may be a little tough or chewy.

11-20. Aromatic fruits. Consider using fresh aromatic fruits in place of sauces and dressings. For instance, mix a small amount of citrus juice with yogurt as a salad dressing. Or sprinkle orange juice over cooked carrots just before serving, or lemon juice over fish.

Grate lime, lemon or orange rind for use in salad dressings, sauces and butters served over hot food.

11-21. Deglazing or meat as a flavoring. Crisp meat particles sticking to the pan after browning meat can be used as a flavoring.

After the browned meat is removed, add a little liquid to the pan and simmer until the particles loosen. Use the seasoned liquid as a base for gravy and sauces or add it to soups and stews.

11-22. Problems. Here are some common problems that may occur when seasoning food:
• *Too much salt.* If the recipe can use a potato, dice a raw peeled potato and add to the mixture. The potato will absorb some of the salt. Depending on the recipe, you can also try adding a little vinegar or a little sugar, both of which tend to neutralize salty mixtures.
• *Too much other seasoning.* There isn't much you can do. But make a note on the recipe to begin with smaller amounts the next time.

• *Too little seasoning.* Add more seasonings, if possible. If you've followed the recipe carefully, it may be a signal that the seasonings have outlived their shelf life and need to be replaced.

• *Bitter flavor.* The herbs and spices may be overcooked. Try adding them a little later in the cooking period the next time.

MICROWAVE COOKING

11-23MW. Drying fresh herbs in the microwave oven. Because the microwave oven works so quickly, it's easy to overdry fresh herbs in the microwave oven. Herbs discolor, scorch easily and lose their aromatic oils. Room drying generally gives the most satisfactory results.

Fruits

BUYING

12-1. Buying fresh fruits. The quality of fresh fruits depends on their maturity and ripeness. Maturity means the fruits have reached their full size. Ripeness means the fruits have softened just enough to have a pleasing texture and full flavor.

Unripened mature fruits will ripen in a few days if allowed to stand at room temperature.

Immature fruits are smaller than their normal size with poor color and texture. Immature fruits will never ripen to full color, texture and flavor.

When buying fresh fruits, look for these characteristics:

• *Firm to the touch.* Test a fruit by pressing it gently. If it gives just a little, it's ripe enough to eat. Don't squeeze it hard—you'll bruise and damage it.

• *Right color.* Except for naturally green fruits such as grapes, green gage plums, limes, pears and certain varieties of apples, a green color means the fruits are underripe. Some oranges turn green after they are picked but this does not affect their eating quality as oranges are fully ripe when picked. Most fruits, however, should have little or no green color. If they are too green, they will not ripen. There are three exceptions—avocadoes, pears and bananas. All three are usually picked green and ripen after they are picked.

• *Well shaped.* Each type of fruit has its own characteristic shape. A misshapen fruit probably has other problems, such as poor flavor or texture.

• *Proper texture.* Fruits should be plump and firm. Avoid any that are dry, withered, too soft or too hard.

- *In the right stage of ripeness.* Overripe fruits lack flavor.
- *Aromatic.* Ripe fruits usually have a pleasant, characteristic aroma. This is a dependable way to select fruits such as pineapple or cantaloupe. However, if fruits have been refrigerated, the aroma may not be noticeable because they are cold.
- *Heavy for their size.* Heaviness usually means the fruits are juicy.

Avoid fruits that are damaged, decayed, mildewed or discolored. Poor quality fruits have lost nutrients and won't keep well. No matter how low the price, they're no bargain.

Some types of discoloration are harmless. Apples and grapefruit sometimes have a brown scale but this does not affect their eating quality.

12-2. Buying canned fruits. Read the labels to be sure you are getting the kind you want.

Buy the form best suited to your needs. If you're serving canned fruit for dessert, you may want the more expensive whole fruit because it looks better. If you're baking a pie or making a molded salad, the less-expensive slices or pieces will do.

Fruit packed in heavy syrup has a high sugar content, so buy fruit packed in its own juices or in water.

See 2-9, "Buying canned food," for general guidelines.

12-3. Buying frozen fruits. Fruits such as cherries, berries, peaches and rhubarb are available frozen. Some may be sweetened with sugar. See 2-11, "Buying frozen food," for general guidelines.

12-4. Buying dried fruits. Dried fruits are packaged in boxes or in plastic bags. Some may also be sold loose by the pound.

Select fairly soft, pliable fruit with a good color. Avoid hard fruit—it's too dry.

12-5. Buying fruit juices. Read the label. Sometimes a fruit juice is mixed with other liquids, such as water. If it is not 100% fruit juice, it cannot be called "fruit juice" on the label. It will be called a "fruit drink" such as "diluted orange juice drink." Or it may have a name that implies it contains fruit juice. The label must tell you the percentage of fruit juice in the drink, such as 10% or 20%.

Since fruit is naturally sweet, avoid fruit juices with added sugar.

STORING

12-6. Storing fresh fruits. Handle fresh fruits gently. They are highly perishable and can be easily damaged if you mistreat them.

Allow unripe fruits to stand at room temperature to ripen. It helps to put the fruits in a brown paper bag. Don't use a plastic bag unless it has a few holes in it for air to circulate. Otherwise, the fruit may start to spoil.

Refrigerate ripe fruits.

Wash all fruits thoroughly before storing, except citrus fruits, berries, grapes and cherries. Dry well.

Citrus fruits such as oranges, grapefruit, lemons and limes can be stored at room temperature, but they'll keep longer if you refrigerate them.

Once bananas ripen, refrigerate them. The skin turns dark and looks unappetizing, but the eating quality remains.

Sort berries and cherries; remove damaged or decayed ones. Return the fruits to their original basket or put them in a shallow bowl. Store in the crisper or refrigerate in a plastic bag or in a covered container. Wash just before serving.

Grapes are sold only ripe. Refrigerate at once and use as soon as possible. Wash just before serving.

Fruits with a strong aroma, such as cantaloupe, should be wrapped in plastic for storage. This will keep the aroma from spreading throughout the refrigerator and flavoring other foods such as milk or fats.

Store cut fruits in an airtight container or wrap in foil or plastic.

Most fresh fruits, except for citrus, should be used within a few days. Their keeping quality will depend on how fresh they were when you bought them, how they were handled and the temperature of your refrigerator.

12-7. Storing canned fruits and juices. Store unopened cans in a cool, dry storage area. Once opened, transfer food to a storage container, refrigerate and use within a day or two.

12-8. Storing frozen fruits and juices. See 3-4, "Freezer storage," for storing frozen foods.

12-9. Storing dried fruits. If packages are unopened, store them in a cool, dry place.

Because dried fruits are naturally high in sugar, opened

packages attract insects. After opening, store dried fruits in airtight containers in the refrigerator.

SERVING FRUIT

12-10. Wash unpeeled fruit thoroughly. Dirt and bacteria may be clinging to the fruit. Some fruits, such as apples, may be waxed.

12-11. Keep cut fruits from turning brown. Fruits with a high acid content, such as grapefruit and oranges, do not turn brown because the acid prevents browning. Most fresh fruits, however, turn brown when cut.

To keep cut fresh fruit from turning brown, coat it with lemon, grapefruit, orange or pineapple juice. You can also buy an ascorbic acid mixture which keeps cut fruit from darkening.

12-12. Serving frozen fruits. Thawed frozen fruits soften and lose their shape when completely thawed. Serve frozen fruits before they are completely thawed. Enough ice crystals should remain so the fruits hold their shape.

12-13. Using canned fruits. Canned fruits to be used in recipes should be drained thoroughly. If you don't have time to drain them, make allowance in the recipe for the additional liquid in the canned fruits.

If fruits are canned in heavy syrup, drain them well even if you're just serving them right out of the can. The syrup is high in sugar and calories.

If fruits are packed in water or in their own juices, serve the liquid along with the fruits.

12-14. Serving dried fruits. Dried fruits make nutritious snacks in place of candy. However, dried fruits are higher in calories than an equivalent amount of fresh or frozen fruit. Dried fruits are concentrated, with about 80% of the water removed during the drying process. It takes about 4 or 5 pounds of fresh fruits to make 1 pound of dried fruits.

CONVENTIONAL COOKING

12-15. Cooking destroys nutrients. Fruits served raw give you the most nutrients. Heat and light destroy nutrients in cooked fruits, such as the vitamin C. However, you may want to cook fruits to add variety to meals.

Fruits can be cooked by poaching or stewing, sauteing, broiling and baking.

12-16. Poaching and stewing fruit. (See 4-4, "Poaching," and 4-5, "Stewing.") Fruits for poaching are generally left whole. Large fruits for stewing are usually cut into smaller pieces.

You can stew fruits in liquid so they hold their shape or you can puree them to make a thick sauce. The result you want determines when you add sugar to the mixture.

Cooking breaks down fruit fiber, making it soft and tender. Sugar helps fruits retain their shape when they are cooked. So does an acidic food, such as lemon juice.

If you want fruits to retain their shape, add a little lemon juice at the beginning of the cooking time. Or add only a small amount of sugar. Fruits cooked with too much sugar may shrivel and shrink instead of remaining plump and tender.

If you want to puree fruits or want a mushy mixture, don't add sugar or a high-acid fruit juice until the fruits are thoroughly cooked and tender.

To poach or stew fruits so they hold their shape, select fruits that are in good condition. Pare them, if necessary. Leave them whole or cut them into fairly large pieces such as quarters. Remove seeds if the fruits are cut.

Cook the fruits slowly in a liquid with a small amount of sugar over low heat until done.

To make a fruit sauce, pare the fruits, remove the seeds and cut the fruits into small pieces so they will cook quickly. Put the fruits in a pan with a small amount of water or fruit juice. Don't use a high-acid juice such as lemon or orange juice. Cover. Cook over medium heat. Stir occasionally to break fruits apart. When done, add sugar and seasonings to taste.

To make a smooth sauce, mash the cooked fruits by putting them through a food mill, strainer or blender.

12-17. Cooking dried fruits. Dried fruits cook faster if they are presoaked, unless package directions specify otherwise. To save nutrients, cook the fruit in the liquid in which it soaked. Presoaking also helps to keep the fruit plump.

12-18. Sauteing fruits. (See 4-15, "Panfrying, sauteing, stir-frying.") Sauteed fruits are generally served as accompaniments to main dishes. Select firm fresh or canned fruits which hold their shape, such as apple, pear and pineapple slices and banana halves. Frozen fruits are generally too mushy to saute.

Saute in a small amount of butter until the fruits are lightly

166

browned. Turn carefully with a pancake turner so the pieces don't break up.

12-19. Broiling fruits. (See 4-21, "Broiling.") Any tender fruits, fresh or canned, that hold their shape may be broiled. These include bananas sliced lengthwise, pineapple slices and grapefruit and peach halves.

Be careful not to let fruits dry out as they broil. To protect them, brush with melted butter. You can also use a topping such as brown sugar or seasoned crumbs to protect them from the direct heat.

12-20. Baking fruits. (See 4-20, "Cooking in dry heat.") You can bake fruits whole, halved or cut into pieces. Several fruits may be baked together in a sweet sauce so their flavors blend, such as bananas and pears in an orange juice sauce.

Apples, probably the most popular baked fruit, are usually baked whole with the skins left on and the cores removed. A sweetened filling, such as sugar and cinnamon, is placed in the cavities. Some varieties of apples bake better than others. Rome is considered one of the top baking apples because it holds its shape.

When preparing apples for baking, cut a thin slit through the skin around the center of the apple. This allows steam to escape from the apple as it bakes and keeps the skin from bursting.

MICROWAVE COOKING

12-21MW. Overcooked fruits. Fruits cook especially fast in the microwave oven so avoid overcooking.

12-22MW. Cover fruits when microwaving. Unless the recipe specifies otherwise, cover fruits when cooking. This allows more even heat distribution.

Vegetables

BUYING

13-1. Kinds of vegetables. Vegetables are classified according to the part of the plant they come from. While all vegetables are high in fiber, stems and skins contain the most. Some parts are higher in calories than others.

Following is a brief summary of the different parts of plants that are eaten and their characteristics:

High water content and low in calories:

• Fruits such as cucumber, eggplant, okra, pepper and summer squash.

• Flowers such as broccoli and cauliflower.

• Stems such as asparagus, celery and the stems of broccoli.

• Leaves such as Brussels sprouts, cabbage, greens, lettuce and spinach.

• Roots such as carrots.

Because these parts store food for the plant, they are high in starch and relatively higher in calories:

• Seeds such as beans, corn and peas.

• Tubers such as potatoes.

13-2. Buying fresh vegetables.

Handle vegetables with care—they bruise easily.

Most fresh vegetables should be used within 2 to 5 days. Root vegetables will last from 1 to several weeks. Buy only the amount you need and can use during the storage life of the vegetable.

Look for these characteristics when buying fresh vegetables:

• *Peak of ripeness.* Vegetables will not ripen in storage. If they're not ripe when you buy them, they'll have poor texture and flavor.

• *Color and texture.* They should have a bright characteristic color and a crispy texture.
• *Good typical shape.* Misshapen ones are usually poor in texture and flavor.
• *Medium size.* The vegetable should feel heavy in relation to its size. Extra-large ones may be overripe, coarse and have poor flavor. Extremely small ones are immature and lack flavor.
Unless you plan to use the tops, buy topless root vegetables such as carrots and beets. Tops draw moisture from the roots, causing the vegetables to wilt.
Root vegetables should not be sprouting. Sprouts mean they have been stored too long.
Don't buy wilted, decayed or damaged vegetables, no matter how low the price. They have lost nutrients and won't last long.

13-3. Buying canned vegetables. Buy the form—whole, sliced or pieces—suitable for your needs. See 2-9, "Buying canned food," for general information.

13-4. Buying frozen vegetables. Frozen vegetables come in small cartons or in large plastic bags, varying in size. Vegetables in cartons are usually frozen in a solid block, so the whole carton must be used. Those in plastic bags are frozen loose. Use whatever amount you want and return the remainder to the freezer. See 2-11, "Buying frozen food," for general information.

13-5. Buying dried vegetables. Most of the moisture has been removed from dried vegetables, which means they can be stored without refrigeration.
The most common dried vegetables are legumes: dried beans, peas and lentils. Over 30 different varieties are available, varying in color, texture and flavor.
Other dried vegetables include chives, mushrooms, onions, parsley flakes, potatoes and sweet potatoes. Since dried vegetables are generally sold in packages, see 2-10, "Buying packaged food," for general information.
Dried legumes are usually packaged in plastic bags or in packages with a window so you can see the contents. Follow these additional guidelines when buying dried legumes:
• Look for good, uniform, bright color. Loss of color means lack of freshness.

• The legumes should be of uniform size. If the sizes within a package vary, you won't get good results—the smaller ones will cook faster than the larger ones.

• Check for visible defects. Foreign materials, cracked skins and small insect holes are signs of low-quality products.

STORING

13-6. Storing fresh vegetables. Except for root vegetables, fresh vegetables are highly perishable. Refrigerate them as soon as you bring them home and store in the crisper or in plastic bags to prevent drying.

Wash before refrigerating only if needed to remove soil. Wash them quickly and shake out the excess water. Never soak vegetables—they lose water-soluble nutrients.

Core iceberg lettuce before storing. Hold the head with both hands, core side down. Hit the core hard against the counter top or any other flat nonbreakable surface. The core will loosen and can be removed easily with your fingers. Run cold water into the hole, turn the head over and let drain. Store in a covered container or plastic bag. The leaves will be ready to use as needed.

Refrigerate root vegetables such as carrots and beets.

Store potatoes and sweet potatoes in a cool, dry area. Do not refrigerate them. The humidity in the refrigerator will cause them to mold and spoil. In addition, the cold temperatures in the refrigerator turn the starch in potatoes into sugar, affecting flavor and texture. The increase in sugar darkens the potatoes when they are cooked.

Potatoes must be stored in a DARK area. Light creates a chemical reaction in the potato, turning it green. This green area is poisonous and must be cut off and discarded. If you don't have a dark storage area, store the potatoes in a paper bag in a cool, dry area. Don't store them in plastic bags—light penetrates the bags and air does not circulate.

Potatoes stored at room temperature will keep only about a week, and may sprout and shrivel. The sprouts on potatoes are also poisonous. Cut off sprouts before using the potatoes.

Store onions in a cool, dry area but not next to potatoes. Onions absorb moisture from potatoes, become moldy and rot. Potatoes sprout faster if stored with onions. Don't refrigerate onions—they mold and decay. Store onions in a loosely woven bag or basket so air can circlate. Do not store them in plastic bags where air cannot circulate.

13-7. Storing canned vegetables. See 3-2, "Dry storage," for guidelines for storing canned food.

13-8. Storing frozen vegetables. See 3-4, "Freezer storage," for guidelines for storing frozen vegetables.

13-9. Storing dried vegetables. Store unopened packages in a dry, cool place. They will keep their quality for months. Once opened, reseal the package tightly or transfer the contents to a tightly closed plastic bag or container with a tight-fitting lid.

Don't mix several packages, especially if you bought them months apart. The older dried vegetables may need a longer cooking time, so you'll get uneven results if you mix them.

13-10. Storing leftover cooked vegetables. Store leftover cooked vegetables promptly in covered containers. If you're going to use them within a few days, refrigerate them. Otherwise, freeze them.

If you have just small amounts of vegetables left over regularly, freeze them in one container and use the vegetable mixture the next time you make soup.

SERVING RAW VEGETABLES

13-11. Clean vegetables carefully. Most vegetable plants are not very tall. Usually the edible parts grow in or close to the ground, which means they carry dirt and harmful bacteria.

Before you eat raw vegetables, scrub them thoroughly to remove dirt and bacteria. Cut off parts that cannot be eaten. Pare if necessary.

If you've grown your own vegetables, you may have to soak them in salted water to remove insects.

CONVENTIONAL COOKING

13-12. General guidelines for cooking vegetables. When properly cooked, vegetables change in several ways. The fiber is broken down, making the vegetables easier to chew. The starch is cooked so the vegetable is easy to digest. The flavor mellows and becomes milder, and the color remains attractive. Only a small amount of nutrients is lost.

If improperly cooked, vegetables lose their shape and texture and become mushy. They lose nutrients and flavor and often turn an unpleasant color.

The results you get in cooking vegetables depend on the

amount of fiber in the vegetable, the amount of heat, length of cooking time and the acids and alkalies in the water or in other foods cooked with the vegetables.

• *Fiber.* Moisture is needed to soften the fiber so it can be eaten. The amount of fiber in the vegetable determines how it can be cooked. High-fiber vegetables such as artichokes can be cooked in liquid but they cannot be baked in dry heat because they don't contain enough moisture to soften the fiber. Some vegetables such as asparagus and broccoli have both high-fiber (stems) and low-fiber (flowers or tips) parts. (See 13-1, "Kinds of vegetables.") This causes difficulty in cooking because the low-fiber parts cook faster than the high-fiber parts.

• *Heat.* Moist heat is needed to soften the fiber and cook the starch in some vegetables. Dry heat methods such as baking and broiling can be used for only a few vegetables that have enough fiber to hold their shape and also enough natural moisture to soften the fiber. Excess heat can overcook vegetables. If overcooked in liquid, vegetables get mushy and lose color, nutrients, flavor and texture.

• *Cooking time.* Vegetables should be cooked until just tender. Cooking them too long overcooks them, often with unpleasant results.

• *Acidic food.* Acidic food slows down the softening of fiber so it takes longer to cook. For example, let's say you're making a stew with a tomato or wine sauce and add sliced carrots and potatoes. The high-fiber carrots will take longer to cook than the potatoes because of the acid in the tomatoes or wine. Acidic food also affects the color of some vegetables. See 13-13, "Color of vegetables determines the cooking method."

• *Alkalies.* Alkalies present in water in the form of minerals can soften some vegetables excessively, sometimes to the point of becoming slimy. In unusually hard-water areas, adding an acidic food such as vinegar or lemon juice to the vegetable cooking water helps to neutralize the alkalies. Alkalies also affect the color of some vegetables. (See 13-13, "Color of vegetables determines the cooking method.")

13-13. Color of vegetables determines the cooking method. The color in vegetables is caused by certain chemicals which are a natural part of the vegetable. These chemicals are affected by heat, acids and alkalies.

Vegetables are generally cooked in liquid according to the method given in 13-15, "Cooking vegetables in liquid." However, the color of the vegetable may require variations in the cooking method or limit the kinds of foods with which it may be cooked.

• *Green vegetables.* Chlorophyll in the vegetables gives them their characteristic green color. Overcooking turns the green to an olive green. Acidic foods such as tomato sauce, lemon juice or wine also turn green vegetables an olive green, even though they are not overcooked. Because alkalies help green vegetables stay a bright green, some people add baking soda to vegetable cooking water to retain the green color. However, baking soda destroys nutrients, so never add it to vegetables. The general rule for cooking most green vegetables is to use a small amount of water and simmer in a covered pan until the vegetables are just tender.

• *White vegetables.* Color pigments known as flavones, present in white vegetables such as potatoes, cauliflower and onions, affect the color when cooked. If overcooked, white vegetables may turn dark. Alkalies cause white vegetables to turn yellow. If white vegetables turn yellow when cooked in hard water, add a pinch of cream of tartar, which is acidic, to the cooking water to keep them white. A general rule for cooking white vegetables is to use a small amount of water and simmer in a covered pan only until done. Potatoes, however, because of their size and the amount of starch they contain, should be cooked covered with water. Ideally, potatoes should be cooked whole with the skins. The skins help retain the nutrients in the potatoes and can be easily peeled off after the potatoes are cooked.

• *Yellow or orange vegetables.* Carotene, a form of vitamin A, is responsible for the yellow or orange color. This color is relatively stable and is not affected by heat, acid or alkalies. However, if vegetables such as carrots are overcooked, the cells break apart and the carotene is lost in the water. This is evidenced by the yellow or orange color of the water. A general rule for cooking yellow or orange vegetables is to use a small amount of water and simmer in a covered pan only until tender.

• *Red vegetables.* Several different chemical compounds in red vegetables are affected by alkalies. Never use baking soda, which is an alkali, in cooking red vegetables. In hard water, or with the addition of baking soda, vegetables such as red cabbage or beets turn blue or green. Because acid helps retain the red color, many recipes for red cabbage and beets include an

173

acidic food such as vinegar, lemon juice or tart apples. Tomatoes are naturally acidic and retain their color when cooked. Since beets are root vegetables, they require long cooking so they should be cooked covered with water with the skins on.

13-14. Cooking strong-flavored vegetables. Some strong-flavored vegetables such as cabbage, cauliflower, turnips and rutabagas should be cooked in a larger amount of water, which absorbs some of the flavor. However, overcooking deepens the flavor, so be careful not to overcook. Cutting the vegetable into small pieces helps to shorten the cooking time. If the cooking water evaporates, add more hot water. Never add cold water—it cools down the entire mixture. The water will have to be brought to the boiling point again, overcooking the vegetables. Cook uncovered.

13-15. Cooking vegetables in liquid. To cook vegetables in liquid, use a pan with a tight-fitting lid to keep water from evaporating. Wash fresh vegetables carefully. Remove unwanted parts. Use a small amount of water—½ to 1 cup of water for 6 servings of young, tender vegetables. Cover the pan and bring the water to a boil.

Turn the heat down and simmer the vegetables only until done. Never boil vegetables—the rolling action of the water breaks them down, causing poor texture and loss of flavor, nutrients and color. See 4-2, "Boiling," and 4-3, "Simmering," for the difference between boiling and simmering.

To test vegetables for doneness, pierce them with a fork or taste a small portion. Vegetables vary in their cooking time, from 3 minutes to 30 or more. Cooking time depends on the thickness of the vegetable and amount of fiber and starch.

Drain the vegetables and serve immediately. Use the cooking water as a sauce for the vegetables—it contains valuable nutrients. Or refrigerate or freeze the cooking water to use later in soups, stews and sauces. If you cooked the vegetable with skins on, such as potatoes or beets, discard the water as it may contain dirt.

Omit salt when cooking vegetables and discover their real flavor. If the flavor is too bland for your liking, experiment with various herbs, spices and other seasonings. (See 11-1, "Kinds of seasonings," and 11-12, "Experiment with seasonings.")

13-16. Steaming vegetables. (See 4-9, "Steaming.") Many people prefer to steam vegetables rather than simmer them.

Place vegetables in the upper compartment of the steamer, cover and steam only until done.

13-17. Frying vegetables. (See 4-15, "Panfrying, sauteing, stir-frying.") Vegetables such as celery, peppers and onions can be sauteed lightly in a small amount of butter before being added to mixtures such as meatloaf or casseroles. Sauteing precooks the vegetables and flavors the butter, which is added to the mixture along with the vegetables.

Potatoes can be fried, either precooked or raw. The raw potatoes will take longer than the cooked.

13-18. Stir-frying vegetables. (See 4-15, "Panfrying, sauteing, stir-frying.") For best results, vegetables must be properly prepared before stir-frying.

Because stir-frying is a quick-cooking method, vegetables must be sliced into thin, uniform pieces for quick, even cooking.

Vegetables that tend to be stringy, such as celery, green beans and broccoli stems, should be cut into thin slices on the diagonal. Slicing on the diagonal helps tenderize tough-fiber vegetables by exposing a larger cut area to the heat. Slices should be about ¼ inch thick.

Remove midribs and stem ends from leafy vegetables such as cabbage and slice them separately.

Other vegetables can be diced or chopped. Be sure all the pieces are of uniform size.

Keep the different kinds of vegetables separate as you slice or chop them.

When stir-frying, have hot water available to add to the fried vegetables so they can steam if necessary. Never add cold water to the vegetables—it cools the pan and slows down the cooking.

When stir-frying vegetables, be sure the pan is hot enough and use only a small amount of oil. Begin with vegetables that take the longest to cook and gradually add the more tender vegetables.

Stir the vegetables continuously and don't overcook them. The inside of the vegetables should remain a little crisp while the outside is cooked until just done.

Near the end of the cooking time, place the lid on the pan for just a short time so the vegetables finish cooking in steam. Some of the vegetables, especially leafy ones, will have enough natural moisture to create sufficient steam. However, if you're cooking high-fiber or high-starch vegetables, you may find it necessary to add a spoon or two of hot water to create steam and complete the cooking.

If you're cooking meat with the vegetables, cook the meat first, remove it from the pan, cook the vegetables and then add the meat during the last few minutes the vegetables cook.

13-19. Baking vegetables. (See 4-20, "Cooking in dry heat.") For baking in the dry heat of the oven, a vegetable must have enough fiber to hold it together as well as enough moisture to create steam. Potatoes, tomatoes, onions and squash can be baked in dry heat successfully. Other vegetables should be baked in a sauce, which provides moisture to tenderize the fiber. A covered pan keeps moisture from evaporating.

Potatoes are generally baked in their skin, which retains moisture. If you like a crisp crust on baked potatoes, don't wrap them in aluminum foil. The foil retains moisture, steaming the potato and softening the skin. Instead, scrub the potatoes thoroughly and cut off any blemishes. Dry the potatoes and rub them with butter. Bake at 425°F for about 45 to 60 minutes, depending on the size of the potato. For an extra thick, crisp crust, increase the baking time by about 5 to 10 minutes.

13-20. Broiling vegetables. (See 4-21, "Broiling.") Tomato slices or halves are about the only raw vegetables that can be broiled successfully. Other vegetables may be broiled if they are cooked first.

When broiling vegetables, brush the tops with melted butter or sprinkle them with buttered crumbs to protect the vegetables from the drying effect of direct broiler heat.

13-21. Scalloped (escalloped) and au gratin vegetables. Scalloped vegetables are generally cut in small pieces, mixed with a sauce and baked. The vegetables and sauce can either be layered or mixed together. High-fiber vegetables should be precooked.

"Au gratin" means that a topping of crumbs is sprinkled over the scalloped dish before it bakes. For added flavor, grated cheese can also be sprinkled over the mixture toward the end of the cooking time. Allow just enough time for the cheese to melt. If you sprinkle it over the mixture at the beginning of the cooking time, the cheese will overcook.

13-22. Cooking dried legumes. Before cooking, pick over legumes. Discard any that are moldy or have insect holes. Wash in cold water, unless the package gives other directions. Soak dried legumes overnight before cooking. Lentils and split peas generally don't need soaking but they give more satisfactory results if soaked. To soak, use 4 cups of water for every cup of legumes. Discard any legumes that float in the water.

If you forget to soak beans, you can still cook them the same day. Cover the beans with cold water and bring the water to a boil. Boil for 2 minutes. Remove from the heat, cover with a tight-fitting lid and let stand for 1 hour. Then cook as directed.

13-23. Heating home-canned vegetables. Always BOIL home-canned vegetables for at least 10 to 15 minutes. This will destroy any harmful toxins that may be present, such as the deadly botulism toxin. Never taste home-canned vegetables without boiling them—even a small amount of botulism toxin can kill.

MICROWAVE COOKING

13-24MW. Amount of water. Use only a small amount of water for fresh vegetables, usually no more than 2 Tablespoons. Generally, water clinging to the vegetables after you wash them provides enough moisture for cooking. Don't add water to frozen vegetables—the melting ice crystals provide enough moisture.

13-25MW. Salt. Don't sprinkle salt over the vegetables. Instead, first dissolve the salt in the cooking water or add it to the vegetables after they are cooked. (See 4-58MW, "Salt.")

13-26MW. Cooking time. To find the cooking time for fresh vegetables, weigh the vegetables after cleaning and washing. On the average, cook 6 to 7 minutes for every pound of vegetable.

13-27MW. Cooking power. Cook vegetables on High power. However, if you're cooking them in a sauce that contains a delicate food such as eggs, milk or cheese, use a lower power. If your oven has only High power, see 4-49MW, "If food overcooks regularly."

13-28MW. Size of vegetables. Be sure the vegetables are uniform in size for even cooking. Tough parts of vegetables, such as broccoli or asparagus stems, should be turned toward the outside edges of the container. (See 4-38, "Oven hot spots.")

13-29MW. Vegetables with skins. If you're cooking vegetables with skins, such as potatoes, pierce the skins to prevent bursting. (See 4-51MW, "To prevent food from 'exploding.' ")

13-30MW. Cooking in plastic pouches. To cook vegetables in plastic pouches, pierce the pouch to prevent bursting. You may want to put the pouch in a dish to catch any liquid that may spill out.

13-31MW. Baking potatoes. To bake potatoes, follow the time schedule in your owner's manual.

Remove the potatoes from the oven before they are completely cooked. Wrap in foil to retain heat and let stand for at least 10 minutes before serving.

If the potato skin shrivels, it means the potatoes have cooked too long. Next time, shorten the microwaving time.

13-32MW. Sweet potatoes. If you have problems microwaving whole sweet potatoes, try wrapping them in plastic wrap. Pierce both plastic and potato skins in several places to prevent bursting. Microwave according to directions in your manual.

13-33MW. Cooking frozen vegetables in the carton. Make a flap out of one of the wide sides of the carton by cutting through on three edges. Put the carton on a paper plate or paper towel to protect the oven bottom because the printing on the carton could transfer to the oven bottom. Microwave 5 to 7 minutes on High power, stirring once to break up the block of vegetables.

13-34MW. Commercially canned vegetables. Remove the vegetables from the can with the liquid and heat in liquid only until hot. Don't overcook.

Never heat vegetables in the can—it could explode.

13-35MW. Heating home-canned vegetables. Never heat home-canned vegetables in a microwave oven. Home-canned vegetables must be boiled for 10 to 15 minutes to destroy any poisonous toxins that may be present, such as botulism toxin. Vegetables cooked for that length of time in the microwave oven will be so overcooked they won't be edible. In addition, the microwave energy pattern is uneven, which could mean that some of the toxin may not be destroyed.

Salads

14-1. Buying salad greens. A wide variety of salad greens is available, each with its own distinct flavor, color, shape and texture.

- *Iceberg lettuce* has a compact head with tightly packed leaves and a mild flavor.
- *Escarole* has dark-green leaves edged in yellow with a mild flavor.
- *Curly endive* adds a dark-green color, lacy texture and tangy flavor.
- *Bibb lettuce* has sweet, tender, deep-green leaves with a mild flavor.
- *Romaine lettuce* has a long head with crisp leaves and a sharp, nutty flavor.
- *Leaf lettuce* has crisp, light-green, curly leaves with a delicate flavor.
- *Fresh young spinach* adds color, flavor and nutrients to a salad.

See 13-2, "Buying fresh vegetables."

14-2. Storing salad greens. See 13-6, "Storing fresh vegetables."

14-3. Drying salad greens. Salad greens and other fresh vegetables must be dry when used in a salad. Moisture dilutes the dressing and keeps it from sticking to the greens.

Wash fresh vegetables carefully to remove dirt and grit and dry thoroughly. To dry greens and other fresh vegetables, put them in a drying basket, strainer or colander and let the moisture drain away. You can also spread them on a layer of clean toweling, cover with another layer of toweling and gently pat dry.

If you've washed the vegetables long before serving, wrap them in clean paper toweling, store in a closed plastic bag and refrigerate until needed.

14-4. Tearing or cutting greens. Whichever method you use depends on your preference and when you plan to use the greens.

Cutting greens with a knife or scissors bruises the edges, which turn brown upon standing. If you're serving the salad immediately, you can cut the greens without fear of brown edges.

Tearing greens does not bruise the edges, thereby eliminating the problem of browning. Tear greens if they are not to be served immediately.

14-5. Parts of a salad. Any salad, except a tossed salad, normally has three basic parts:

• *Base.* The base serves as a lining between the salad and the bowl or plate. The base generally consists of a layer of torn lettuce, lettuce leaves or a lettuce cup. To make a lettuce cup, wash and core Iceberg lettuce. (See 13-6, "Storing fresh vegetables.") Gently remove the outer lettuce leaves so that each retains its cup shape. Be careful not to break them. The lettuce cup makes an ideal base for salads served in a mound such as Waldorf, tuna or chicken salad. Hollowed-out fruit shells, such as pineapple quarters, cantaloupe halves and avocado halves, make attractive bases for salads.

• *Body.* The body is the main part of the salad, placed on the base. You can use any food for a salad, from a mixture of fruit and greens to cold cooked meats.

• *Dressing.* The dressing is a sauce which adds a distinct flavor to the salad. Dressings should always be compatible with the body of the salad. If you're serving a tart fruit salad, use a slightly sweet salad dressing. If the body of the salad is relatively mild, avoid overpowering dressings.

There are three basic types of dressings:

French dressing is made of oil, vinegar and seasonings. You can vary the flavor by using different oils, vinegars and seasonings. (See 11-1, "Kinds of seasonings.")

Mayonnaise is a rich dressing made with salad oil, egg yolk, vinegar or lemon juice, sugar and seasonings.

Cooked dressing is made with eggs, milk or water, and seasonings, thickened with flour. It is often called "Salad Dressing" on the label.

You can buy many different varieties of prepared dressings but most are a variation of one of the three basic types. Most salad dressings have an oil base, which adds a considerable number of calories to what might otherwise be a low-calorie salad.

Yogurt makes a nutritious, flavorful salad dressing, relatively low in calories. Buy the plain low-fat yogurt and flavor it with seasonings, depending on the kind of salad with which it will be used. Yogurt blends well with the ranch-type dressing mix normally made with buttermilk. For a fruit salad, mix yogurt with a little honey, lemon or lime juice and grated lemon or lime rind. For ham salad, mix yogurt with mustard and a little honey. (See 11-1, "Kinds of seasonings.")

For a low-calorie salad, sprinkle fresh lemon juice on the salad instead of a dressing.

14-6. Putting a salad together. Wash and dry all fresh vegetables and fruits thoroughly. If you're using canned foods, drain them well.

If you're on a close time schedule, prepare greens and other foods for the salad a few hours ahead of time. Refrigerate separately in covered containers.

If you're preparing a salad other than a tossed or chef's salad, arrange the base on the plate or in the bowl. A tossed vegetable salad doesn't need a base.

Arrange other foods on the base. Frequently, the ingredients are cut into small pieces and mixed with the dressing, such as potato or tuna salad. If large pieces of food are used, arrange them attractively on the salad plate. Putting a salad together gives you a chance to use your creativity. But avoid contrived designs—strive to make the arrangement look natural.

If the salad contains greens, add the dressing just before serving. If the dressing is added too early, it will wilt the greens.

Instead of spooning the dressing on the salad, serve it in a bowl or pitcher so people can help themselves. Dieters will appreciate your consideration—they can help themselves to as much or as little as they like.

Beverages

CONVENTIONAL COOKING

Coffee

15-1. Grinds. Follow the recommendations in the owner's manual accompanying your coffeemaker for the type of grind to use. Read the labels on coffee containers carefully to be sure you buy the kind of grind recommended.

15-2. Storing ground coffee properly. The flavors in coffee are volatile and are released as soon as the coffee is ground. Ground coffee stored in a paper bag loses its flavor quickly.

Store coffee in an airtight container, such as a can or a jar with a tight-fitting lid. Keep the ground coffee in the refrigerator or freezer for maximum storage.

Generally, ground coffee will retain its freshness about a week if properly stored in the refrigerator.

15-3. Grinding your own coffee. For maximum flavor, grind coffee beans yourself just as you need them.

Be sure the coffee grinder is always CLEAN. Coffee beans contain oil which clings to the grinder and can become rancid and develop an off flavor. The coffee you grind will pick up this off flavor.

Follow the instructions in the owner's manual and clean the coffee grinder carefully after every use.

15-4. Making fresh coffee. Follow the directions in your owner's manual for using your coffeemaker.

Be sure the coffeemaker is clean. Oils in coffee stick to the inside of the coffeemaker and are difficult to remove. They become rancid quickly and develop an off flavor which affects the flavor of freshly made coffee. Ceramic and glass coffeemakers are a little easier to clean than metal.

Scrub the inside of the coffeemaker with hot soapy water, using a brush for hard-to-reach areas. Rinse thoroughly to get rid of all soapy water. If you have an electric coffeemaker, follow manufacturer's directions for cleaning. Don't immerse an electric coffeemaker in water.

Use freshly drawn cold water. Measure the water, allowing ¾ cup (6 ounces) cold water for every cup of coffee. Most coffee cups do not hold a full measuring cup (8 ounces) of liquid. If you're measuring water by the markings on the coffeepot, test them first before relying on them. Many of these markings are inaccurate.

Measure coffee accurately. No matter what kind of coffeemaker you use, the proportions of water and ground coffee are always the same. Use 2 level Tablespoons of ground coffee for every ¾ cup of cold water. If you prefer weaker coffee, dilute it with hot water after the coffee has been made at full strength. If you begin with less ground coffee, the brew will be bitter if cooked for the same length of time.

Brew the coffee for the recommended time for your coffeemaker. The finer the coffee grind, the less brewing time it needs to extract the flavors. As a rule, regular or percolator coffee brews 6 to 8 minutes, drip coffee 4 to 6 minutes and fine or vacuum coffee 1 to 4 minutes. If you have an automatic coffeemaker, check the brewing time with a timer to be sure it is correct. As soon as the coffee is brewed, remove the coffee grounds.

Boiling or overcooking makes the coffee bitter.

15-5. Iced coffee. Ice cubes dilute coffee. To keep coffee the same strength when it is iced, use either of the following methods:

• Use 3 Tablespoons of ground coffee for every ¾ cup cold water. The extra strength allows for dilution by the ice.

• Make ice cubes out of regular strength coffee. To make iced coffee, use regular strength coffee and coffee ice cubes.

15-6. Reheating coffee. Never reheat coffee—it becomes bitter. You can keep it warm on a low setting on top of the range or in an automatic coffeemaker.

Tea

15-7. Buying and storing tea. Experiment with the wide assortment of teas available including herb teas, which are caffeine-free.

Store tea in a tightly closed container in a cool, dry area. If improperly stored, it loses its flavor quickly.

15-8. Making hot tea. Use a ceramic or glass teapot. Pigments in regular tea react with metal and give the tea a bitter flavor. They also create a light film over the surface of the tea that clings to the inside of the cup as you drink. Preheat the teapot by rinsing it out with hot water.

In another pot, bring fresh cold tap water to a full rolling boil. If you use reheated water, the tea will have a flat taste. Only boiling water can extract the full flavor from the leaves.

Measure the tea into the teapot according to directions on the package or use the recommended number of tea bags. The amount needed will vary with the type of tea. Loose tea can be placed in a tea infuser or tea ball made of stainless steel, which has the least metallic reaction with the tea.

As soon as the water boils, pour it over the leaves or bags in the teapot. Let the tea brew for about 3 to 5 minutes. Never boil tea—it gets bitter. If you steep it too long, it may get cloudy. If you have a tea cozy (a teapot cover made of thick fabric), cover the teapot to keep the water hot.

Don't judge the strength of tea by its color. Some varieties may have a light color and a strong flavor while others brew to a very dark color with a light flavor.

Remove the tea bags. If you use loose tea leaves, stir and strain the tea.

15-9. Hard water. If you live in a hard-water area, the minerals in the water may make the tea cloudy with a film on the surface. To minimize the problem, add a few drops of lemon juice to the brewed tea.

15-10. Iced tea. To make iced tea, use about 50% more tea than you do for hot tea. The extra strength allows for dilution by melting ice cubes.

When the tea has steeped, remove tea leaves or tea bags and allow the tea to come to room temperature. Pour over the ice when ready to serve.

Never chill tea in the refrigerator—it becomes cloudy.

15-11. Sun tea. With the sun tea method, tea is brewed in cold water in a jar which stands in the sun.

To make sun tea, use 4 tea bags for every 2 quarts of water. Remove the paper tags from the bags. Pour cold water into a large jar with a lid. Add the tea bags, cover tightly and stand the jar in the sun for about 6 hours. The time will vary depending on where you live and the time of year.

If you prefer a stronger tea, add more tea bags

Hot cocoa

15-12. Making cocoa. If you try to stir plain cocoa into a liquid, it will cook into lumps. When making hot cocoa, mix the cocoa with the sugar first. Then make a smooth paste by adding a little liquid to the cocoa mixture. Add the paste to the remaining liquid and cook.

To remove lumps, strain the cocoa through a fine sieve. If you need to add more cocoa for additional flavor, add a little of the liquid to the cocoa-sugar mixture, as described above.

MICROWAVE COOKING

15-13MW. Boil-overs. Beverages may boil over when cooked in the microwave oven. Use a container that is large enough to allow the liquid to foam up without spilling over the sides.

15-14MW. Reheating beverages. When reheating beverages, stir them vigorously before placing them in the microwave oven.

A beverage that stands for even a short time develops a very smooth surface that acts almost like a film or skin. If you reheat a beverage without stirring it, the smooth surface could prevent steam from escaping and the beverage will "explode" out of the container.

15-15MW. Temperature probe. If your oven has a temperature probe, use it for heating beverages to the exact temperature you enjoy for drinking.

Soup

CONVENTIONAL COOKING

Stock

16-1. Ingredients for stock. Stock is generally used as a foundation for soups and sauces. Stock can be made from meat, poultry, fish or vegetables or any combination of these ingredients. Use meat or poultry stock as a base for soups or other dishes that cook for any length of time. Use vegetable and fish stocks in recipes that cook 30 minutes or less. If cooked longer, vegetable and fish stocks lose their flavor.

For stock liquid, use water or leftover vegetable cooking water. Never use cooking liquid from cured meats such as ham, tongue or brisket, which contain additives. Cooking water from cured meats is also highly salted.

Ingredients used in making stock should be mature with well-developed flavors. You can use mature poultry such as stewing hens, mature vegetables, bones and less-tender cuts of meat such as beef shank. Be sure some of the meat bones contain marrow, which adds a delicious flavor to the stock.

Avoid starchy foods such as peas, potatoes, pasta and rice—they make the stock cloudy. It will also sour rapidly if stored. Starchy foods can be added when you make soup from the stock.

The basic stock ratio is about 2 cups of water for every cup of meat and bones.

16-2. Seasonings. Use flavorful vegetables such as onion, parsley, celery, leek and carrots, along with herbs and spices such as whole peppercorns and bay leaf and thyme, marjoram and savory. Experiment with different seasonings to vary the flavor of the stock.

Seasonings should be subtle, never overpowering. If you use too much seasoning to start with, your stock may be ruined. As stock simmers, it evaporates and the flavor becomes more concentrated. Always begin with small amounts of seasoning —you can always add more toward the end of the cooking time. Add herbs and spices during the last 30 minutes of cooking. (See 11-14, "Don't overcook herbs and spices.")

If you flavor stock with wine, use less salt than you normally would. Wine accents the salt flavor.

16-3. Cooking the stock. Use a large enough pot to hold all the ingredients and water.

The purpose in making stock is to extract the flavorful juices from the ingredients. Expose as much cut surface as possible. Have the butcher crack bones, even if they're small. Clean vegetables and cut into small pieces. Trim excess fat off meat and poultry and cut or chop into small pieces.

For a light, mild-flavored stock, use light-colored meat such as poultry and veal. Beef will give a slightly darker, more flavorful stock.

For a dark stock, use beef and beef bones. Brown some of the meat in a small amount of fat. You can also roast the pieces at 425°F for a short time until the outside is brown. Pour off all fat before adding the browned meat to the stock pot. Browning adds a desirable darker color and distinctive flavor but don't brown too many of the pieces. Because browning forms a crust on the meat that keeps the juices inside, the stock won't have as rich a flavor if all the meat is browned. Don't flour the meat before browning—the starch in the flour will make the stock cloudy.

Bring the stock to a boil. Lower the heat and simmer the stock slowly—don't boil it. The more slowly it cooks, the more flavors are extracted from the ingredients.

A scum forms as the stock begins to cook. For a clear soup, skim off the foam during the first 30 minutes of cooking and discard it. Use a long-handled spoon, strainer or skimmer. For a brown stock, some chefs feel that skimming off the scum is not necessary.

Cover the pot partially, leaving it slightly open on one side. This allows for evaporation, which helps to concentrate the flavors.

The cooking time for stock varies. Cook it until the flavors have been extracted from all the ingredients—at least 2 hours. A longer cooking time is preferable, especially if you use large bones.

16-4. Straining the stock. To remove particles of food and bone floating in the stock, strain it after it has cooked. Rinse a cheesecloth or a linen towel in cold water and wring it out. Line a large sieve with the wet cloth. Ladle the stock into the sieve carefully and let it drip through into another pot. Cool the strained stock in the refrigerator.

16-5. Degreasing the stock. To degrease means to remove excess fat from the stock. As the stock cools, the fat floating on the surface solidifies. Remove the fat before clarifying, serving or storing the stock.

If you plan to use the hot stock immediately, you can siphon the grease off the top with a meat baster—a tapered hollow tube with a rubber bulb at one end.

16-6. Reducing the stock. Reducing the stock means to boil it so some of the liquid evaporates, giving the stock a more pronounced flavor.

To reduce stock, pour the degreased stock into a pot. Boil slowly, uncovered, until the stock is one-third or one-half of its original volume. Taste occasionally and stop boiling when the flavor is to your liking.

If the stock is reduced too much, the flavor may be stronger than you like. Add a little hot water or other liquid to dilute it.

16-7. Clarifying the stock. If you want a clear stock, it must be clarified with egg whites.

For 1 quart of stock, add 1 egg white, beaten until just foamy, and 1 crushed egg shell. Use medium heat and bring the stock to a boil. Then simmer about 10 minutes or until the egg white rises to the surface as a foam. Remove from heat and let stand 10 minutes to settle. Strain as described in 16-4, "Straining the stock."

16-8. Storing stock. Refrigerate stock in a covered container if you plan to use it within 3 or 4 days. If you want to keep it longer, freeze it in small containers so you can thaw out only the amount you need. Frozen stock will keep about 3 months.

Soups

16-9. Number of servings. 1 quart of soup will give about 6 servings of an appetizer soup. For a heartier, main-dish soup, 1 quart will give about 4 servings.

16-10. Broth, bouillon, consomme.
Broth is another name for clear stock when it is served as a soup.
Bouillon is also a clear soup but with a definite meaty flavor such as beef or chicken.
Consomme has the strongest flavor of the three. It is generally made from beef, veal or chicken stock or a combination of the three. The stock is clarified and sometimes meat, vegetables and seasonings are added.
Broth, bouillon and consomme are often used as ingredients in recipes. If you don't have the homemade versions, use the canned varieties. Because canned varieties are generally saltier than the homemade versions, cut down on the amount of salt used in the recipe or eliminate it altogether.

16-11. Hearty main-dish soups. To make a hearty main-dish soup, remove the meat and strain and degrease the stock. (See 16-4, "Straining the stock," and 16-5, "Degreasing the stock.") It's not necessary to clarify it.
Cut the meat into bite-size pieces and return to the stock. Add whatever vegetables and grains you like. Season and cook until the vegetables and grains are tender.

16-12. Pureed vegetable soups. Thick, hearty soups can be made from pureed vegetables. Almost any vegetable can be cooked in stock and then pureed.
The easiest way to puree is to put the cooked mixture through a blender. Add seasonings, if needed.
To turn a pureed soup into a cream soup, mix the puree with cream, half-and-half or yogurt.
Pea soup, a popular pureed vegetable soup, traditionally uses a ham bone for flavoring. However, because of modern curing methods, ham bones add nitrates and other additives, along with excess salt, to the puree. Consider using other seasonings in place of the ham bone.

16-13. Cream soups. A cream soup generally is made with a thin white sauce combined with pureed, chopped or diced vegetables.

A bisque is a cream soup made with shellfish. However, sometimes the word "bisque" is also used for vegetable cream soups, especially if chopped or diced vegetables are added.

Cream soups curdle easily. The following precautions may help prevent curdling:

• Use fresh milk in making the white sauce. Milk is more apt to curdle as it ages.

• Avoid oversalting—salt tends to curdle cream sauce.

• Serve the soup as soon as it is ready. Holding cream soup for even a short time before serving may make it curdle.

16-14. Chowders. Basically, a chowder is a thick soup containing diced bacon or salt pork, diced potatoes, seafood and vegetables. New England or Boston chowder has a milk base. New York or Manhattan chowder contains tomatoes but no milk. When preparing New England or Boston chowder, follow the precautions given in 6-8 to 6-13 for cooking milk.

16-15. Storing soups. Refrigerate leftover soup immediately in a covered container. Use within 3 days. For longer storage, freeze the soup and use within 3 months.

Cream soups may not freeze satisfactorily, depending on the ingredients used. Some may curdle when thawed. Experiment with a small amount before making up a large batch for the freezer.

MICROWAVE COOKING

16-16MW. Heating canned soup. Never heat soup in the can—it may explode and the metal may damage the oven. Pour the contents into a cup or bowl for heating.

16-17MW. Stir soup. Stir soup halfway through the cooking time to distribute the heat more evenly. If not stirred, the soup closest to the outside of the container heats faster than the center. The soup in the center of the container may erupt.

16-18MW. Reheating soup. When reheating soup, stir it vigorously before placing it in the microwave oven. See 15-14MW, "Reheating beverages."

16-19MW. Temperature probe. When using the temperature probe for soups, heat cream soup to 140°F and water-base soups to 160°F. Heating cream soup to a higher temperature may curdle it.

Meat

BUYING

17-1. Composition of meat. Meat has four basic parts: muscle, connective tissue, fat and bones. Each has special characteristics that affect the tenderness, quality and price of meat as well as the cooking methods that can be used.

• *Muscle* is made up of protein fibers.

• *Connective tissues,* also a protein, bind the protein fibers together and also bind them to the bones. Connective tissues determine the tenderness of the meat—the more connective tissues in a cut, the less tender it is. The parts of the animal that receive the most exercise have the most connective tissue. Since the back and loin of an animal get the least exercise, they are generally more tender than the legs, shanks, neck and shoulder.

Meat has two types of connective tissues: collagen and elastin. Collagen is a white, fairly thin tissue between layers of muscle. It softens when it is cooked slowly in moist heat or liquid.

Elastin is a thick, yellowish-white connective tissue that is rubbery in texture even when cooked. It is generally cut away from the meat before cooking since the only way to tenderize it is to pound, cube, dice or grind it.

The tenderness of a cut of meat is your clue to the proper cooking method. Tender cuts of meat can be cooked in dry heat. Less-tender cuts of meat need long, slow cooking in moist heat or liquid to soften the connective tissue.

• *Fat* gives meat its flavor and juiciness. It has nothing to do with tenderness. Meat has two types of fat. One type is in the form of layers of fat between the muscles. The other type is in the form of small flecks of fat throughout the muscle, known as marbling. The more marbling in meat, the more flavorful and juicy it is.

• *Bones* make up the skeletal structure of the animal. Different parts of the skeletal structure have differently shaped bones, which help in identifying cuts of meat. (See 17-4, "Tenderness of meat.") Some bones contain marrow, a tender portion in the center and highly prized by gourmets. Because marrow is high in fat and protein, with a delectable flavor, marrow bones are essential ingredients for soup stock. Shin and knuckle bones are high in collagen, which softens and turns into a gel when cooked. Soups made with these bones will thicken and gel when they are chilled.

17-2. Kinds of meat. There are four basic kinds of fresh meat:

• *Beef* comes from mature cattle over one year old. It has a firm texture and is usually a deep, bright red color with creamy white fat. However, when exposed to air for a time, the bright red turns dark. When buying beef, look for hard, creamy white fat. Yellow fat generally means the meat came from an older animal, which is less tender. It could also mean the animal was fed on grass rather than on grain. Hamburger is beef which has been ground to make it tender. Generally, hamburger contains up to 30% fat.

• *Veal* comes from immature cattle, about 4 to 8 weeks old. Low in fat, veal has a very mild flavor. Most cuts of veal are not tender. When buying veal, look for a delicate pink color.

• *Lamb* refers to young sheep up to a year old. It is sometimes called "spring lamb." Lamb has a delicate flavor and a gray-pink color with white fat. Older animals are sold as mutton, which has a much stronger flavor, is a deeper red color and has a larger amount of fat than lamb. Since mutton comes from a full-grown animal, comparable cuts of mutton are larger than the same cut of lamb. New Zealand lamb is generally smaller than lamb grown in the United States and is always sold frozen. Tenderness depends on the part of the animal the cut comes from.

• *Pork* is meat from young swine between 5 and 7 months old. All pork cuts are tender. When buying pork, look for grayish-pink flesh with white fat. Pork is also available smoked and cured. Smoked pork is actually exposed to smoke, such as smoked ham hocks. Cured pork has been treated with curing ingredients such as salt, sugar and sodium or potassium nitrate or nitrite. These ingredients give cured pork a typical flavor and red color. Ham can be purchased "fully cooked" or "cook before eating." Fully cooked ham means the ham has been cooked; it may be warmed before serving or eaten as it comes from the package. Cook-before-eating ham must be cooked to an internal temperature of 160°F. Follow the instructions on the wrapper.

• *Variety meats.* Variety meats include the animal organs such as liver, kidneys, brains, heart, tongue, tripe (stomach of cattle), sweetbreads (thymus glands) and chitterlings (small intestines of young pigs).

• *Sausage and other cured meats.* A wide assortment of cold cuts, sausages and other cured meats is available. Read labels carefully for cooking and serving instructions. Cold cuts as a rule can be eaten without any cooking. However, sausages and other cured meats may have to be cooked or heated before serving.

17-3. Meat grades. Government meat grades are your guides to the quality of the meat you buy. Generally, the higher the grade, the more expensive the meat and the more fat it contains. Grading is voluntary except where required by local ordinances.

Beef, veal and lamb are graded, but pork is not. Since pork comes from young hogs, most cuts are the same in eating quality.

The meat grade, in the form of a shield, is stamped on the carcass in a harmless fluid. The stamp does not have to be cut off before cooking.

The quality of the meat is determined by the maturity of the carcass, the amount of marbling and the color, firmness and texture of the lean portion of the muscle.

Of all the grades, only the three top ones are sold in retail markets. These are:

• *Prime.* The top grade, it contains the greatest degree of marbling. Only a small percentage of this grade is sold in retail markets. Most is sold to restaurants.

• *Choice.* High in quality, the meat has enough marbling but not as much as prime. This grade is most commonly sold in supermarkets.

• *Good.* The least expensive of the three grades, the meat has less marbling and less flavor than the two top grades.

17-4. Tenderness of meat. Tenderness is determined by

193

the part of the carcass from which the cut comes. (See 17-1, "Composition of meat.") Your clue to tenderness is the shape of the bone, which helps you identify the part of the carcass:

• *Long, thin, flat bone* appears in shoulder, chuck and hip cuts. These cuts are not tender, except for the sirloin cut.

• *Backbone with rib bone or T-bone* is found in loin and rib cuts. All are tender.

• *Round bone* appears on cuts from either front or back legs. Cuts from front legs and shoulders are called arm and shank. These cuts are not tender. Cuts from the back legs are called leg, round or ham. Veal, lamb and pork cuts from the back legs are usually tender. Beef generally is not tender, but that may depend on the grade.

• *Breast and rib bones* are found in breast and brisket cuts. These cuts are not tender.

17-5. Names of cuts. A meat carcass is first cut into large pieces called primal or wholesale cuts, such as chuck, rib or loin. These are then cut into smaller pieces called retail cuts, such as an arm chuck roast, spare ribs, loin chops and short ribs.

The meat industry has adopted a nationwide uniform meat labeling system, which is used by many stores. This system consists of about 300 standard names for cuts. The name of each cut has three parts:

• *The type of animal*—beef, veal, lamb, mutton or pork.

• *The name of the primal or wholesale cut,* such as chuck, rib, loin or round. This name tells you the part of the carcass the cut comes from. It's another clue to the tenderness of the meat and how to cook it—dry heat or moist heat.

• *The retail cut* such as arm roast, shoulder steak or chop.

Use of the uniform meat labeling system is voluntary. Some stores continue to use other names to identify cuts of meat. If you're in doubt as to which part of the animal you're buying and how to cook it, ask your butcher.

17-6. Guidelines for buying meat. A serving of meat means 3 ounces of cooked meat, without bone or fat. Some people may want more than one serving. Use these guidelines to estimate the number of servings in meat:

• *Boneless meat,* such as ground meat, meats for stews and soups, boneless roasts and steaks and liver and other variety meats—allow ¼ to ⅓ pound per serving. 1 pound makes 3 to 4 servings.

• *Small bones in meat,* such as steaks, chops and roasts— allow ⅓ to ½ pound per serving. 1 pound makes 2 to 3 servings.

• *Bony meat* such as spare ribs, short ribs, oxtails and lamb riblets—allow ¾ to 1 pound per serving. 1 pound makes slightly more than 1 serving.

If the meat is high in fat, it will give fewer servings.

Read the meat label to be sure you're buying the type of meat you want. Check the name of the cut carefully so you'll use the proper cooking method. Is it a cut that requires long, slow cooking in moist heat or a tender cut that can be broiled quickly in dry heat? You can ruin a good cut of meat with the wrong cooking method.

If the meat is prepackaged, check the package for odor and color of the meat.

Compare price per serving for different kinds and cuts of meat that can be used in your recipe. (See 2-6, "Price per serving.")

Don't buy packages that have been opened.

Consider other good sources of animal protein, such as fish, poultry, cheese and eggs.

When you're through shopping, get the meat home and into the refrigerator as soon as you can. If you stop on the way home for other shopping or errands and let the meat stay in a warm car for any length of time, the quality will deteriorate.

STORING

17-7. Storing meat. If meat is prepacked in plastic wrap, store it in the original wrapper for not more than 2 days. If it is packaged in market wrapping paper, rewrap the meat loosely in waxed paper, plastic or foil. Market wrapping paper absorbs moisture and sticks to the meat.

Variety and ground meats should be used within a day or two.

If you plan to keep fresh meat longer than its refrigerator life, freeze it for storage. (See 3-4, "Freezer storage.") If the meat is prepacked in plastic wrap, rewrap it in freezer wrap. The plastic wrap is porous and is not intended for freezing meat.

Processed meats in vacuum packaging are best stored in the original package, both before and after the package is opened. Use before the expiration date stamped on the package.

Read label directions for storing unopened cans of meat.

Some may be stored in a cool, dry place while others require refrigeration.

All canned meats should be refrigerated after the cans are opened. Transfer the meat to a covered container or wrap in plastic wrap or foil.

17-8. Defrosting frozen meat. Defrost meat in its freezer wrapper in the refrigerator. The amount of time it takes to defrost in the refrigerator varies, depending on the temperature in the refrigerator, the size of the meat and how well the meat is frozen. As a rule, a large roast will take 4 to 7 hours for each pound, a small roast will take 3 to 5 hours for each pound and a 1-inch steak will take about 12 to 14 hours to defrost.

Don't defrost meat at room temperature. The surface of the meat will defrost first and may start to spoil before the rest of the meat has thawed.

17-9. Refreezing defrosted meat. If the meat has partially thawed and still contains ice crystals, it can be refrozen. However, refreezing affects the quality—the meat will lose some flavor and texture.

If the meat has completely thawed, inspect it closely. If it has no off odor or off color, use it immediately or cook it and then freeze it. If you have any doubts about the quality of the meat, discard it.

17-10. Spoiled uncooked meat. If uncooked meat has started to spoil, it shows signs of loss of quality:
• The color changes to a dull gray.
• The meat has an off odor.
• If the meat was kept in an unopened package, the meat surface may feel slippery.

If you have any doubts about the quality of the meat and its freshness, throw it out—don't take chances.

CONVENTIONAL COOKING

17-11. General guidelines to meat cookery. Because meat is a protein food, it must be cooked at moderate temperatures only until done. The proper cooking method brings out the best in a cut of meat. The protein becomes firm as it coagulates, fat melts, connective tissue softens and the meat becomes tender and juicy.

On the other hand, if improperly cooked in dry heat, meat

will be tough, chewy and hard to digest. If overcooked in moist heat, it can be mushy and flavorless.

Tender cuts of meat (see 17-4, "Tenderness of meat") can be cooked in dry heat—roasted, broiled, grilled over an open fire, panbroiled or panfried. When cooking meat in dry heat, your use of seasonings is limited. Recipes often call for rubbing seasoning into a roast. However, seasoning rubbed into meat penetrates the surface only slightly.

Less-tender cuts of meat (see 17-4, "Tenderness of meat") require long, slow cooking in moist heat to soften the connective tissue. They can be braised, stewed or boiled. Meat cooked by any of these methods absorbs flavors from the liquid, enabling you to use assorted seasonings and vegetables to vary a recipe.

17-12. Degree of doneness. Tender cuts of beef, including hamburger, which are cooked by any dry-heat method, can be cooked to different degrees of doneness—rare, medium or well done. Rare means the inside is just heated but it has a bright red color. The outside is cooked and crisp. Well-done meat is cooked completely throughout. Medium is halfway between.

Lamb can be cooked rare, but most people enjoy it well done.

Fresh pork and veal should always be cooked well done to develop their flavors since both are, by nature, very mild. Fresh pork must always be cooked to well done to prevent trichinosis—an intestinal illness caused by undercooked pork. If you broil or grill pork, be sure it is cooked throughout.

Meat cooked in moist heat is always cooked until it is well done, giving it time to tenderize and develop flavors.

If meat is cooked by a dry-heat method, you can tell if it is done by any of several methods:

• *Recommended cooking time.* Keep track of the time the meat cooks. Most recipe books and owner's manuals for ranges have timetables for roasting, broiling and grilling meat.

• *Internal temperature.* Use a roast meat thermometer to tell you the internal temperature of a roast. As the meat roasts, its internal temperature increases. The internal temperature is different from the temperature at which the oven is set.

• *Appearance.* Make a small cut in the meat, either near the center or close to a bone. Check the color of the meat and the juices flowing from the cut.

• *Texture.* Experienced cooks can determine doneness of broiled meat by pressing down on it with a blunt instrument such as a spoon. Meat that is done has a firm texture while uncooked meat feels more springy.

17-13. Meat tenderizers. Less-tender cuts of meat may be tenderized by several different methods:

• Commercial meat tenderizers contain protein-digesting enzymes from plants such as papayas, figs and pineapple. Tenderizers can reduce the cooking time for less-tender cuts of meat by about 25%. Be sure to follow package instructions carefully. Using meat tenderizer improperly can result in mushy, crumbly meat.

• Mechanical methods such as grinding, pounding or cutting tenderize meat by breaking down and cutting the connective tissues and tough fibers. Less-tender cuts of meat can be pounded with a meat tenderizing hammer or ground into hamburger. Thin cuts such as flank steak are made partially tender by scoring—making rows of shallow cuts about an inch apart.

• Add acidic food to the cooking liquid, such as tomatoes, vinegar, wine and fruit juices. Sometimes meat is marinated in an acidic food mixture. While marinating may tenderize a thin slice of meat, it only penetrates slightly below the surface of thicker cuts and only if the meat is allowed to marinate at least overnight. Generally, marinating for an hour or so may help to flavor meat rather than tenderize it.

17-14. Roasting meat. Roasting and baking mean the same: cooking a food uncovered in the oven. The word "roast" is generally applied to meat while "bake" refers to baked products such as breads and cakes. However, some meats such as ham are baked. Baked or roasted, the process for cooking meats in dry heat in the oven is basically the same. (See 4-20, "Cooking in dry heat.")

Roasting is usually used for large, tender cuts of meat such as loin, rib and leg roasts. Small cuts dry out before they cook completely.

Use moderate oven temperatures for roasting meat: 300°F to 325°F for beef, veal and lamb and 325°F to 350°F for pork. Higher temperatures cause excess loss of juices and shrinkage.

The only possible exception is a beef tenderloin roast, which is often roasted at 425°F and served rare. Since the beef tenderloin is thinner than most roasts, the higher temperature helps to give a crisp, flavorful crust but cooks the interior just to the rare stage.

Pork loin roasts should be cooked at 325°F so they can cook well done to the center.

Never cover the meat. Use a shallow roasting pan, large enough to hold the meat and drippings. Avoid pans with high sides which may hold in moisture and keep the dry heated oven air from circulating around the roast.

If you cover the meat, either with a pan lid or foil, or place the meat in a plastic cooking bag, you are no longer roasting —you are cooking the meat in moist heat. This is an acceptable method, even for tender cuts. However, you won't get the crisp outer crust with its distinctive flavor, typical of dry-heat roasting.

To roast meat, place the meat on a rack. This keeps the meat out of the juices and fat. If the meat rests in drippings, it fries rather than roasts. Some meats, such as rib roasts, have a natural bone structure that can serve as a base to hold them out of drippings so a rack is not needed.

Place the meat fat side up. This allows the fat to baste the roast, adding flavor and juiciness. If the meat is very lean, baste the top occasionally with the drippings or place strips of bacon or suet on top of the roast.

Add seasonings, including vegetables, to the drippings for a more flavorful gravy.

It's a little difficult to time a roast to exact doneness because of the variables involved—shape and size of the roast, whether it is boneless or with bones, temperature of the roast when put in the oven and accuracy of the oven thermostat. A timetable can only serve as a guide. Following are approximate cooking times for roasts:

Beef rib with bones—30 minutes per pound for rare, 38 minutes per pound for medium and 40 to 45 minutes per pound for well done.

Boneless beef rump roast—28 to 30 minutes per pound for medium to well done.

Veal leg—30 to 35 minutes per pound.

Veal loin, lamb leg and shoulder—30 to 35 minutes per pound.

Pork loin—35 to 40 minutes per pound.

The surest way to check the doneness of the roast is to use a roast thermometer. Insert the thermometer in the fleshiest part of the roast, away from bone and fat. When the thermometer reaches the desired internal temperature, remove the roast

from the oven. Following are internal temperatures for roasts:
BEEF
    Rare—140°F
BEEF AND LAMB
    Medium—160°F
BEEF, LAMB, FRESH PORK AND VEAL
    Well done—170°F
CURED AND SMOKED PORK
    Follow label directions.

If you don't have a meat thermometer, judge doneness by the appearance of the meat and juices. (See 17-12, "Degree of doneness.")

If a roast is overcooked, the pan juices will usually evaporate and the remaining drippings will scorch.

Allow the roast to stand about 15 to 20 minutes before carving. The standing period makes the meat firmer and easier to carve. Because of the heat in the roast, the internal temperature will continue to rise about 5 more degrees during the standing time. You may want to remove a beef roast when it is slightly underdone to make up for the slight increase in temperature during standing.

If you're not ready to serve the roast, you can keep it warm in the oven at 160°F.

17-15. Broiling meat. (See 4-21, "Broiling.") Broil only tender cuts of meat such as hamburger; lamb chops; liver; and beef porterhouse, club, sirloin and rib steaks. Pork chops can be broiled but be sure they are thoroughly cooked in the center. Cured meats such as bacon and ham can also be broiled.

Steaks and chops should be at least 1 inch thick while a ham slice should be at least ½ inch thick. If you broil thinner slices, they dry out before they have a chance to brown. Thinner slices are best panbroiled.

Trim off excess fat. With a sharp knife, cut through or score the remaining fat and connective tissue around the edge of the meat. Make the cuts at about 1-inch intervals. Fat and connective tissue shrink as they cook and the meat curls. The part that curls up will be closer to the heat and may overcook. Cutting through fat and connective tissue keeps the meat flat as it cooks.

Wipe the meat completely dry. Moisture clinging to meat keeps it from browning and getting crisp.

If meat has a great deal of fat, pour a little water into the bottom pan to keep the fat drippings from smoking.

Don't season meat before broiling. Salt draws out juices, preventing browning and crisping.

As the meat broils, the outside sears, keeping juices inside. About halfway through the broiling time, turn the meat. Add salt and other seasonings before turning, but do not salt the raw side that is yet to broil.

Broil the other side until done as you desire. Test for doneness. (See 17-12, "Degree of doneness.") Season and serve hot.

Excess spattering and smoking mean the heat is too high. Move the rack to a lower position.

Don't broil a frozen cut of meat. While it can be done, the results are not satisfactory. As the meat thaws under the broiler, it gives off moisture which prevents browning and crisping.

17-16. Grilling meat outdoors. (See 4-22, "Outdoor grill.") Meat tender enough to be broiled can be grilled on an outdoor grill. Thick roasts can also be cooked on some grills. Follow the manufacturer's instructions for your grill.

If desired, marinate the meat for at least an hour or so in a flavorful sauce before cooking. Baste the meat with the sauce as it cooks.

Rub the grid with suet or salad oil to keep meat from sticking to the bars. When placing the meat on the grid, allow space between each piece so it can brown.

If you're roasting meat on a rotisserie or covered grill, use a drip pan to prevent smoking or flaming. You can make a disposable drip pan from heavy-duty aluminum foil. Place the pan directly under the roast, a little to the back of the grill. Build the charcoal fire around the drip pan.

17-17. Panbroiling meat. (See 4-14, "Panbroiling.") Tender cuts less than an inch thick can be panbroiled. Score the fat and connective tissue around the edge. When browned, turn. Thicker cuts may have to be turned twice before they are done. To test for doneness, see 17-12, "Degree of doneness."

17-18. Panfrying meat. (See 4-15, "Panfrying, sauteing, stir-frying.") Tender cuts of meat can also be panfried in shallow fat. As a rule, start out with about ⅛ inch of fat in the pan. Use less if the meat is high in fat. If the meat is breaded or batter dipped, start out with ¼ inch of fat since the breading will absorb some of the fat.

For even browning, use a heavy aluminum or cast-iron skillet. Stainless steel pans sometimes develop hot spots which heat unevenly.

Don't try to fry too many pieces at one time. Meat gives off moisture and steam as it fries. If you have too many pieces, the excess steam will keep the meat from getting crisp.

17-19. Stir-frying meat. (See 4-15, "Panfrying, sauteing, stir-frying.") Very thin slices of raw meat are fried quickly in a small amount of oil in a wok or skillet. Generally, the meat is fried first and removed from the pan. Then vegetables are fried and steamed and the meat is added for final heating. The meat can also be partially cooked, vegetables added, and the entire mixture cooked quickly until the desired doneness.

Meat for stir-frying must be very thinly sliced. The easiest way is to partially freeze a boneless cut of meat. The partially frozen meat is much firmer than an unfrozen piece and is easier to slice. Use a sharp, heavy butcher knife or cleaver and a cutting board.

17-20. Braising meat. (See 4-7, "Braising.") Braising is used for less-tender cuts of meat.

Tender meat with mild flavor, such as pork, is frequently braised in a seasoned sauce to enhance its flavor. Very thick or stuffed pork chops are braised to be certain they are cooked through to the center.

Flavors can be varied by using fruit and vegetable juices as all or part of the liquid.

Braised meat is always cooked to well done. Test for doneness with a fork. If the fork can be inserted and removed easily, the meat is done. Recipes give approximate cooking times for braised meat because actual time varies depending on the cut, size and shape of cut, grade of meat and the type of liquid.

For instance, if the recipe calls for adding water as a liquid and you decide to use tomato juice or wine, the meat will cook faster because of the acidic food. (See 17-13, "Meat tenderizers.")

17-21. Stewing meat. (See 4-5, "Stewing.") Less-tender cuts of meat make delicious stews. The meat can be browned for added flavor and a darker gravy. Generally, water is used as the liquid for meat stews.

Vegetables such as tomatoes, carrots and potatoes are added close to the end of the cooking time for the meat. If added too soon, the vegetables overcook and become mushy. But if you're thickening the stew with cooked vegetables, add them early enough to overcook and break down into a puree. (See 10-21, "To thicken with vegetables.")

Different kinds of vegetables are generally added at different times, depending on the cooking time each needs. Whole carrots, for instance, take longer to cook than diced potatoes. If you're making up your own recipe, check a vegetable cooking chart in a basic cookbook to determine cooking times for the vegetables you're using. Keep in mind that each time you add a cold vegetable to the stew, the liquid will need time to warm up. Begin adding the vegetables early enough so that the combined cooking time for the vegetables won't overcook the meat.

The meat should remain covered with liquid. If the liquid begins to cook down, add a little hot liquid. The liquid can be thickened in different ways. See Chapter 10, "Thickeners."

17-22. Red color in cooked pork. Even though it is cooked well done, pork sometimes has a red color. The color is caused by chemicals naturally present in liquids and vegetables cooked with the meat. Chemicals present in heating and exhaust gases in the oven may also cause the red color.

17-23. "Fell" on lamb. The fell is a paper-like covering on lamb. Generally, it is removed by the butcher from small cuts such as steaks and chops. However, it is left on roasts because it helps to retain the shape of the meat. It also holds in moisture, which helps speed up the cooking.

Don't remove the fell from a lamb roast until the meat is cooked.

17-24. Cooking frozen meat. If possible, thaw frozen meat before broiling. See 17-15, "Broiling meat."

To roast frozen meat, add about one-third to one-half to the cooking time given in the recipe, depending on the size of the cut.

Less-tender cuts of meat will cook in moist heat in about the same time given in the recipe, whether they are frozen or thawed.

17-25. Gravies. Meat can be served with gravy, which is made from the drippings in the pan and has a definite meat flavor. Gravy can be thickened or unthickened. Meat served "au jus" means it is served with unthickened pan juices.

In either case, remove as much of the fat from the meat juices as possible. You can do this in several ways:

• Use a baster to remove fat floating on the surface of the drippings.

• Pour off all the pan drippings into a small pan and place the pan in a bowl of ice water. The fat floating on the surface solidifies. You can also place the pan in the freezer for a short time. Remove all but about a Tablespoon or two of the fat.

Return the drippings to the pan. Gradually bring the mixture to a boil and deglaze the pan. Scrape off all the flavorful bits of meat and crust remaining in the bottom of the pan. These give a wonderful flavor to the gravy. Simmer, allowing the liquid to evaporate until you have the desired flavor. Add more seasonings, if necessary. To thicken, see 10-3, "To thicken with all-purpose flour."

If drippings consist only of grease and no meat juices, you can still make a flavorful gravy by using a liquid such as a vegetable or fruit juice or wine to deglaze the pan.

MICROWAVE COOKING

17-26MW. Thaw frozen meats completely. Before microwaving them, thaw frozen meats completely. When defrosting, foods get hotter on the bottom than on the top, so turn large pieces of meat over as they defrost.

To defrost, use about 5 minutes for every pound at the defrost setting. Follow this with a carryover time of 5 minutes for every pound. Alternate defrosting and carryover cooking until the meat has thawed.

17-27MW. Roasts for microwave cooking. Select tender, boneless roasts, about 3 to 5 pounds, with a uniform shape, for best microwave results. Bones reflect microwaves, resulting in uneven cooking.

If a roast has an uneven shape, shield thinner parts with a small smooth piece of foil during the first half of the microwave period. Secure the foil to the meat with a wooden toothpick if necessary. Don't let the foil touch any part of the oven interior or other pieces of foil. Remove the foil halfway through cooking when you rotate and turn the meat.

Roasts, as a rule, must be both rotated and turned halfway through the cooking period. (See 4-42MW, "Turning and stirring.") Otherwise, they won't cook evenly.

17-28MW. Browning. As a rule, meats microwaved for

more than 10 minutes will turn a dark brown. However, roasts do not develop the crisp outer crust and flavor characteristic of those prepared in dry heat.

17-29MW. Meat with fat. If meat is fat, cover loosely with paper towel or wax paper to prevent spattering.

17-30MW. Use a microwave meat thermometer. Never use a regular meat thermometer in a microwave oven. A standard roast meat thermometer contains mercury, which is incompatible with microwaves. If your microwave oven does not have a temperature probe, buy a special meat thermometer for microwave cooking.

17-31MW. Ground meat. To brown ground meat easily, put a heat-proof plastic colander in a large glass bowl. Place ground meat in the colander.

If the meat is frozen, thaw it first—microwave on the defrost or low setting for 6 or 7 minutes for every pound and allow carryover time of 6 or 7 minutes for every pound.

When defrosted, cook on high. Break up the clumps regularly. The fat will drip through the colander into the bowl below. Stop cooking when the meat is still slightly pink as carryover cooking will complete the browning. Stir the meat when you remove it from the oven.

17-32MW. Less-tender cuts of meat. Less-tender cuts will be done quickly in the microwave oven but they will be tough because the connective tissue has not had enough time to tenderize. (See 17-1, "Composition of meat," and 17-4, "Tenderness of meat.") Less-tender cuts of meat must be cooked on lower power settings, with ample carryover time allowed to tenderize the connective tissue. Follow the recommendations in your microwave oven owner's manual for cooking less-tender cuts of meat.

17-33MW. Overcooked meat. Be careful not to overcook meat in the microwave oven. Overcooked meat gets hard, tough and chewy and may be impossible to eat.

When sausage begins to overcook, the casing splits.

17-34MW. Carryover time for a roast. Remove the roast from the oven, cover with a foil tent, and allow about 15 to 20 minutes of carryover time.

17-35MW. Meatloaf. When microwaving meatloaf, shape

the meat into a round ball or use a ring mold. If you shape the meat into a long loaf, the edges will overcook.

17-36MW. Drippings. Remove drippings from the pan frequently. They attract microwaves and slow down cooking.

17-37MW. Bacon. If bacon cooks unevenly, buy a different brand. Different curing processes can affect the way bacon cooks in the microwave oven. If cooking more than 3 or 4 pieces, rearrange them halfway through the cooking time so they cook more evenly.

Poultry

BUYING

18-1. Grades. Poultry sold through interstate commerce must be inspected for wholesomeness. Through a voluntary program, poultry is also graded. The inspection mark and grade shield usually appear either on the wrapping or on the wingtag.

Grades for poultry have been established by USDA. Grade A is the highest, and indicates a fully fleshed and meaty bird with an attractive appearance. Grade B poultry is less attractive, lacks meatiness and is seldom found in supermarkets.

18-2. Tenderness. The tenderness of the bird is determined by its age and class. Class indicates the cooking method to use for best results, such as "broiler." The following terms appear on poultry labels to designate age and class:

CHICKENS
- *Rock Cornish*—under 2 pounds; tender; usually roasted.
- *Broiler or Fryer*—2 to 3½ pounds; tender.
- *Roaster*—2½ to 5 pounds; tender; best for roasting.
- *Capon*—4 to 7 pounds; male chickens which are surgically desexed; fine flavor and more white meat than chicken; best for roasting.
- *Stewing Chicken, Hen or Fowl*—4½ to 6 pounds; plump, meaty, mature hen; best cooked in liquid, such as braised, stewed or simmered.

Allow about 1 pound of chicken for each serving.

TURKEYS
- *Fryer or Roaster (very young turkey)*—4 to 8 pounds.
- *Young Turkey, Young Hen or Young Tom*—8 to over 24 pounds.

• *Mature or Old Turkey*—8 to over 24 pounds.

Allow an average of about 1 pound of turkey for each serving. The larger the bird, the more meat it will have in proportion to bone and fat. That means you'll get more servings per pound from a larger bird, such as one weighing 18 pounds, than you will from a smaller bird weighing 8 or 10 pounds.

DUCKS

• *Duckling, Young Duckling, Broiler or Fryer*—3 to over 5 pounds.

• *Roaster Duckling*—3 to over 5 pounds.

• *Mature or Old Duck*—3 to over 5 pounds.

Ducks have more fat than chickens or turkeys. Allow about 1½ pounds for one serving.

GEESE

• *Young Goose*—4 to over 14 pounds.

• *Mature or Old Goose*—4 to over 14 pounds.

Allow about 1 to 1½ pounds for one serving, depending on the size of the bird. Larger birds will have more meat per pound in proportion to bone than smaller birds.

POULTRY PRODUCTS

Poultry is available in halves and pieces. Some, such as turkey, are available as boneless rolled roasts.

Cured poultry products are also available, such as chicken frankfurters and turkey hams and pastrami.

18-3. Guidelines for buying poultry.

Read the label to be sure you're buying the kind of poultry you want.

Check the color of the flesh. A yellowish skin usually means fat underneath the skin. A bluish skin generally indicates a lack of fat.

Note the condition of the skin. Look for a fine-textured, smooth skin, free of bruises. It should be unbroken and clean of all feathers and hairs. Breaks in the skin will allow juices to escape when the poultry cooks.

If the poultry is frozen, be sure the package is not broken. A break in the package exposes the poultry to air, resulting in freezer burn.

Frozen poultry should be hard.

Consider buying pieces if whole poultry gives more servings than you want.

STORING

18-4. Storing in the refrigerator. Wrap fresh poultry

loosely in wax paper and refrigerate immediately. If it is pre-packaged in plastic, store it in its original wrapper. Use fresh poultry within one or two days.

When you open prepackaged poultry, you may notice a strong aroma. This is considered normal and should disappear within a few minutes. If the unusual odor continues, return the package to the store.

Never stuff a bird and refrigerate it for roasting on the following day. Because a stuffed bird is thick and compact, the inside takes a long time to cool and harmful bacteria flourishes.

If you're on a tight time schedule, clean the bird and refrigerate it. Prepare the stuffing but don't add the liquid. Refrigerate the stuffing. When you're ready to roast the bird, add the liquid to the stuffing and finish stuffing and trussing the bird.

When storing leftovers, remove the stuffing from the cavity and refrigerate separately. Use leftover poultry and stuffing in a day or two. For longer storage, freeze leftovers.

18-5. Storing and defrosting frozen poultry. Store frozen poultry in the freezer immediately.

To defrost frozen poultry, place in a pan in the refrigerator. For birds under 5 pounds, allow about 2 hours of thawing time for each pound. Larger birds may take several days:

> 4 to 12 pounds—1 to 2 days
> 14 to 20 pounds—2 to 3 days
> 20 to 24 pounds—3 to 4 days

You can also thaw poultry in cold water for 2 to 6 hours, depending on its size. The poultry should be in its original freezer wrapper with no breaks or tears in the wrapping.

For larger birds, the safest method is to thaw them in the refrigerator.

Thawing time will vary greatly, depending on the temperature in the refrigerator, how hard the bird is frozen, the size and shape of the bird and the amount of fat in the bird.

Never thaw a frozen STUFFED turkey. It must be roasted frozen.

CONVENTIONAL COOKING

18-6. Cooking poultry. (See 4-24, "Protein cooking.") Because poultry is a protein food, it must be cooked at moderate temperatures only until done. Overcooking poultry in dry heat makes it tough and dry. If overcooked in moist heat, poultry loses flavor and gets mushy.

18-7. Roasting poultry. (See 4-20, "Cooking in dry heat.") Frozen commercially stuffed poultry must be roasted frozen according to package directions.

Frozen unstuffed poultry must be thawed before cooking. That's the only way you can remove the bag of giblets from the cavity and wash out the cavity.

To prepare a bird for roasting, remove the bag of giblets from the body or the neck cavity. Wash the bird thoroughly in cold running water and drain well. Do this just before you plan to roast the bird. Don't keep the bird at room temperature for any length of time—harmful bacteria will begin to grow.

To stuff the bird, spoon the dressing into the bird loosely to allow room for expansion. Stuff the neck cavity also. If you prefer not to stuff the bird, rub the inside with seasoning. Place aromatic vegetables such as carrots, celery, leeks, onions, garlic or parsley in the cavity for flavor.

Sew the body cavity closed with a large needle and cotton thread, but avoid synthetic thread—it might melt when heated. You can also insert small metal sewers along the body cavity opening and lace cotten string around the pins.

Truss the bird. Your main goal is to make the bird as compact as possible so it cooks evenly and is easy to handle. Tie cotton string around the tail and secure the legs to the tail. Use a skewer to fasten the neck flap over the neck opening. You can also sew it down with a large needle and cotton thread.

To secure the wings, tie them close to the body with cotton string. Or fold the wings toward the back so the tips rest on the back—the wings will stay in this position.

To roast poultry in dry heat, place it breast-side up on a shallow rack in a roasting pan large enough to hold the drippings. Be sure the rack is high enough to keep the bird out of the juices and to allow heat to circulate evenly around the bird. Brush turkey or chicken skin with melted butter. Ducks and geese have enough natural fat.

If you have a roast meat thermometer, insert it so the bulb is in the center of the inside thigh muscle or the thickest part of the breast meat. If the bird is stuffed, insert the thermometer into the center of the stuffing. Be sure the bulb does not touch bone or fat. If you're roasting a frozen commercially stuffed turkey, don't attempt to insert a roast meat thermometer—the bird is too hard.

Baste chicken or turkey occasionally. Ducks and geese have ample fat under the skin which self-bastes as it melts.

When the poultry is about two-thirds cooked, cut the string at the tail to release the legs. This allows heat to reach the heavy-meated part so it can brown. If excess browning occurs, cover the area with a loose tent of foil or a cloth moistened with fat or oil.

To judge cooking time, estimate the time the bird should cook from the roasting timetable. Unless they specify otherwise, timetables generally give roasting times for stuffed birds. Add about half an hour to your estimate to give yourself a little leeway in case you misjudge the cooking time. Allow the bird to stand about 15 minutes after cooking for easier carving.

ROASTING TIMETABLE FOR STUFFED POULTRY

Pounds	Hours
CHICKEN, WHOLE (Broiler, Fryer, Roaster)	
1½ to 2½	1 to 2
2½ to 4½	2 to 3½
TURKEY, WHOLE	
6 to 8	3 to 3½
8 to 12	3½ to 4½
12 to 16	4½ to 5½
16 to 20	5½ to 6½
20 to 24	6½ to 7
TURKEY PIECES, HALVES, QUARTERS	
3 to 8	2 to 3
8 to 12	3 to 4
BONELESS POULTRY ROASTS	
3 to 9	2½ to 3½
DUCKS	
4 to 6	2 to 3
GEESE	
8 to 10	3½ to 4½

OVEN TEMPERATURE: 325°F

INTERNAL TEMPERATURE: 180°F to 185°F

If you're roasting an unstuffed bird, deduct about 3 minutes of cooking time for every pound.

If you "roast" poultry in aluminum foil or in a special heavy-duty plastic cooking bag, the cooking time is usually shorter. Begin testing for doneness about three-fourths through the cooking time.

If you're using the special heavy-duty cooking bag, follow directions on the package carefully. If you miss a step, the bag may burst in the oven, spattering grease and possibly igniting.

To roast self-basting turkeys, follow the directions on the wrapping.

Poultry halves, quarters or pieces may also be roasted. Follow the directions given for roasting a whole bird.

18-8. Stuffing for poultry. Allow about 1 cup of stuffing for each pound of poultry. If you have stuffing left over, bake it in a greased and covered casserole for about 30 to 45 minutes, depending on the amount.

Bread cubes usually form the base for the stuffing. You can use any type of bread, from white to whole wheat or corn bread. Some stuffings are made with rice instead of bread. In addition to a wide variety of seasonings, you can add oysters, chestnuts, cooked and chopped giblets, sausage, nuts and fruit.

To cook the neck and giblets for stuffing, cover with cold water, season, cover the pan and simmer for about 45 minutes. You can use the broth as a liquid for the stuffing.

The stuffing can be either moist or dry, depending on personal preference. Add more liquid to the stuffing if you prefer it moist. Juices from the bird will add moisture to the stuffing during roasting.

18-9. Broiling poultry. (See 4-21, "Broiling.") Very young chickens, turkeys and ducks can be broiled. Split the poultry in half lengthwise or cut into quarters or pieces. The broiling time will vary, depending on the size of the bird.

To broil chicken, place the chicken skin side down on the broiler grid. Brush with melted fat or oil. Season. Place broiler pan so the top of the chicken is about 4 inches below the heat. About halfway through the broiling period, turn the chicken, using tongs. Brush with melted fat or oil and season. Continue broiling until done. Total broiling time will be about 40 minutes, depending on the size of the pieces.

To broil turkey, place the turkey pieces skin side down in a broiler pan—do not use the grid. Brush the turkey with melted fat or oil. Season. Place the pan in the broiler so the top of the turkey is about 9 inches away from the heat. About halfway during the cooking period, turn the turkey pieces skin side up with tongs. Baste with the juices in the pan. Season. Continue broiling until done. Total broiling time will be from 80 to 90 minutes, depending on the size of the pieces.

To broil ducks, follow directions given above for chicken. However, don't brush ducks with fat or oil—they have enough natural fat of their own.

18-10. Panfrying poultry. (See 4-15, "Panfrying, sauteing, stir-frying.") Use this method for tender poultry only.

If you wish, coat lean poultry such as chicken with seasoned flour or crumbs before frying. (See 4-19, "Breading food for frying.")

Have about a half inch of cooking oil or fat in a large, heavy skillet. Heat over medium-high heat until a cube of bread will sizzle. Begin with the large, meaty pieces such as the breast and thigh. Place in the hot fat skin side down. Add remaining poultry. If you have too many pieces, they may not get brown and crisp. Instead of cooking all of them at once, divide them into batches. Keep the cooked batch warm in the oven.

Smaller pieces will take a shorter time to cook than larger ones. Fry small poultry such as chicken for 15 to 30 minutes and larger poultry such as turkey for 45 to 60 minutes. Larger pieces may take longer. To cook larger pieces, cover the skillet.

When the pieces are done on one side, turn them over with tongs. Remove pieces as they are done.

18-11. Oven frying poultry. Oven frying uses much less fat than panfrying and still gives a flavorful, crisp crust.

To oven fry poultry, prepare poultry as for pan frying. (See 18-10, "Panfrying poultry.")

Place chicken or duck in a large, shallow roasting pan, skin side up. Place turkey skin side down. Brush with melted fat or oil. If you wish, coat chicken with seasoned crumbs before baking. Bake at 350°F.

Bake chicken and duck uncovered for about 1 to 1¼ hours. Do not turn.

Bake turkey uncovered for about 1½ hours. About halfway during baking, turn pieces over and baste.

18-12. Braising poultry. (See 4-7, "Braising.") Any bird that is too tough to cook in dry heat can be cooked in moist heat.

To braise poultry, cut the poultry into pieces. If you prefer, you can braise a whole bird. Brown the pieces, although it is not necessary. Add a small amount of liquid and seasonings. Add herbs and spices during the last 30 minutes of cooking.

Cover and cook as directed in the recipe. If you're making up your own recipe, cook over low heat or in the oven at 350°F until tender. The cooking time will depend on the size of the pieces and tenderness of the bird. Generally, allow about 1½ to 2½ hours.

If you're braising whole poultry in the oven, uncover the pan during the last half hour of cooking so the bird can brown.

18-13. Stewing poultry. (See 4-5, "Stewing.") Use this method for mature, less-tender birds.

To stew poultry, cut it into pieces. Place in a deep pot and add just enough water to cover. Season. Bring to a boil, reduce the heat to simmer and simmer until tender. It usually takes 2 to 3 hours.

If you wish to add vegetables, add them near the end of the cooking time according to the time each vegetable will take to cook. Be careful not to overcook the vegetables. Add herbs and spices during the last 30 minutes of cooking.

18-14. Doneness tests. You can test poultry for doneness in several ways:
• Poultry roasted in dry heat—use a meat thermometer.
• Whole poultry—move the drumstick gently. It should twist easily in the thigh joint. Use a clean dish cloth or towel when grasping the drumstick to protect your hand from the heat.
• Poultry pieces—halves: move the drumstick, as described above; smaller pieces: pierce a thick piece, such as the breast meat near the shoulder joint, with a fork. If it pierces easily and the juices flowing out are clear and not pink, the poultry is done.

18-15. Fat in poultry. Most of the fat in poultry is located right under the skin. You may also find pads of fat inside the body and neck cavities.

If you're diet conscious, remove the skin from cooked poultry before eating it, and you'll remove most of the fat. Don't remove the skin before cooking—it adds flavor to the poultry and keeps it from drying out as it cooks.

Chicken fat has its own mild, distinctive flavor and can be used as a fat in recipes. It must be rendered because it's perishable and turns rancid quickly, even when refrigerated. To render chicken fat, pull the fat out of the cavity before cooking the chicken. Dice the fat along with any uncooked skin. Place in a heavy skillet and cover with cold water. Boil, uncovered, until the liquid evaporates. If you wish, add chopped onion or garlic for flavor. Cook until the solid pieces are brown and shriveled. Cool slightly and drain off the fat. Strain it through a strainer lined with cheesecloth.

Refrigerate the rendered fat in a tightly closed container and use within 2 or 3 weeks. If you want to keep it longer, freeze it and use within 2 months.

Many people consider the leftover browned skin and pieces, sometimes called cracklings, a delicacy. They can be used to flavor casseroles and cooked vegetables. This same method can be used to render other fats such as duck fat and beef suet.

18-16. Pink color in cooked poultry. Cooked poultry sometimes has a pink color due to a chemical reaction between exhaust gases in the oven and substances in the poultry. It happens in both gas and electric ovens.

Even though the meat is pink, it is safe to eat if the poultry passes the signs of doneness and has cooked for the estimated time.

18-17. Dark bones in cooked poultry. Sometimes the bones in cooked poultry, along with surrounding meat, turn a dark color. This is characteristic of frozen poultry. During freezing and thawing, blood cells in the bones break down. Cooking turns the red blood to brown, but the dark color has no effect on flavor.

MICROWAVE COOKING

18-18MW. Defrosting frozen poultry. Leave the frozen poultry in the original wrapper, unless it is foil. In that case, remove the foil and rewrap the poultry in paper or plastic. Remove metal ties from wrapping. Use the defrost setting until the poultry is defrosted, following directions in your owner's manual.

If your oven does not have a defrost setting, use the lowest power. Alternate 2 minutes of microwave heating and 2 minutes of carryover cooking.

Turn and rotate a whole bird. Separate parts frequently. Make certain the poultry does not begin to cook as it defrosts.

Since giblets defrost more quickly than other parts, remove them as soon as they are slightly pliable. Bonier parts, such as wings, also thaw more quickly than meatier parts.

When properly defrosted, poultry feels moist and still cold but it is pliable, not hard and stiff.

18-19MW. Tying the bird for microwaving. Tie the legs and wings close to the body to make the shape as even as possible. Use cotton string. Don't use any synthetic string or thread—it may melt or catch fire.

Pat the bird dry before roasting.

18-20MW. Piercing the skin. Whether you're microwaving a whole bird or pieces, pierce the skin to keep air bubbles from forming and bursting.

18-21MW. Using a roasting rack. To cook the poultry more evenly, put it on a roasting rack designed for use in a microwave oven.

18-22MW. Salt. Do not salt the surface. You may, if you wish, rub the skin with unsalted oil or melted shortening.

18-23MW. Roasting a whole bird. Begin by placing the bird breast side down on the roasting rack. This is the opposite of the method used when roasting in a conventional oven.

If the bird weighs less than 10 pounds, rotate the bird and turn it over breast side up about halfway through the microwaving time.

Larger birds will need to be turned and rotated several times. Follow the directions in the owner's manual for your microwave oven.

18-24MW. Poultry pieces. When microwaving poultry pieces, place meatier parts near the outside of the dish and bonier parts toward the center. Tuck giblets under the breast. Begin by placing the pieces skin side down. Halfway through the cooking time, turn them skin side up.

18-25MW. Breading. If you're breading chicken for microwaving, don't use flour—it gets gummy. Use crumbs—either plain or mixed with seasoning.

18-26MW. Covering poultry. To distribute the heat more evenly, cover poultry loosely during the first half of the cooking time with wax paper or plastic wrap. Uncover it during the last half of the cooking time, after you have turned and rotated it, so it browns better.

18-27MW. Shield certain parts. Some parts of the poultry may overcook quickly, such as wing tips and legs. Shield them with small, smooth pieces of aluminum foil. Fasten the foil to the poultry with wooden toothpicks—don't use plastic picks as they may melt or ignite. Be sure the foil does not touch any part of the oven interior.

18-28MW. Adding color. Microwaved poultry will darken if it is cooked for more than 15 minutes, but it does not get crisp. To increase color, baste it with a browning sauce. You can buy commercially prepared browning sauces or make your own. Mix butter (not margarine) with brown sugar and honey or butter with soy sauce and paprika.

18-29MW. Removing drippings. Remove fat and juices as they accumulate in the pan. A baster is the easiest way to do this. Fat and juices left in the pan slow down cooking because they attract the microwaves. Save the juices for gravy or soup.

18-30MW. Chicken livers. Don't overcook chicken livers— they get tough and chewy. Cook them on a lower power. If your oven has only High power, put a cup of water in the oven with the livers to absorb some of the microwaves. Pierce them before cooking.

18-31MW. Carryover cooking. For carryover cooking, remove the poultry from the microwave oven. Cover loosely with a tent of aluminum foil to retain the heat.

18-32MW. Stuffing. If you're roasting poultry with stuffing, make a dry stuffing. Because liquids evaporate only slightly in a microwave oven, poultry juices will add moisture to the stuffing.

Precook vegetables used in the stuffing, such as celery or onions.

Pack the stuffing very lightly into the cavity to make room for rapid expansion as it cooks.

19 🍴 *Seafood*

BUYING

19-1. Kinds of seafood. Seafood is a general name for edible creatures living in either fresh or salt water. You'll find two general types of seafood in the marketplace: fish and shellfish.

Fish have fins, a back bone and a bony structure that is part of the backbone. Hundreds of different kinds of fish are available, from white meat to dark. White fish generally have the lowest number of calories.

Shellfish have a hard outer shell, no backbone or bones and a soft body. They include shrimp, lobsters, crabs, clams, oysters and scallops.

19-2. Forms of fish. Fish is available in many different forms:

• *Whole.* Fish just as it is caught; scales must be removed and insides taken out; head, tail and fins may be cut off when bought; 1 pound makes 1 serving.

• *Drawn.* Fish is cleaned on the inside only; you must scale it and cut off fins; 1 pound makes 1 serving.

• *Dressed.* Fish is cleaned and scaled; head, tail and fins are cut off; ready to cook; 1 pound makes 2 servings.

• *Steaks.* Slices of fish about ¾ to 1 inch thick, cut across the fish; a part of the backbone is in the steak; ready to cook; 1 pound makes 3 servings.

• *Fillet.* Sides of fish cut away from the backbone; usually boneless and ready to cook; 1 pound makes 3 servings.

• *Chunks.* Large pieces of fish cut across the fish; ready to cook; 1 pound makes 3 servings.

• *Blocks.* Frozen blocks of fish fillets and pieces; 1 pound makes 3 servings.

• *Sticks and portions.* Cut from blocks of frozen fillets; covered with batter; follow package instructions for cooking; 1 pound makes 4 servings.

• *Canned.* Some fish, such as herring, tuna, salmon and sardines, are available in cans or jars. 1 pound makes 6 servings.

• *Cured.* Some fish such as herring and salmon are available cured and smoked.

19-3. Forms of shellfish.

Some shellfish can be purchased live, such as lobsters and crabs, but they must be kept live until cooked.

Shellfish vary greatly in the number of servings per pound. On the average, 1 pound of cooked shellfish without the shells makes about 4 servings.

•*Lobsters* can be purchased live, frozen, canned or cooked. A live lobster shell is green or brown, but turns a bright red when cooked. Generally 1 small lobster or half a large lobster makes 1 serving. A 2½ pound lobster makes about 2 cups of cooked lobster.

• *Crabs* can be purchased live, frozen, canned or cooked. About 2 or 3 small crabs make one serving.

• *Shrimp* are sold fresh, frozen or cooked. Only the tail section of the creature is eaten. Shrimp vary in size. Prawns are jumbo-size shrimp—2 or 3 are enough for one serving. "Green" shrimp is raw shrimp with the shell. 1 pound of green shrimp makes about 3 servings. 2 to 2½ pounds of green shrimp give about 2 cups of cooked, shelled shrimp.

• *Oysters* are sold live in the shell, shucked (shell removed), frozen and canned. Generally, 1 quart of undrained, shucked oysters makes about 6 servings.

• *Clams* can be purchased live in the shell, shucked, frozen and canned. 6 to 8 shucked clams generally make 1 serving. If you're steaming clams, allow about 1 quart of unshucked clams per serving. 8 quarts of clams in the shell make about 1 quart shucked.

• *Scallops* are the edible parts of the muscle found in the scallop shell. Scallops are sold only without the shell, either fresh or frozen. 1 pound raw scallops makes about 3 or 4 servings.

19-4. Buying fresh fish.
Fish is highly perishable so be

sure fresh fish is really fresh when you buy it. Look for the following characteristics, typical of fresh fish:
- Firm flesh, springy to the touch.
- Fresh and mild aroma. A strong fishy odor means the fish is not fresh.
- Red gills, free from slime.
- Bright, clear, round eyes. The eyes should not be sunken.
- Shiny, bright-colored skin.
- No dried edges.

19-5. Buying fresh shellfish.
- *Shrimp:* Green shrimp should have a fresh aroma and good color. Cooked shrimp should have a mild aroma with a good pink color and should be deveined—the black strip along the back of the shrimp should have been removed before the shrimp were cooked.
- *Lobsters and crabs:* Live ones should be lively. Cooked lobsters and crabs should have a pleasant aroma and good color. Cooked crabmeat should have no ammonia odor.
- *Oysters:* Live oysters in the shell should have tightly closed shells. Discard any oysters with slightly open, cracked or broken shells. Shucked oysters should be plump, shiny and creamy in color. Shucked oysters are packed in their own thick juices. The juices should be clear, not cloudy and free of any sour or unpleasant odor.
- *Clams:* Live clams sold in the shell should have tightly closed shells. If the shells are slightly open, touch them—they should close immediately. Throw out clams that float or any with damaged shells. Shucked clams should be plump and shiny with a fresh aroma. They are packed in their own thick juices, which should be clear, not cloudy and free of any sour or unpleasant odor.
- *Scallops:* Fresh scallops vary in size. They should have a slightly sweet aroma and be free of any liquid.

19-6. Buying frozen seafood. (See 2-11, "Buying frozen food.") Look for packages that are frozen solid and feel hard, with little or no odor. The packages should be tightly sealed so no air can get in. If the seafood is visible, look for good color for the type you're buying and no discoloration.

19-7. Buying canned cured seafood. (See 2-9, "Buying canned food.") Read labels to be sure you're buying the product you want. Compare cost per serving.

STORING

19-8. Storing fresh seafood. Fresh seafood is highly perishable and must be refrigerated. Use within a day or two. Don't put live salt-water lobsters in fresh water—they can live only in salt water. If you have purchased live seafood and it dies in storage, don't use it; discard it.

19-9. Storing frozen seafood. Store in the freezer. If frozen seafood has accidentally thawed, do not refreeze it. Use it immediately. (See 3-4, "Freezer storage.")

19-10. Thawing frozen fish. Thaw frozen fish in the refrigerator, allowing 24 hours for a 1-pound package. Never thaw fish at room temperature or in warm water—the outside will thaw too quickly and begin to spoil.

To speed up thawing, immerse the package of frozen fish in cold water. Be sure the package is waterproof.

Follow package directions for commercially frozen fish. Some may be cooked without thawing.

Frozen steaks and fillets which are not breaded may be broiled, fried or poached without thawing.

19-11. Storing canned and cured seafood.
Read the label on canned seafood for storage directions. Some unopened cans may be stored in a cool, dry area, but others may need refrigeration.

Once cans are opened, remove the contents, store in a tightly covered container and refrigerate. Use within a day or two.

Cured seafood should be refrigerated and used within a few days.

Be safe. If any canned or cured seafood has an off odor or off color, don't eat it.

CONVENTIONAL COOKING

19-12. Cooking seafood. Because it is a protein, seafood must be cooked at moderate temperatures.

Since seafood has little or no connective tissue, it cooks in a relatively short time. As a general rule, cook fish 10 minutes for every inch of thickness. However, the cooking time will vary depending on the temperature of the fish, cooking method and size and shape of fish.

Because fish is tender, it is generally cooked by dry heat methods such as baking, broiling, grilling on an outdoor grill or frying. However, it can also be cooked in moist heat—poached, stewed or steamed.

Most fish is relatively lean. When cooked in dry heat, it must be protected from drying out. Brush it with oil or melted butter or cover with a sauce or buttered crumbs when baking, broiling or grilling.

When overcooked in dry heat, seafood gets tough, dry and chewy and loses its flavor. When overcooked in moist heat, shellfish can get tough and rubbery; fish becomes mushy and falls apart.

19-13. Preparing seafood for cooking.

• *Fish.* Be sure the fish is clean. For broiling or frying, wipe it dry. Inspect fillets carefully to be sure all of the bones have been removed. If you're cooking frozen fish that must be thawed, time the thawing so the fish is thawed when you start to cook. If it's thawed sooner than you need it, keep it refrigerated. Cook thawed frozen fish within 24 hours.

• *Shellfish.* If you're cooking shellfish in the shell, be sure they are clean. Clams and oysters should be well scrubbed. Before shucking clams, scrub and wash them several times in cold water. To help remove the sand, soak them in a salt-water solution made of 1 gallon of water and ⅓ cup of salt. Green shrimp must be deveined: shell and remove the sand vein, a black strip just under the skin along the back of the shrimp. If you cook shrimp with the shells on, devein them after cooking.

19-14. Fish odors.
Because acidic foods help get rid of fish odors, many fish recipes include an acidic liquid such as vinegar, dry white wine or a citrus juice. This explains why lemon is such a popular garnish for fish.

If you're bothered by fish odors on your hands, rub them with a piece of lemon or rinse them in vinegar.

19-15. Substitutions.
If you can't find the exact type of fish called for in a recipe, you can substitute other kinds. Here's a chart of equivalents to help you make substitutions:

2 cups cooked flaked fish = 16 ounces cooked fish fillets,
steaks or blocks
1 pint shucked clams = 18 clams in shells
= 2 7½-oz. cans minced clams

1 cup cooked, flaked crab meat = 1 7½-oz. can crab meat
= 1 6-oz. package frozen crab meat
= 8 to 10 ounces king crab legs in shell
1 cup cooked lobster meat = a 16-oz. whole lobster
= an 8-oz. lobster tail
= 1 5-oz. can lobster
24 oysters in shells = 1 pint shucked oysters
1 cup cooked shelled shrimp = 12 ounces raw shrimp in shells
= 8 ounces raw shelled shrimp
= 1 4½-oz. can shrimp

19-16. Test seafood for doneness. Following are guidelines for determining whether seafood is done:

• *Fish:* Raw fish is translucent with watery-looking juices. As it cooks, the juices turn a milky color and the flesh turns opaque. When all the flesh has turned opaque, the fish is cooked. In addition, when fish is done, the flesh separates easily into flakes and falls away from bones. To test for doneness, pierce with a fork. If the fish flakes easily and the color is opaque, it is done.

• *Lobster and crab* cooked in the shell turn a bright pink when they are done.

• *Shucked oysters* are done when they are plump with slightly curled edges.

• *Whole clams* are done when the shells open.

Serve seafood as soon as it is cooked. If you try to keep it warm before serving, it will lose its quality.

19-17. Baking fish. (See 4-20, "Cooking in dry heat.") Baking is one of the easiest ways to cook fish. Whole fish may be stuffed for baking. You can also stuff fillets by spreading them with stuffing and then rolling them up.

Frozen fish can be baked without thawing but you may have to increase the baking time slightly.

Use a well-oiled baking dish. To keep the fish from drying, brush it with melted butter or oil, pour a sauce over it, or top with buttered crumbs. Season the fish. If you plan to brush the fish with oil or butter, mix the seasoning with the fat.

Bake fish uncovered until done at 350°F. Two pounds of fresh or thawed fillets or steaks will take about 20 to 25 minutes. Test fish for doneness before removing from oven.

19-18. Broiling fish. (See 4-21, "Broiling.") Fish for broiling should be at least an inch thick. Thinner fish will dry out before it is cooked.

To broil fish, oil the grid of the broiler pan. Place the fish skin side down in a single layer on the grid. Brush with seasoned oil, melted butter or a sauce.

Place the broiler pan in the broiler so the fish is about 4 inches from the heat. Thicker pieces should be placed farther from the heat.

Broil for about 10 to 15 minutes or until done. Baste occasionally. Turn thick pieces about halfway during the broiling period and baste. Continue broiling until done. Thinner pieces do not have to be turned.

19-19. Panfrying fish. (See 4-15, "Panfrying, sauteing, stir-frying.") Panfrying is probably the most common method of cooking fish. You can panfry small whole fish, fillets and steaks.

Generally, panfried fish is breaded to keep it from drying out as it cooks. (See 4-19, "Breading food for frying.")

To panfry fish, heat about one-eighth of an inch of fat in a large, heavy skillet. The fat should be hot enough to make a bread cube sizzle. If you use an electric skillet, set the thermostat at 350°F.

Place a single layer of fish in the hot fat, leaving ample space between fish. Don't overload the pan—it'll take too long for the fat to reheat. Instead of frying immediately, the fish will soak up the fat. If you overload the pan, you'll also create too much steam and the fish will be soggy instead of crisp.

Fry about 4 to 5 minutes or until brown. Turn the fish carefully, using tongs and a pancake turner. Don't use a fork—it could scrape the breading off or break up the fish.

Fry on the second side until done.

Remove from skillet and let drain on absorbent paper, such as paper towel, to remove extra fat. Serve hot.

If you're frying fish without breading, be careful not to overcook.

19-20. Oven frying fish. (See 4-20, "Cooking in dry heat.") Oven frying gives the same results as panfrying, but without as much fat added to the fish.

To oven fry fish, bread the fish as you would for panfrying. Place breaded fish in a shallow, well-oiled baking dish. Pour a small amount of seasoned oil or melted butter over the fish.

Bake at 500°F. This is one of the few exceptions to using moderate temperatures for cooking fish or any other animal protein. In this case, the breading keeps the fish from drying out and the high temperature gives a crisp, flavorful brown crust. The crust, in turn, keeps the juices sealed in, resulting in a tender, moist fish with a crispy brown crust.

Bake for only 10 to 15 minutes. Near the end of the baking time, test for doneness.

19-21. Braising fish. (See 4-7, "Braising.") Since fish is tender, it does not need moist heat to tenderize it. However, to vary flavor, fish is frequently braised in a sauce or with other foods, such as vegetables.

When braising fish, use a container with a tight-fitting lid or cover it with aluminum foil to keep the moisture inside.

19-22. Cooking fish in liquid. (See 4-2, "Boiling"; 4-3, "Simmering"; 4-4, "Poaching"; and 4-5, "Stewing.") Fish is cooked in liquid to make fish stews and chowders. Don't boil the mixture—simmer it gently and only long enough to cook the fish and blend the flavors. If overcooked, the fish will fall apart and lose its identity. The mixture may also develop an extra-strong fish flavor.

Shellfish such as lobster and crabs are often "boiled." Be careful not to overcook, or the meat will be tough and rubbery.

Poaching is another method of cooking fish in simmering liquid. Generally, a flavorful liquid, called "court bouillon," is prepared, using a liquid base, seasonings, vegetables and an acidic liquid such as lemon juice, vinegar or dry white wine. Since fish is tender, it needs to be handled carefully when cooked to retain its shape. If you enjoy poached fish, you can buy a special fish poacher which helps keep the shape of the fish intact.

To poach fish, use a wide, shallow pan such as a skillet. Barely cover the bottom with liquid such as water, milk or leftover vegetable cooking water. Add the following: seasonings and diced vegetables for flavor and an acidic liquid such as lemon juice, tomato juice, vinegar or dry white wine. Place the fish in the mixture. For easier handling, tie the fish in a clean white cloth such as cheesecloth. Cover the pan and simmer until done, usually about 5 to 10 minutes. Remove the fish carefully and keep warm. Reduce the liquid to taste and serve as a sauce with the fish. (See 4-2, "Boiling.")

19-23. Steaming fish. (See 4-9, "Steaming.") When steaming fish, use a court bouillon (see 19-22, "Cooking fish in liquid") in the bottom of the kettle to generate steam. It not only adds flavor to the fish but the acidic food also minimizes the fish odor.

To steam fish, bring the liquid to a boil. Place the fish on the rack. Cover the pan tightly and steam for 5 to 10 minutes or until the fish tests done.

MICROWAVE COOKING

19-24MW. Seafood cooks quickly. Seafood is tender and cooks quickly, making it ideal for microwaving. Because seafood rarely browns when cooked conventionally, lack of browning in the microwave oven is acceptable.

19-25MW. Defrosting frozen seafood. Defrost frozen seafood before microwaving. Thaw in its original package—open the package slightly or make a 1-inch slit in the package with a knife. To defrost, allow 2 to 3 minutes per pound on Low power and then allow to stand an equal length of time. Be careful—if you defrost seafood too long in the microwave oven, it begins to cook.

19-26MW. Preparing seafood for microwaving. Wash in cold water. Pat dry with a paper towel. Press out any excess moisture.

19-27MW. Even cooking. For more even cooking, place the larger and thicker pieces of seafood near the edge of the baking dish.

19-28MW. Adding color. You can add color to seafood by topping it with buttered crumbs or dusting with paprika.

19-29MW. Cooking time. As a rule, cook seafood about 4 minutes for each pound on High, then hold 2 or 3 minutes. Add more cooking time if necessary. If other foods are cooked with the seafood, such as vegetables, add more cooking time.

Be careful not to overcook seafood—it gets dry and tough and develops a strong odor and flavor.

19-30MW. Cover seafood. Cover seafood with wax paper or plastic if you want it steamed. If you want it to dry slightly, cover with a paper towel or leave uncovered.

Cover the seafood during carryover cooking to retain heat and moisture. Uncover if excess moisture accumulates.

19-31MW. Crumb coating. If seafood has a crumb coating, do not cover the pan. The coating on the seafood will help to keep it moist. A covered pan gives a soggy coating.

19-32MW. Test for doneness. (See 19-16, "Test seafood for doneness.") Begin to test for doneness several minutes before the end of the cooking time. Be sure fish flakes in the center, not just at the edges.

19-33MW. Reheating seafood. You can reheat seafood quickly in the microwave oven but be careful not to overcook it. If the seafood is in a sauce, it is less likely to overcook.

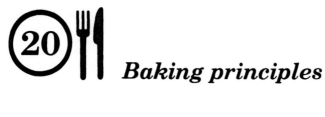

Baking principles

INGREDIENTS USED IN BAKING

Flour

20-1. Purpose of flour. Flour makes up the structure of any baked product. When liquid is added, the flour particles absorb it, swell and stick together.

The proteins in the flour make up gluten, which gives baked products their framework. Except for gluten flour, refined white wheat flour has the most gluten.

Whole grain flours vary in gluten, depending on the kind of grain. As a rule, most recipes for whole grain breads also call for either white flour or gluten flour to provide the necessary gluten for the framework. Baked goods made entirely of whole grain flour rise very little and tend to be heavy and compact.

As the dough is mixed or kneaded, the gluten develops. The amount of gluten developed depends on how long the dough is mixed or kneaded. The gluten helps form an elastic mesh that is composed of tiny cells. The cells trap air or gas created by the leavening.

When the product is heated, the air or gas expands. If the flour is high in gluten and the dough has been well mixed or kneaded, the dough is elastic and expands easily as the gases expand. The greater the expansion, the coarser the texture. If the product has been mixed just enough to blend ingredients, such as mixing a cake, the gluten has not been developed. The cake batter expands only slightly as the gases expand, giving the product a finer texture. Of course, other ingredients also influence the coarseness of the texture.

If you compare a white yeast bread with a yellow cake, both made from all-purpose flour, you'll notice a difference in the grain. The yeast bread is coarse—you can see the cells or air spaces. A layer cake, on the other hand, is so fine grained that it's difficult to see the little air spaces.

As the product bakes, the proteins and starch in the flour set, giving the baked product its final shape.

20-2. Kinds of flour. The more common types of flour can be purchased in most supermarkets. Specialized flours, such as gluten, are available in specialty shops and health food stores.

Whole grain flours are made from the entire grain kernel. Refined white wheat flours contain most of the protein and carbohydrate of the grain but the germ and bran are removed during milling.

The germ is the sprouting section inside the kernel from which a new plant can grow. It contains minerals, B vitamins, oil and fat. Because of the oil and fat in the germ, whole grain flours turn rancid and develop an off flavor when not properly stored. The bran or outside covering of the grain contains fiber and B vitamins. During processing, the bran is removed along with the nutrients it contains.

To compensate for the removal of nutrients in milling, white wheat flours are enriched—certain vitamins and minerals are added to them.

Following is a brief summary of the variety of flours available in the marketplace:

• *All-purpose flour.* A white flour made from wheat, it is bleached to give it a pure white color. All-purpose flour is suitable for most general household cooking and baking. Buy only flour that is enriched.

• *Bread flour.* A special white flour milled for making bread, it is generally available only to commercial bakers. It is higher in gluten than all-purpose flour.

• *Cake flour.* This is a soft white flour especially milled for cakes. It is lower in gluten than all-purpose flour.

• *Cornmeal.* See 9-5, "Buying other grains."

• *Cracked wheat flour.* It is made from cracked whole wheat kernels rather than ground.

• *Gluten flour.* This is a starch-free, high-protein flour made from hard wheat. It is used frequently in whole grain breads when gluten is needed. As a rule, 13 Tablespoons of gluten flour equal 1 cup of all-purpose flour. Gluten flour can generally be purchased in health food stores.

• *Graham flour.* See whole wheat flour.

• *Instant, instant-blending or quick-mix flour.* This is a

grainy, all-purpose flour especially formulated to blend easily into liquids without lumping. It is used primarily for making sauces and gravies and is usually sold in a shaker-top container. Do not substitute this flour for all-purpose flour in baking.

• *Pastry flour.* A finely milled, low-gluten flour, it is used for quick breads and pastries. It is more readily available in certain areas than in others.

• *Presifted flour.* This is white, all-purpose flour which has been sifted many times in processing. It can generally be used without sifting except for tender cakes and some recipes where even a slight excess of flour could cause a failure. As a rule, presifted flour gives a different texture to baked products. If you use pre-sifted flour for baking cakes, many food experts suggest that you sift it first. Most well-known brands of flour are presifted. However, most generic and many store brands of flour are not presifted and are much lower in cost than presifted.

• *Rice flour.* This is a flour made from rice. It makes a delicately textured cake, especially if several eggs are used. Don't confuse rice flour with waxy rice flour, sometimes called mochika or sweet flour. (See 10-22, "Less common thickeners.") The waxy rice flours are used mainly as thickeners but should not be substituted for all-purpose flour. As a rule, 1 cup of all-purpose flour equals ⅞ cup rice flour (1 cup minus 2 Tablespoons). Rice flour is generally available in health food stores.

• *Rye flour.* A coarse flour made from ground whole rye, it contains most of the nutrients of the whole grain.

• *Self-rising flour.* This is a flour to which leavening, such as baking powder, has been added along with salt, both in correct proportions for all general baking. If stored too long, the leavening tends to weaken. Do not use self-rising flour for making yeast bread.

• *Semolina flour.* A durum-wheat flour used by commercial bakers for pasta, it has a higher gluten content than all-purpose flour. The gluten helps commercially made pasta hold its shape when cooked. Homemade pasta made with all-purpose flour may not keep its shape as well as commercially made pasta.

• *Soy flour.* Made from soy beans, it has both a high protein and high fat content. Because of its distinctive flavor, it is generally used in combination with all-purpose flour. To substitute for 1 cup of all-purpose flour, combine 2 Tablespoons of soy flour with ⅞ cup all-purpose flour. You can use soy flour up to 20% of the weight of the flour in any recipe. Because of its high fat content, soy flour gives a heavy brown crust. If used as a substitute for part of the all-purpose flour, reduce baking temperatures about 25 degrees.

• *Stoneground flour.* This indicates that whole grain flour is milled by an old-fashioned method which gives a heavier, coarser flour.

• *Unbleached all-purpose flour.* It is made from refined white all-purpose flour which has not been bleached, resulting in a slightly gray color. Omitting the bleaching does not make this flour any more nutritious than the bleached flour. However, the unbleached flour does not contain bleaching additives. Unbleached flour tends to give a slightly coarse baked product.

• *Whole wheat flour (also called graham flour).* A coarse flour made from ground wheat kernel, it contains most of the nutrients of the kernel.

• *Whole wheat pastry flour.* It is a more finely ground whole wheat flour and is used in baking quick breads and cookies. It is available in health food stores.

20-3. Buying flour. Read the label carefully to be sure you're buying the kind of flour you want. Flour packages look alike. Therefore, it's easy to accidentally pick up the wrong package. You might find you bought self-rising flour when you wanted all-purpose.

Use whole grain flours wherever possible. They give you more flavor and nutrients.

Remember that convenience costs money. Generic or the store's house brand all-purpose flour may not be presifted but it will cost less.

Inspect flour bags carefully. The bags are made of heavy paper which damages easily. If flour spills out of the bag, choose another one.

20-4. Storing flour. Store flour in a cool, dry place. After opening the bag, put the flour in a tightly covered container to keep it free from dirt, moisture and pests.

Once a package of whole grain flour is opened, refrigerate it unless you plan to use it shortly. If you store it in a dry storage area too long, the oils may turn rancid, giving the flour an off flavor.

Liquids

20-5. Liquids in baking. Liquids help the flour form the structure of the baked product. They also make possible many of the chemical changes which take place in the mixture.

Water and milk are the most common liquids in baking. Milk adds nutrients to the baked product, gives flavor and richness and helps the crust to brown.

Other liquids include fruit juices, vegetable cooking liquid, vegetable juices, yogurt and sour cream.

Normally, one kind of liquid can be substituted for another. However, when substituting, keep in mind that an acidic liquid can affect the result of the product. See Section 20-10, "Chemical leavening agents."

20-6. Weight of water. Occasionally, an international or quantity food service recipe may give the quantity of water by weight:

    1 ounce water = 2 Tablespoons
    8 ounces water = 1 cup
    1 pound water = 2 cups

Leavening agents

20-7. Purpose of leavening agents. Leavening agents produce air or gas, which is trapped by the cells in the mixture. When the product is heated, the air or gas expands and the product rises.

There are four types of leavening agents—air, steam, chemicals and yeast.

20-8. Air as a leavening. Air can be trapped in mixtures in many ways—by sifting flour, creaming fat and sugar, beating egg whites and beating batter. Follow recipe directions carefully. Beating batter for a specific length of time or eggs until they are creamy yellow incorporates air into the batter. If you take shortcuts, you may not get the best results.

20-9. Steam as leavening. To use steam as a leavening agent, the mixture must have a relatively high amount of water or other liquid.

The product must be baked at a high enough temperature to turn the liquid into steam, which in turn causes the product to rise. Cream puffs and popovers are a good example of products using steam as leavening.

20-10. Chemical leavening agents. There are two basic kinds of chemical leavening agents—baking soda and baking powder.

Baking soda must be used with an acidic food such as sour milk. The alkali in the baking soda combines with the acid in the liquid to form carbon dioxide—a harmless gas. When the mixture is heated, the carbon dioxide expands and the product rises.

Recipes using buttermilk, yogurt, sour cream or any other form of acidic milk call for baking soda to neutralize the acid and act as a leavening. If you're substituting any form of acidic milk or cream for the liquid in a baked recipe, be sure to use baking soda as part of the leavening agent.

Many foods are naturally acidic. If one is used in a recipe, baking soda is generally used as all or part of the leavening. Some of the naturally acidic foods include honey, molasses, brown sugar and citrus fruits and juices.

Baking powder is a combination of baking soda and a dry acid. When mixed with a liquid, it gives off carbon dioxide gas. There are three kinds of baking powders—tartrate, phosphate and double-acting or S.A.S. (sodium aluminum sulfate).

Tartrate baking powder is a combination of baking soda, cream of tartar and tartaric acid. As soon as it is mixed with liquid, it reacts instantly and gives off carbon dioxide. This means the batter must be baked immediately after mixing.

Phosphate baking powder reacts more slowly than tartrate but gives up a good part of its carbon dioxide when the batter is still cold. The rest is generally released when the mixture is baked.

Double-acting baking powder combines the qualities of tartrate and phosphate powders. It releases some carbon dioxide in the cold mixture but most of it is released when the mixture starts to bake. Most recipes use the double-acting baking powder. However, if a recipe specifies one of the others, be sure to follow the instructions.

20-11. Yeast. Yeast is a microscopic plant which reproduces rapidly if it has warmth, food and moisture. Sugar is usually added to the mixture to make yeast grow. As the yeast grows, it gives off carbon dioxide gas, which acts as a leavening. Yeast gives baked products a distinctive flavor and aroma.

Yeast can be bought as active dry or compressed.

• *Active dry yeast* is sold in a small packet and does not need refrigeration. A packet contains about 1 Tablespoon of dry yeast.

• *Compressed yeast* comes in individually wrapped cakes weighing 3/5 of an ounce. Because it is perishable, it must be refrigerated.

A packet of dry yeast (1 Tablespoon) can be used interchangeably with a 3/5-ounce cake of compressed yeast. However, some recipes require the dry yeast so follow directions carefully.

20-12. Buying baking powder and yeast.

• *Baking powder.* Read the label carefully to be certain you're buying the kind you want. Check the expiration date on the container.

• *Yeast.* Compressed yeast is stored in the refrigeration section of the supermarket. Active dry yeast is usually kept in the baking supplies section. Check the date on either package.

20-13. Storing baking powder and yeast.

• *Baking powder.* Store in a cool, dry cabinet. Once the container is opened, be sure to put the lid back on tightly. If the lid is loose and moisture from the air gets into the container, the baking powder begins to lose its leavening power. Even though the date on the container indicates it's still usable, it will not give satisfactory baking results. Don't attempt to use baking powder if it has passed the expiration date stamped on the container.

• *Yeast.* Refrigerate compressed yeast and use before the date shown on the wrapper. Fresh compressed yeast is a light creamy gray but turns brown as it ages. If the cake of yeast is brown around the edges, even though the date on the wrapper indicates it is fresh, it may have been improperly stored. See 21-14, "Using yeast," for a freshness test for yeast.

Fats

20-14. The purpose of fat.
Fat makes the product tender by coating the gluten and keeping it from over-developing. It also adds richness and flavor and helps to brown the crust.

The most popular fats in baking are butter, margarine, vegetable oil, lard and shortening. Although each fat gives a slightly different flavor and texture, almost any fat can be used in baking. Bacon drippings, for instance, are often used in corn bread.

20-15. Butter and margarine. Butter is fat from cream. It can be bought either lightly salted or unsalted (sweet) and comes in grades AA, A and B. Grade B is made from sour cream and is highly prized by some people for its unusual flavor.

Recipes sometimes call for clarified butter. Clarifying removes the salt and milk solids. To clarify butter, heat the butter slowly over low heat—don't let it brown. With a spoon, skim off the white froth that rises to the top. Pour off the clear yellow butter. Be careful not to mix it with the curdled-looking white residue. Clarified butter will keep in the refrigerator for several weeks.

Margarine is made from hydrogenated vegetable oil. For baking, you can use regular margarine as a substitute but don't use the soft variety unless the recipe specifies it. Soft margarine contains oil, which requires a different mixing method than solid fats. See 20-16, "Cooking oil."

20-16. Cooking oil. Cooking oil is made from vegetables such as olives, corn, cottonseeds, soybeans, peanuts or safflower seeds. Olive oil has a distinctive flavor and usually is not used for baking unless the recipe specifies it.

As a rule, you can substitute oil for melted shortening. However, don't substitute oil for a solid fat in baking and don't substitute a solid fat when the recipe calls for an oil. In either case, you could have a failure—the mixing method for recipes using solid fat differs from the mixing method used for recipes containing oil.

20-17. Other fats. Lard and shortening are also used in baking.

• *Lard* is fat from pork. Leaf lard is lard that comes from the layers of fat around the kidneys and is preferred for baking. Lard tends to give a flakier texture to pie crusts and biscuits. Don't use leaf lard in cakes because it produces an undesirable texture. Some lard is hydrogenated and is so labeled; it does not give the same flakiness to pastry that leaf lard does. However, hydrogenated lard may be used in cakes. To substitute hydrogenated lard for butter in cakes, use about 20% less lard.

• *Shortening* is a hydrogenated solid, white fat made from vegetable oil. It has very little flavor and is used mainly for cooking and baking.

20-18. Buying fat. Read the label carefully to be sure

you're buying the kind of fat you want. For example, if you're buying lard for biscuits or pie crusts, be sure to buy the leaf lard and not hydrogenated lard.

20-19. Storing fat.

• *Butter, margarine, lard.* Store these in the refrigerator. If you don't plan to use them within a week or two, freeze them in their original containers.

• *Cooking oil.* Store in a cool, dry cabinet if you plan to use the oil within a month. However, if the area is warm, the oil may become rancid. For safer storage, refrigerate oil. It becomes thick and cloudy when refrigerated but will return to its normal consistency if left at room temperature for about half an hour.

• *Shortening.* Store in a cool, dry area. Don't refrigerate unless instructions on the label state otherwise.

Sweeteners

20-20. Purpose of sweeteners. Sweeteners give flavor and also help the crust to brown.

Sugar, honey, molasses and corn syrup are the most common sweeteners used in baking.

20-21. Sugar. Sugar helps to slow down the development of gluten. It also raises the temperature at which the gluten sets as it bakes, thus giving the gluten more time to expand.

• *Granulated sugar* is white table sugar, available as fine granules or cubes. It is made from sugar cane or sugar beets.

• *Brown sugar* is granulated sugar with molasses added for flavor and color. Dark brown sugar has a stronger flavor than light brown sugar.

• *Powdered or confectioner's sugar* is granulated sugar which has been ground to a fine powder and mixed with a little cornstarch to keep it from caking.

20-22. Honey. Honey is produced by bees from nectar in flowers. Honey has a distinct flavor, depending on the flowers from which it was produced.

Honey has greater sweetening power than sugar. 1 cup honey = 1¼ cups sugar.

If you want to use honey in baking, you'll get best results by following recipes developed specifically for honey. You can substitute honey for sugar in recipes, but other modifications in the recipe may also be needed. Honey, for instance, increases browning so the baking temperature may have to be lowered 25°F.

If you're determined to experiment, you can usually substitute honey for sugar in quick and yeast bread recipes and in puddings and custards. In cookies, substitute honey for one-third to one-half of the sugar. In cakes, you can substitute honey for about 40% of the sugar. If the cake does not call for baking soda, add a pinch of soda to counteract the acidity of the honey.

If the honey is not mixed well with the shortening and liquids, baked goods will have a soggy top layer.

Honey is heavy—1 cup of honey weighs 12 ounces.

20-23. Molasses. There are three different kinds of molasses:

• *Unsulfured molasses* is made from the juice of sugar cane.

• *Sulfured molasses* is a byproduct of several of the intermediate steps in refining cane sugar. The sulfur is used in the refining process and the sulfur fumes are retained in the molasses as sulfur. Whether the molasses is light or dark depends on the manufacturing process.

• *Blackstrap molasses* is the end byproduct of refining sugar cane. It has a somewhat strong flavor.

Molasses is not as sweet as sugar. 1 cup molasses = ¾ cup sugar. Generally, you can use molasses in place of sugar for a distinctive flavor. However, don't replace more than 50% of the sugar with molasses.

When you're substituting molasses for sugar in a recipe, you'll have to do some experimenting since other modifications must be made.

• For each cup of molasses you use, reduce the other liquid in the recipe by 5 Tablespoons.

• Add ½ teaspoon baking soda for each cup of molasses you add. This will counteract the acidity of the molasses.

• If the recipe calls for baking powder, omit it or use only half the amount called for.

20-24. Corn syrup. Corn syrup is a solution of dextrose, a sugar, mixed with water. It is used most commonly in making cooked frostings as it helps prevent the formation of undesirable crystals. Corn syrup is available as light or dark.

Don't substitute corn syrup for sugar in baking—you could have a failure.

20-25. Non-caloric sweeteners. Many non-caloric substitutes for sugar are available. If you want to use them in baking, write to the manufacturer for recipes using that particular product or follow the directions on the package.

Since non-caloric sweeteners give baked products a different flavor, you may want to experiment with different brands.

20-26. Storing sweeteners.

Store all sweeteners in tightly closed containers in a cool, dry area.

Even in an airtight container, powdered sugar may cake. Sift it before using to remove the lumps.

When storing liquid sweeteners such as honey, wipe the container with a damp cloth to remove any sweetener. Traces of liquid sweetener on jars or storage shelves attract insects.

Refrigerate syrups and honey after the jar has been opened. When refrigerated, honey crystallizes. To reliquify, put the container of honey in warm water.

Store brown sugar in a plastic bag or in an airtight container. If it hardens, put a piece of cut fruit in the container. Or if you prefer, cover the top of the sugar with foil or plastic wrap and then add a damp paper towel. Cover tightly. The sugar will absorb the moisture from the cut fruit or damp towel. Remove the fruit or towel when the sugar softens.

Other ingredients

20-27. Eggs as ingredients. Eggs serve a number of purposes in baking. They help to emulsify batters and keep them from separating. When beaten, eggs trap air, which acts as a leavening agent. Cream puffs, for instance, depend on the leavening action of air beaten into the eggs. Eggs add flavor and richness and give the product a tender texture.

20-28. Flavorings. Many kinds of seasonings and flavorings can give distinctive flavors to baked products. These include spices, flavor extracts, chocolate, nuts, fruit and juices.

If you make substitutions in a favorite recipe, be prepared for possible changes in texture and appearance as well as in flavor. For instance, nuts and fruit added to a cake will make it heavier. Salt helps to develop gluten, especially in yeast breads.

Remember, if you add any acidic food such as fruit and the recipe does not contain baking soda, add a pinch of soda to counteract the acidity of the food.

CONVENTIONAL BAKING

20-29. Ingredients. Use only fresh, top-quality ingredients for baking. The final product—its texture, aroma and flavor—will be only as good as the ingredients you put into it.

20-30. Pan materials. The type of material from which a baking pan is made affects the amount of heat that is transferred from the baking pan to the product. Unless they state otherwise, recipes normally are written for bright metal pans such as aluminum or stainless steel. If you're using a different type of pan material for baking, you will probably have to make an adjustment in the oven temperature.

Dull metal pans retain a little more heat than bright shiny ones, so lower the oven temperature about 10°F.

Glass and ceramic pans retain even more heat than dull metal pans. Lower the temperature 25°F.

If you're using special pans such as cast iron or stoneware, or pans with a dark finish, follow the manufacturer's directions.

20-31. Preparing pans for baking. Pans must be properly prepared for baking. Otherwise you may have difficulty removing the baked product from the pan.

Follow recipe directions for preparing pans. Some recipes call for greased pans, others for ungreased pans. If a recipe calls for a "buttered" pan, it means a greased pan.

Use only unsalted shortening for greasing pans. The salt in butter or margarine creates an excessively brown crust that sticks to the pan. If you want to use butter for greasing a pan, use sweet or clarified butter. (See 20-15, "Butter and margarine.")

When greasing a pan, use your fingers, a paper towel or wax paper. Be sure corners and the areas where the sides and bottom meet are thoroughly greased. A baked product is most likely to stick to the pan in those areas and may break apart when you try to remove it.

Some recipes call for greased and floured pans, which makes the product easier to remove. To grease and flour a pan, grease it thoroughly. Sprinkle about 2 Tablespoons of flour into the pan. You may need more or less, depending on the size of the pan. Holding the pan in both hands, turn it to different angles to spread the flour evenly over the bottom and sides. Tap the pan gently to help spread the flour. When the flour is spread evenly over the pan, turn the pan upside down over a large piece of waxed paper and tap gently to remove excess flour. Don't put this flour back in the flour container and don't use it for recipes. It may have some shortening sticking to it, which could affect the recipe. Save it for flouring pans or for flouring or breading food.

A recipe may call for lining the bottom of the pan with paper. This is a common procedure for rich cakes such as fruit cake or a fruit bread, which may stick to the pan even if it is greased and floured. Never use wax paper to line the pan. The wax melts as the product bakes and is absorbed by the crust. Use parchment paper.

To line a pan with parchment paper, cut a piece of the paper to fit only the bottom of the pan. To get the right size and shape, place the pan on the paper. Trace around it with a pencil and then cut the paper. Grease the pan thoroughly. Fit the paper into the bottom of the pan. If the bread or cake is extremely rich, you may want to grease the paper, too.

If cakes don't contain shortening, such as angel food cakes, the pans are not greased. The batter for unshortened cakes rises by clinging to the sides of the pan as the batter expands. If the pan is greased, the cake will not be able to cling to the pan and will not rise as well.

20-32. Pan placement in the oven. A conventional oven bakes with heated air which circulates gently through the oven. The success you have in baking a product depends to some degree on the way the pans are placed in the oven.

The air must be allowed to circulate freely. Position racks so pans are in the center of the oven. Leave at least a 1-inch space between the pans and oven walls for air circulation.

Be sure the pans don't touch each other or the sides, tops, bottom or door of the oven. If pans touch each other or any part of the oven walls or door, they create a hot spot—a concentration of heat which makes the baked product overbrown in that area.

The way you place the pan in the oven depends on the number of pans you are using:

• One pan. Place it in the center of the oven.
• Two pans. Place each on a separate rack in corners diagonally opposite to each other.
• Three pans. Place two pans on the top rack in diagonally opposite corners. Place the third pan on one of the opposite

corners on the lower rack but not directly under the pans on the upper rack.
• **Four pans.** Place two pans on the upper rack in diagonally opposite corners. Place the other two pans on the other opposite diagonal corners on the lower rack but not directly under the pans on the upper rack.

Always wipe off sides and bottoms of pans before placing them in the oven. Food particles adhering to the pans will burn and will be hard to scrub off.

20-33. Baking. Unless otherwise stated, preheat the oven. Turn it on to the recommended temperature at least 10 minutes before putting the food in to cook.

If you suddenly have failures with oven recipes you've used successfully in the past, suspect the oven. Place an oven thermometer in the oven along with the food and check the temperature periodically. As a rule, the oven temperature fluctuates about 25°F to 30°F below and above the temperature selected on the thermostat. However, it should average out to the temperature selected.

20-34. Removing baked products from pans. Usually all baked products should be removed from the pans as soon as they are taken out of the oven. However, there are several exceptions:
• The recipe may give other directions. Sometimes a quick bread or a bar cookie must cool in the pan.
• Cakes without shortening, such as angel food cake, are cooled in the pan. The pan must be turned upside down during cooling; otherwise, the cake will fall. Some angel food cake pans have supports about an inch high to hold the pan upside down. If the pan has no supports, turn it upside down and fit the tube over the neck of an empty beverage bottle. Be sure the bottle is empty. If you fit a hot pan over the neck of a full bottle, the heat will warm up the contents and may create enough inside pressure to explode.
• Unless the recipe states otherwise, pies should be cooled in the pan before cutting to allow the filling to thicken.

To remove cakes and quick breads from the pan, run a spatula around the sides of the pan between the cake and the pan. Don't use a knife—you might cut into the sides of the cake. Place a wire cake rack over the top of the cake. Hold the cake and rack securely with pot holders. Turn the cake and rack upside down. Place the wire rack on a level surface such as a table or counter. Lift off the cake pan. If the pan was properly prepared, it should lift off easily. The cake layer is now upside down. Quickly place another wire rack on the cake. Grasp both wire racks with both hands and turn them so the cake layer is right side up. Work gently—don't squeeze the cake layer between the two racks. Remove the top wire rack and allow the cake to cool.

To remove yeast bread from the pan, turn the baking pan over on its side on a wire rack. Gently ease the bread out with a clean pot holder. With clean pot holders, turn the bread right side up on a wire rack and allow to cool.

Follow recipe directions for removing cookies from pans. Some recipes direct that the cookies be allowed to stay on the baking sheet for several minutes before removing. This resting time allows the cookies to harden sufficiently so they can be handled without breaking.

To remove cookies, use a wide spatula and handle the cookies gently. When warm, they are extremely fragile and may fall apart. Place them on a wire rack to cool. Depending on the type of cookie, you may have to wipe off the spatula with a paper towel occasionally to remove gummy traces of cookie and shortening. Cookies can stick to the gummy residue and break apart as you try to slide them onto a cooling rack.

MICROWAVE BAKING

20-35MW. Adapting a conventional recipe. If you're adapting a conventional recipe for microwaving, find a similar microwave recipe, if possible. If not, you may have to reduce the liquid slightly since baked products do not dry out in the microwave oven as they do in conventional baking. If the recipe has no liquid, try adding a little more flour, if necessary. Decrease the leavening by one-third.

20-36MW. Flouring baking pans. Don't flour baking pans. The flour will become gummy because moisture collects on the bottom of the pan as the product bakes.

20-37MW. Lining baking pans. Line baking pans with paper toweling to absorb some of the moisture.

20-38MW. Softening brown sugar. Put hardened brown sugar in a glass bowl. Add a few drops of water and microwave on High power for 10 to 15 seconds. Store the softened sugar in an airtight container.

Breads: quick and yeast

21-1. About breads—quick and yeast.
Quick breads are so called because they're quicker to make than yeast breads. Quick breads use baking powder or baking soda as a leavening and are baked as soon as they are mixed. They include pancakes, waffles, muffins, biscuits, loaf breads and coffee cakes. They are usually made by one of two basic mixing methods—the biscuit method and the muffin method.

Yeast breads use yeast as a leavening. The dough generally must be allowed to rise twice before it can be baked. Therefore they take much longer to prepare than quick breads. Yeast breads are made by either the conventional mixing method or by the rapid mix method.

Breads are made from either batters or doughs. There are two kinds of batters—pour and drop.

• *Pour batters* are thin and can be poured into a baking pan, such as crepes, pancakes and waffles.

• *Drop batters* are thick enough to be dropped from a spoon and hold their shape, such as drop biscuits.

• *Doughs* are so thick they can be shaped by hand, such as tortillas or yeast breads.

QUICK BREADS

21-2. Pour batters. Pour batters for quick breads are generally made by mixing sifted dry ingredients with combined liquid ingredients.

The batter should be well mixed but not overmixed. Overmixing develops the gluten and makes the pancakes or waffles tough.

If pancake batter has enough liquid and fat, it can be thoroughly mixed without overdeveloping the gluten. The ideal ratio for pancake batter is 1 cup of liquid to 1 cup of flour plus 2 Tablespoons of butter for every cup of liquid. This ratio permits sufficient mixing without gluten development.

Crepe batter is thinner than pancake batter. It has more liquid in relation to flour—about 1½ cups liquid to 1 cup of flour. If the batter is too thick, the crepes will be thick. Let crepe batter stand for about a half hour after mixing to allow the flour to absorb the liquid and make more tender crepes.

Waffle batter is similar to pancake batter, but a little richer, with more butter, eggs and sugar. Generally, waffle batter has more flour than liquid, sometimes as much as 1½ cups of flour to every cup of liquid. Because waffle batter needs to be well mixed, it can be easily overmixed. Gluten develops more slowly in cool batter, so when mixing waffles use ingredients right from the refrigerator.

21-3. Baking crepes and pancakes. Proper baking gives tender, flavorful crepes and pancakes. If overbaked, either at too high a temperature or for too long a time, crepes and pancakes get dry and hard and may have a burned flavor.

To bake crepes: Use a skillet that handles easily and grease it lightly. Heat the skillet until a drop of water dropped on the surface sizzles. If the skillet isn't hot enough, the batter will not spread—the crepes will be thick and may stick to the pan. Pour 1 to 2 Tablespoons batter in the center of the skillet. Working quickly, tilt the skillet so the batter covers the bottom evenly. The layer should be thin—about ⅛ inch. If the batter is too thick to spread thinly, add a little more liquid before you continue baking. Cook about 1 minute. Shake the pan to keep the crepe loose. Lift the edges of the crepe with a spatula. When it is browned in a lacy pattern, turn it over and brown the other side for a few seconds. Slide the crepe out onto a warm plate and fill as desired. Crepes may be frozen and reheated after defrosting. To freeze: Separate each crepe with a sheet of wax paper so they will pull apart easily while still frozen. Remove wax paper before thawing.

To bake pancakes: Grease the griddle lightly. Heat until a drop of water dropped on the surface sizzles. If the water erupts and disappears, the griddle is too hot. If you're using a thermostatically controlled griddle, set the temperature at about 425°F. Pour the batter onto the griddle until it spreads out to the size you want. Bake until bubbles in the batter begin to break and the edges begin to dry just slightly. Lift slightly with a spatula—the bottom should be nicely browned. Turn quickly but carefully with a spatula. Continue baking until the second side is nicely browned. Remove and serve immediately.

21-4. Baking waffles. If the batter is thick and rich and baked long enough to evaporate the moisture, the waffles will be crisp and tender, as they should be.

If waffles are limp, they have not been baked long enough or the temperature was too low. The recipe could have too much liquid in relation to the flour. (See 21-2, "Pour batters.")

Bake waffles until they stop steaming and are a golden brown. If the waffles are golden brown but continue to steam, the batter contains too much liquid and the waffles will be limp.

21-5. Mixing biscuits. Properly made biscuits are well shaped, tender and flaky, free from yellow or brown spots with a well-blended, pleasing flavor. You can make either drop or rolled biscuits.

Drop biscuits can be mixed the same as rolled biscuits or they can be mixed by the muffin method. (See 21-9, "Muffin method of mixing.") The dough for drop biscuits has a little more liquid in proportion to flour and sometimes uses oil instead of solid fat. Because the mixing method and ingredients may differ, drop biscuits generally do not have the same flaky texture as rolled biscuits. If you wish to give drop biscuits a more symmetrical shape, bake them in muffin tins instead of dropping them onto a baking sheet.

The mixing method for rolled biscuits helps to make them flaky. The fat is cut into the flour so that very thin layers of fat are coated with flour. Then the liquid is added. The secret to tender, flaky biscuits is to mix the dough with the liquid just long enough to blend ingredients but not so long that too much gluten develops or the fat begins to melt. When the biscuits bake, the fat melts, resulting in a tender, flaky texture.

To mix rolled biscuits, measure dry ingredients accurately and sift them together into a mixing bowl. If the ingredients are improperly measured, the biscuits will have poor flavor, appearance and texture. If too much flour is used, for instance, the biscuits will be dry. Too much baking soda will create dark spots in the crust.

Measure cold fat. Be accurate. Too much fat causes an irregular shape, poor color and heavy, crumbly texture. Too little fat gives a tough texture. Be sure the fat is cold so that it retains its texture as it is worked into the flour. If the fat is at room temperature, it will be too soft to form the flaky layers. Don't substitute oil for solid fat in rolled biscuits. Oil cannot be cut into flour to give a flaky texture.

Add the cold fat to the flour and cut it into the flour, just as you do when making pie crust. Use two knives or a pastry blender. Cut the fat into the flour until the mixture looks like coarse crumbs. If the flour-fat mixture is either overmixed or undermixed, the biscuits will not be flaky.

Add cold milk. The cold helps the fat stay solid. If you add too much liquid, the biscuits will have an irregular shape and coarse texture. If you use too little liquid, excess flour may appear on the crust and the biscuits will be dry.

Using a fork, mix until the dry ingredients are moistened and then stir quickly to blend the ingredients thoroughly. If you're making rolled biscuits, the dough should "clean" the sides of the bowl—that is, it should be firm enough not to stick to the sides of the bowl. If you're making drop biscuits, the thick batter should hold its shape when mounded, but it will not clean the sides of the bowl. If you overmix the dough, the biscuits will be heavy with an irregular shape and a tough, coarse texture. If undermixed, the biscuits wil have an uneven color and poor flavor.

Rolled biscuits must be kneaded and cut. See 21-6, "Kneading dough," and 21-7, "Rolled biscuits." Drop biscuits need only be dropped onto a baking sheet.

21-6. Kneading dough. Kneading serves two purposes: It helps mix the ingredients more thoroughly and it develops gluten.

To knead dough, turn it out onto a lightly floured board. Use only enough flour to keep the dough from sticking to the board. If you use too much flour, the baked product could become tough and dry.

Gently fold the dough over in half toward you. Be careful not to tear the dough apart.

With the heels of both hands, push down on the edge of the dough nearest you. Push firmly but not so hard that you break the dough apart. If the dough sticks to your hands, dust them with a little flour.

Give the dough a quarter turn to your right. Repeat the folding and pushing process.

Knead the dough only for the time specified. Remember, as

you knead, gluten develops. Some doughs are kneaded for only seconds while others require 8 to 10 minutes of kneading. It depends on how much gluten must be developed.

21-7. Rolled biscuits. The dough for rolled biscuits must be kneaded, rolled and cut.

Turn the dough out onto a lightly floured surface. Knead quickly and gently. Don't knead biscuit dough more than 30 seconds or you'll develop too much gluten and the heat from your hands will begin to melt the fat. As a result, the biscuits will be heavy and compact with an irregular shape and coarse texture. If the dough isn't kneaded enough, the ingredients won't be thoroughly blended. The biscuits will have an uneven color, poor flavor and a rough texture.

Roll the dough out gently with a lightly floured rolling pin until it's about ½ inch thick. Use only enough flour on the board and rolling pin to keep the dough from sticking. Too much flour makes the dough hard, resulting in a tough rather than tender biscuit. It will also add excess flour to the crust. Use gentle, light strokes, rolling from the center to the outside. Try to keep the dough a circular shape—you'll have the least waste when cutting. If the dough isn't evenly thick, you'll have lopsided biscuits. Unevenly shaped biscuits generally bake unevenly with a poor color.

Cut the dough out with a biscuit cutter dipped in flour. Cut straight down through the dough. Don't use a twisting or turning motion—it might pull the dough out of shape, resulting in lopsided biscuits with a rough edge.

Biscuits can be cut in other ways, too. Cut them into squares with a sharp knife dipped in flour. Work carefully so you don't tear the dough or pull it out of shape. You can also use shaped cookie cutters if they are deep enough not to flatten the dough.

Leftover dough can be quickly patted together, rerolled and cut. However, it will not be as tender and flaky as the original biscuits because of excess handling.

Lift the biscuits with a wide spatula onto an ungreased baking sheet, spacing them about 1 inch apart. If you space them close together, their crusts may be a little less crispy. For extra browning and flavor, brush the tops with milk or melted butter.

Place pans in oven. (See 20-32, "Pan placement in oven.") If pans are improperly placed, the biscuits will bake unevenly, with uneven color and shape.

Bake rolled biscuits at 425°F for 12 to 15 minutes, depending on their size. Follow recipe instructions for drop biscuits, as the temperature and time will vary. If biscuits are underbaked, the crust will be pale and the biscuits heavy and unusually moist. If overbaked, the crust will be excessively brown and the biscuits too dry.

21-8. To test biscuits for doneness.

• *Rolled biscuits* will be lightly browned on top with light, creamy-colored sides. They should be double in size with a nice, even shape and straight sides.

• *Drop biscuits* will have an irregular shape but should be lightly browned and double in size.

21-9. Muffin method of mixing.
The muffin method of mixing, used for most quick breads, gives a tender, slightly coarse texture. Some quick breads are mixed by the cake method (see 22-9, "Conventional method of mixing a cake"), resulting in a finer-textured product.

To mix quick breads by the muffin method, measure the dry ingredients accurately. Too much flour gives the products an irregular shape and tough, dry, crumbly texture. It also creates tunnels. Too much sugar gives a dark, sticky crust. After measuring, sift the dry ingredients together into a mixing bowl. If you're using a whole grain flour, don't sift the dry ingredients but mix them together in a bowl so they are well blended. By mixing the dry ingredients thoroughly, you'll avoid overmixing the batter.

Measure the fat and liquid accurately. Too much fat gives an irregular shape while too little gives a tough texture. Not enough liquid creates an irregular shape and tunnels. Too much liquid gives too smooth a crust.

Mix the liquid ingredients together thoroughly. Generally, the eggs are beaten with milk or other liquid and either oil or melted butter. Be sure the liquid ingredients are well mixed. If they're not, the color will be uneven and the product will be too moist with a tough, coarse crust.

Pour the liquid ingredients all at once into the dry ingredients. Work quickly and with just a few strokes mix the liquid and dry ingredients. For best results, use a large wooden spoon. Stir gently for no longer than 20 seconds. The dry ingredients should be just moistened. The batter will not pour but will stick together and look very lumpy. If the batter is overmixed, muffins will have tunnels and peaked tops. Properly mixed loaf breads will have a crack down the center, but if overmixed they will have rounded or flat tops without a crack. Overmixing also gives a heavy product with a coarse texture and a tough crust.

Gently spoon the batter into greased and floured muffin tins or loaf pans. Be sure muffin tins are no more than two-thirds full. If the muffin tins are too full, the batter overflows during baking. Instead of having rounded tops, the muffins will be flat with tunnels.

21-10. Baking muffins and loaf breads. Follow recipe directions.

Oven temperatures are important when baking muffins. If the oven temperature is too low, the muffin top will be peaked instead of rounded. If it is too high, the gluten will set too quickly, resulting in a muffin with an irregular shape and cracked top.

If overbaked, both muffins and breads will have an irregular shape, an excessively dark, tough crust and a dry texture with tunnels. If underbaked, the product will be heavy with a pale crust and a moist, crumbly texture.

21-11. To test muffins and loaf breads for doneness:
• *Muffins* should be lightly browned with rounded tops.
• *Loaf breads* should be lightly browned with a crack down the center. The bread should be starting to pull away slightly from the sides of the pan. Tap the top gently—it should be firm.

As a rule, muffins should be removed from the pans immediately, unless the recipe states otherwise. Muffins are best served fresh and warm, although they may be reheated.

Follow recipe instructions for removing loaf breads, since some must cool slightly in the pan. Loaf breads should be allowed to cool completely before cutting. Cooling helps blend flavors and firms the texture so the bread can be sliced more easily. Some nut and fruit breads slice more easily if they are wrapped in foil and refrigerated for at least 12 hours before cutting.

YEAST BREADS

21-12. Kinds of yeast breads. There are five basic kinds of yeast doughs, but many variations of each:
• *Basic white bread* is made from flour, yeast, salt, sugar, fat and water. It gives the typical loaf of white bread, some-

what lean, with a crisp crust. To make a richer bread, milk can replace part or all of the water.

• *Sweet white bread* has more sugar than basic white bread. For added richness, milk replaces all or part of the water. Butter and eggs give richness, tenderness and flavor. Nuts and fruit may be added.

• *Whole grain bread* is made from the same basic ingredients as white bread except that whole grain flour such as whole wheat or rye replaces part or all of the white flour. Each type of whole grain flour gives bread its own characteristic flavor, fragrance and texture. If only whole grain flour is used, some gluten flour is usually added to the mixture because whole grain flour does not produce enough gluten. Whole grain breads tend to more compact and heavy than white breads, depending on the amount of whole grain flour used.

• *Batter breads* are made of the same ingredients as white bread. However, more liquid is used, making a batter instead of a dough. The batter is allowed to rise twice—once in the bowl and the second time in the pan or casserole in which it is baked. The only step omitted is kneading. Batter bread tends to have a somewhat coarse, dry texture and dries out much more quickly in storage than standard yeast breads.

• *Sourdough bread* has a distinctive sour, yeasty flavor. Instead of using yeast as a leavening, it uses sourdough "starter." The starter is a mixture of yeast, water and flour, which is allowed to stand for 4 to 7 days or until it has fermented. As the starter is used up to make bread, it can be replenished.

21-13. Kinds of yeast dough. Yeast doughs can be soft or stiff. Soft dough makes a more tender bread which rises more rapidly. Stiff dough makes a firmer bread with a harder crust. A stiff dough takes a little longer to rise than a soft dough.

The ratio of flour to liquid determines whether the dough is soft or stiff. The more flour in relation to liquid, the stiffer the dough.

21-14. Using yeast. Yeast needs food in the form of sugar and flour in order to grow. It also needs moisture and warm temperatures. How the yeast is used depends on the type of yeast—fresh or dry—and the mixing method—conventional or rapid mix.

For the conventional method of mixing, soften or dissolve either fresh or dry yeast in warm water before adding to the liquids. Use water—yeast will not dissolve in other liquids, such as milk. Softening or dissolving activates the yeast and starts it growing. If the water is too cool, the yeast will not grow well. If too hot, it kills the yeast.

Dissolve compressed fresh yeast (see 20-11, "Yeast") in a small amount of warm water at 85°F, without stirring, for about 8 to 10 minutes.

Dissolve active dry yeast in water at about 105°F to 110°F. It requires slightly warmer water than compressed yeast. "Baby bottle temperatures" are too cool for dry yeast. The water should feel quite warm if dropped on your wrist. Starch in the dry yeast provides food. As the yeast grows, it foams, indicating it's alive. A non-foaming yeast normally signifies it is "dead." However, due to recent changes in processing, some dry yeasts do not foam when dissolved in warm water. The starch in some brands is no longer released in water. The yeast has nothing to grow on and therefore doesn't foam, even though it is alive.

If you have any doubts about the reliability of yeast, add ½ teaspoon sugar to the yeast and warm water mixture. If the yeast is alive, it will start to foam within 10 minutes. If it doesn't, discard it and use a fresh package.

Heat the fat, sugar and liquid. If milk is the liquid, scald the mixture. Cool the mixture slightly so it is still warm. Add the dissolved yeast to the warm liquid. If the liquid is too hot, it kills the yeast.

For the rapid mix method, use only active dry yeast. Combine the undissolved yeast with part of the flour and the sugar and salt. Heat the fat and liquid to 120°F or 130°F, add them to the dry ingredients and mix with an electric mixer. Finally, mix in the rest of the flour. If you use too much flour in the first stage of mixing, the yeast will not dissolve and grow and the dough will not rise.

If you converted a standard recipe to the rapid mix method and it does not rise properly, the mixture may not have enough liquid for the yeast's growth. When converting recipes to the rapid mix method, be sure to include the water formerly used to dissolve the yeast.

21-15. Amount of flour. Yeast bread recipes generally do not give exact amounts of flour. Usually they specify a range, such as 4 to 4½ cups. The reason is that flours vary in the amount of liquid they can absorb.

In humid weather, flour absorbs moisture from the air and

cannot absorb as much liquid as it normally might. But in dry weather, the flour might require more liquid than normal. Certain types of flour may need more liquid than others.

Add enough flour to the mixture to make the type of dough specified in the recipe—soft or stiff (see 21-13, "Kinds of yeast dough"). As you mix the flour into the dough, it begins to form a ball. When the dough begins to cling together and leaves the sides of the bowl "clean" or free of dough, you have added enough flour.

If you add too little flour, the dough will be difficult to handle. As you knead the dough, you will have to continue adding flour until it reaches the proper consistency.

If you add too much flour, the dough will be too stiff to rise properly. The top of the loaf will crack during baking. The baked bread will be heavy and compact with a thick crust. It will be dry with a coarse crumbly grain.

21-16. Never use cold ingredients. Liquids used to dissolve the yeast must be the temperature specified in the recipe. See 21-14, "Using yeast."

Never add cold liquids to yeast doughs. The yeast will stop growing and the bread will not rise.

Other ingredients used in making yeast dough, such as the flour and sugar, should be at room temperature.

21-17. Kneading yeast dough. See 21-6, "Kneading dough." When you knead yeast dough, use as little flour as possible, just enough to keep the dough from sticking to the work surface. Excess flour gives a tough crust and a dry, heavy bread. If the dough sticks to your hands, dust them occasionally with a little flour.

Don't pound the dough as you knead—pounding will not mix the ingredients and develop gluten. Push it gently away from you.

As you knead the dough, its surface develops a coating, which keeps it from sticking to the work surface or to your hands. At this point, you should not have to add any more flour. Avoid breaking through the coating—wherever there is a break, the dough will stick to the work surface or to your hands. You'll have to add more flour, which may result in too stiff a dough.

Bubbles of gas form as you continue to knead. This is a sign that gluten is developing, allowing the cell walls to stretch as carbon dioxide gas is formed by the growing yeast. If the gluten is not developed properly, the cell walls break down and the bread cannot rise.

Knead yeast dough for about 8 to 10 minutes to give gluten ample time to develop. At the end of the kneading time, the dough will have changed from a sticky, rough mixture to a silky smooth, elastic ball.

If the dough is not kneaded enough, it will not rise properly. The bread will have dark streaks because of improper mixing. The baked loaf will crumble easily because the ingredients were not thoroughly mixed. It may sink in the middle or the top may crack. The baked bread will be dry and coarse.

If the dough is kneaded too much, it will be difficult to shape. As you try to roll or pat it out, it will keep springing back because the gluten is too strong and elastic. The shaped loaf will not rise properly, and the bread will have holes in it.

21-18. Letting dough rise. Letting dough rise allows the yeast to continue to grow and flavors to develop. Yeast grows best at room temperatures of 75°F to 85°F. If the area is cooler than that, you can use several methods to increase the heat:

• Fill a large bowl half full of hot water. Place a wire rack on the bowl. Set the bowl of dough on the rack above the hot water and cover the bowl with a clean, dry towel.

• If you have a gas oven with a continuous burning pilot light, set the bowl in the oven. Do not turn on the thermostat. The pilot light provides just enough warmth for proper rising.

• If you have a microwave oven with a low power setting, see 21-28MW, "Yeast breads."

If the area is drafty, the dough may not rise properly. Don't place the bowl of dough on a radiator or furnace outlet—those areas are too hot for proper rising.

The bread must rise twice—once after it is kneaded and the second after it is shaped. For the first rising, after you have kneaded the dough, place the dough in a large, lightly greased or oiled bowl. The dough must rise to twice its size so the bowl should be large enough to hold that amount.

Grease the top of the dough to keep it from drying out. Do this by gently rubbing the dough against the oiled bowl so the surface of the dough is oiled. Then turn the ball over so the oiled surface is on top. If dough dries, it forms a crust which turns into heavy streaks throughout the bread. If a crust does form, even though the surface is oiled, remove and discard it. Dark streaks can also develop in the bread if the bowl is too heavily oiled or greased.

Very lightly press plastic wrap on top of the dough to help prevent drying. Oil alone will not keep the dough from drying. However, it will help keep the plastic from sticking to the dough. Cover the bowl with a clean, dry cloth.

Let the dough rise until double in bulk. To test, gently press two fingers into the surface. If the dent you made in the dough remains, the dough is ready to shape. If the dent springs back up, the dough should rise a little longer. Normally, it should take the dough about 1 to 1½ hours to rise. However, doughs made with whole grain flour will take longer.

Allow the dough to rise again after it is shaped and placed into baking pans. Cover the top with a dry towel and let rise until double in bulk.

If the dough has not been allowed to rise for the proper length of time, either during the first or second rising, the crust will be thick. The bread will be heavy, compact and too moist, with a coarse grain.

If the dough is allowed to rise too long, the bread will not rise more as it bakes. The baked bread will crumble easily. It will have a coarse grain with large holes and a yeasty smell with a sour flavor. If allowed to rise too long during the final rising, the bread will fall.

If the rising temperature is too low, the dough will not rise properly. The bread will be small and compact with a poor flavor.

If the rising temperature is too high, the bread will not rise more as it bakes. The baked loaf will crumble easily and have a sour flavor.

21-19. Punching dough down. When the dough has doubled in bulk at the end of the first rising, it must be punched down. Punching down lets excess gases escape, making it easier to shape the dough.

To punch dough down, push your fist down in the center of the dough as far as you can. Pull the dough away from the sides of the bowl. Press the dough down toward the center to form a ball. Turn the dough out on a lightly floured board or pastry cloth.

Some people feel that letting the dough rest about 10 minutes makes it easier to shape.

21-20. Shaping yeast bread. Bread is generally shaped into a loaf and baked in loaf pans.

Divide the dough as specified in the recipe. Usually the

dough is divided evenly in half. Use scissors or a sharp knife to cut the dough apart. Do not tear it—you damage the strands of gluten. If you have a scale, weigh each piece out to be sure all are about the same size.

Flour the work surface lightly. Use as little flour as possible when you roll out the dough. Excess flour makes the bread tough and leaves a coating of flour on the crust.

With a rolling pin, roll the dough into a rectangle about 12 inches long and 8 inches wide. Be sure it is the same thickness throughout. Roll out all the bubbles in the edges. Press the air out—air or bubbles left in the dough will make large holes in the bread.

Roll up the dough. Begin with the 8-inch edge farthest away from you. Roll the dough up tightly toward you. Work carefully, making sure no air is trapped as you roll the dough. Trapped air creates large holes in the bread.

After the bread is rolled, seal the ends by turning the roll so the seam is on top. With your fingers, pinch the seam edge to the roll so it stays closed. Turn the roll seam side down. Hold your hands straight up and down so the palms face each other. With the bottom edges of your hands, press down on both ends of the roll, about ¼ inch inside the edge. This will pinch and flatten the uneven ends of the dough. Turn the flattened ends underneath the roll. Turn the roll upside down and pinch the ends to the roll. Turn the roll seam side down.

The loaf should be evenly shaped. As it rises, it retains its original shape. The baked loaf will be the exact shape as the unbaked.

You can give yeast dough many different shapes. Bread can be made into long loaves, braids or rounds. Rolls can be shaped into cloverleaves, sailors' knots or crescents. The shape is limited only by your imagination. Yeast dough is pliable and fun to work with. Once you become accustomed to handling it, you'll discover numerous ways of shaping it.

21-21. Preparing pans. (See 20-31, "Preparing pans for baking.") As a rule, pans for baking bread should be well greased so the bread comes out easily. Flouring the pans helps keep the bread from sticking.

Follow recipe instructions for preparing the pans.

Be sure you use the proper pan size. If the pan is too large, the top of the bread will not brown properly. If the pan is too small, the bread will have an odd shape and may droop over the sides of the pan.

21-22. Baking temperatures. Follow the exact temperatures specified in the recipe. Yeast doughs bake at different temperatures, depending on the ingredients used. Plain doughs made of flour, water, fat, yeast, salt and a little sugar usually bake at higher temperatures. Rich doughs using eggs and milk need lower temperatures to allow the interior to bake without the exterior browning excessively.

If the oven temperature is too low, the crust will be thick. The inside of the baked loaf will be moist and coarse grained and the bread will crumble easily.

If the oven temperature is too high, the center of the bread will pop up or "mushroom." The crust will dry and get too dark before the inside of the bread is baked.

21-23. Placing pans in oven. (See 20-32, "Pan placement in oven.") If you have only 1 or 2 loaves, place them in the center of the oven. Don't allow pans to touch each other or the sides of the oven. If they do, the bread will rise unevenly.

Don't crowd pans in the oven. If you try to bake too many pans at one time, the bread will not brown on the sides.

21-24. To test yeast bread for doneness. Look at the bread near the end of the baking period. If the bread is done, the top will be nicely browned.

Remove the loaf from the pan and tap the bottom and sides. If it sounds hollow, it is done.

If the bread isn't done, continue baking.

21-25. Cooling yeast bread. (See 20-34, "Removing baked products from pans.") Remove the bread from the pans immediately. Cool the bread on a cooling rack so air circulates around it. If bread is cooled on a solid surface such as a counter or in the baking pan, the bottom will get soggy.

Don't wrap bread for storing until it has completely cooled. If it is slightly warm when wrapped, the crust will be soft rather than crisp.

Don't cool bread in a drafty spot, such as in front of an open window. The bread cools too rapidly and the top of the crust may crack.

21-26. Adding wheat germ or soy flour to yeast dough. You may want to add wheat germ or soy flour to yeast dough for extra nutrition, even though the recipe doesn't call for it. If wheat germ or soy flour is not used in the right proportions, it can keep yeast bread from rising properly.

If you want to add wheat germ or soy flour, use only those recipes which list them as one of the ingredients.

MICROWAVE BAKING

21-27MW. Quick breads. Quick breads baked in a microwave oven have a heavier, coarser and more uneven texture. They will not brown, but a topping can be added to cover the raw-dough appearance. Use toppings such as frosting or cinnamon and sugar.

If you prefer, choose a recipe that gives a darker dough, such as one using whole wheat flour. The lack of browning will not be as noticeable.

21-28MW. Yeast breads. Yeast breads bake most successfully in conventional ovens. However, several steps in preparing yeast doughs can be done successfully in microwave ovens:

• If your oven has an automatic temperature control, use it to heat the liquids to the proper temperature.

• If you have a low temperature setting, let yeast dough rise in the microwave oven. Follow the manufacturer's recommendations. In some ovens, dough will double in size in 15 minutes at the low setting. Turn the pans halfway through the rising time. Other ovens recommend 10 minutes on 1 or Low and 10 minutes' carryover time. Occasionally, feel the dough and the bottom and sides of the bowl. If they feel too warm, let the dough stand for a few minutes, then microwave again. If the dough is microwaved too long, it begins to cook. If you are letting shaped loaves rise in the microwave oven, be sure to use glass loaf pans. When you bake the loaves in the conventional oven, lower the baking temperature by 25°F to compensate for the glass baking pans.

21-29MW. Reheating breads and rolls. Breads and rolls are very porous so they reheat rapidly. Defrost them before reheating.

Wrap the rolls or bread in a napkin or paper towel to absorb some of the moisture. If you put the rolls on a flat surface, the bottoms become soggy because of trapped steam.

If reheated too long, breads and rolls get tough and chewy.

STORING

21-30. Storing breads. Breads do not get stale as quickly if they are kept in a breadbox at room temperature instead of in the refrigerator. However, in hot, humid weather, refrigerate bread to help keep mold from growing.

Bread may be frozen for long-term storage. See 3-4, "Freezer storage."

㉒ ¶¶ *Cakes*

22-1. Kinds of cakes. Cakes are classified according to the type of leavening they use and the way they are mixed. There are two basic kinds of cakes: shortened and foam cakes.

• *Shortened cakes* are also called butter cakes. A fat such as butter or solid shortening is used and the cake is leavened with baking powder. Shortened cakes can be prepared by a conventional method of mixing or by a faster method known as the quick-mix or one-bowl method.

• *Foam cakes* are light, airy cakes that rely on air beaten into egg whites or into the batter for leavening. There are three basic kinds of foam cakes—angel food, sponge and chiffon. Each differs a little and is made by a slightly different method. Angel food cake relies primarily on air beaten into egg whites for leavening and contains no fat. Sponge cake also relies on air beaten into egg whites, but it also uses egg yolks, which add fat to the mixture. Chiffon cake is a combination of shortened and foam cakes—it contains beaten egg whites and egg yolks but it also has oil and baking powder. Cakes made with oil or melted fat usually have special mixing methods.

A recipe for a cake is like a chemical formula. The amount of each ingredient is in a certain proportion to other ingredients. If the proportion or the ratio of one ingredient to another is changed, you could have a failure.

SHORTENED CAKES

22-2. Ingredients. The basic ingredients in shortened cakes are fat, sugar, salt, eggs, flour, baking powder and liquid. Each ingredient performs specific functions and contributes a certain characteristic to a cake.

If ingredients are improperly measured, the cake may turn out to be a failure. At minimum, it may still be edible but it may not be as good as you'd like it to be. (See 5-8, "Measuring ingredients.")

Follow recipe instructions carefully when baking a cake. If you take shortcuts, you may have a failure.

22-3. Shortening vs butter in cakes. (See 20-14, "The purpose of fat.") Shortening is 100% fat but butter is only 80% fat, the remaining 20% being liquid. Because of the higher fat content, a cake made with shortening tends to have a softer, spongier texture and more volume than one made with butter. However, a cake made with butter has more flavor and color, although it is a little less tender.

If a recipe calls for shortening and you want to substitute butter, add just a little more butter. Since butter contains salt, reduce the amount of salt in the recipe.

If you measure fat improperly and use too little, the cake will have a firm rather than tender texture. If you use too much fat, the cake won't rise very much and will sink in the center. It will be soggy with an uneven grain and a solid, compact texture.

22-4. Sugar. (See 20-21, "Sugar.") Besides adding sweetness, sugar makes a cake more tender by slowing down the development of gluten in the flour as the cake is mixed. As the cake bakes, the sugar makes the protein in the flour set more slowly, giving the cake a longer time to rise and resulting in greater volume.

If you measure improperly (see 5-8, "Measuring ingredients") and use too little sugar, the crust will have a pale color. The cake will have a dry texture with tunnels.

If you use too much sugar, the crust will be too brown. The cake will sink in the center and will have a crumbly texture.

22-5. Eggs. (See 20-27, "Eggs as an ingredient.") Eggs add richness, flavor, color and moistness.

If the eggs are beaten before being added to the creamed mixture, air is trapped in the foam and serves as a leavening.

As the cake bakes, the protein in the eggs coagulates, adding to the structure of the cake.

Too few or too small eggs result in a lack of richness, flavor and color as well as a dry texture.

Too many or too large eggs create tunnels in the baked cake.

22-6. All-purpose vs cake flour. Cake flour not only contains less gluten but its gluten also forms a tender, delicate structure. All-purpose flour has more gluten and gives a cake a coarser and less-tender texture.

Be sure to use cake flour if it is specified in the recipe. If you want to substitute all-purpose flour, use only ⅞ cup all-purpose flour for every 1 cup of cake flour called for in the recipe. (See 5-6, "Substitutions.")

Most modern cake recipes use all-purpose flour. If a recipe calls for "flour" without specifying a particular kind, it usually means all-purpose flour.

If you measure improperly (see 5-8, "Measuring ingredients") and the cake has too little flour, it will fall during baking. The cake will have a compact, gummy texture.

If you use too much flour, the cake will be heavy with a solid, compact grain and a tough texture. The top will crack or form peaks during baking.

22-7. Baking powder vs baking soda. (See 20-10, "Chemical leavening agents.") Double-acting baking powder is normally used in cake recipes.

If an acidic ingredient such as buttermilk, fruit juice or chopped fruit is used in the cake, baking soda is used for leavening to counteract the acid. The average ratio is ¼ teaspoon soda for every cup of flour.

If you're using an old recipe, it may call for dissolving the soda in liquid. This is no longer necessary. Baking soda made in early days did not dissolve easily and had to be helped by dissolving it in warm or hot liquid. Today's baking soda is finely ground so it can be sifted with the dry ingredients. If you dissolve baking soda in the liquid, it begins to react immediately. Most of the gases are lost before the mixing is completed and the cake will not rise properly. If you sift the baking soda with the dry ingredients, it does not begin to react until the liquid is added, which is usually the final stage of mixing the cake. Much more of the gases are available to help the cake rise.

Too little baking powder results in a cake with poor volume. Too much baking powder gives a coarse texture and an off flavor. The cake may fall during baking.

22-8. Liquids. (See 20-5, "Liquids in baking.") If you add too little liquid, the cake will sink in the center and have an uneven grain.

If you add too much liquid, the cake will not rise sufficiently and will have a solid, doughy texture.

22-9. Conventional method of mixing a cake.

Assemble all the ingredients and equipment. (See 5-4, "Organize your work.")

Cream the fat and sugar until they have a smooth texture and a light color. If the fat is cold, you may have to cream it first before adding the sugar. Butter or shortening at room temperature creams the easiest. Proper creaming is a vital step —it combines the fat and sugar into a mixture filled with very fine air bubbles needed for both a fine texture and volume. You can cream either by hand or with a mixer. A mixer does the job more quickly but there's also the danger of overcreaming when using a mixer. If the mixture looks frothy and curdled, you've overcreamed it. The oil has separated from the butter, which can result in a cake with a coarse texture and smaller volume.

Beat in the eggs. Recipes vary as to how eggs are beaten into the creamed mixture. Sometimes they are all added at once, sometimes one at a time and sometimes they are beaten first and then added. Follow the directions in the recipe. If eggs are beaten before they are added, they entrap air which adds to the leavening process and aids in greater volume. When adding eggs, be sure to beat until they are thoroughly blended with the fat-sugar mixture. If eggs are either overbeaten or underbeaten, the cake will not rise well and will be compact.

Sift the dry ingredients together.

Add the dry ingredients and the liquid to the creamed mixture alternately, beginning and ending with the dry ingredients. Usually, the dry ingredients are added in thirds and the liquids in halves. If you add the liquid last, the mixture will separate and curdle, giving the cake a poor texture. Mix the ingredients only until well blended. Run a rubber scraper around the inside of the bowl to loosen particles of creamed mixture or flour so the entire mixture will be well blended. The batter should be thick and smooth. The entire process of adding dry and liquid ingredients should take a relatively short time.

If the batter is undermixed, the cake will not rise properly. It will be heavy with a coarse texture and tunnels.

If the batter is overmixed, the cake will be tough and compact with a coarse grain.

22-10. One-bowl or quick-mix method of mixing a cake.

As a rule, the one-bowl method makes it possible to use a higher proportion of sugar and liquid to flour than you can with the conventional method. If you attempt to use the one-bowl method of mixing for a recipe that was originally developed to be mixed by the conventional method, you could have a failure. If you mix a conventional cake by the one-bowl method and it doesn't work, next time increase the sugar and liquid just slightly.

While this method saves time, the cakes do not have as fine a grain or texture as those mixed by the conventional method. They also get stale faster.

To make a cake by the one-bowl method, combine the flour, sugar, shortening and part of the milk in a large mixing bowl. For optimum results, the ingredients should be at room temperature.

Blend by hand or with a mixer. This method is ideal for the mixer since it's a little difficult to mix the ingredients thoroughly by hand. If not mixed well, the cake will not rise properly, will have a coarse texture and will lack flavor.

Mix in the remaining ingredients. The batter should be thick and smooth. As with the conventional method, don't overmix the batter. Overmixing will cause the same problems that occur when a cake is mixed by the conventional method. (See 22-9, "Conventional method of mixing a cake.")

22-11. Pans. (See 5-15, "Pan substitutions," and 20-31, "Preparing pans for baking.") Use the same size pans specified in the recipe and prepare them as directed.

Fill the pans a little over half full. If pans are too small and you have too much batter in the pans, it will overflow and the cake will not rise properly. If the pans are too large and you have too little batter, the cake won't brown or rise properly and will be dry.

Be sure the pans are in good condition. If they are uneven or dented, the cake will be out of shape. The batter will bake to the same contour as the pan.

If you want to use a mold, measure it to determine if it is close to the same size specified on the recipe. Using a standard liquid measuring cup, pour water into the pan called for in the recipe. Do the same with the pan you plan to use. If both use close to the same amount of water, they are interchangeable. (See 5-15, "Pan substitutions.")

If the shape of the pan is markedly different from the one recommended in the recipe, it may change the baking time. For example, if you're substituting a deep mold for two 9-inch layer cake pans, the baking time for the cake will increase considerably. Begin to test the cake shortly after the initial baking time and let it continue to bake until it passes the test for doneness.

22-12. Baking cakes. (See 20-32, "Pan placement in oven.") Follow the recipe for baking temperatures.

Begin to check the cake a few minutes before the earliest time specified in the recipe. Variations in the temperature of ingredients and the temperature in the oven affect baking time. The time given in the recipe is merely a guide—test the cake for doneness before removing it from the oven. (See 22-13, "Testing cakes for doneness.")

If the oven temperature is too low, the cake will have a pale crust and may sink in the center. It will have an uneven grain and be soggy inside.

If the oven temperature is too high, the top of the cake will peak or crack. The cake will not rise properly and the crust will be too brown. Although the cake will be done on the outside, it will still be soggy on the inside.

If the oven temperature is accurate but the cake is not baked long enough, the crust will be pale, the cake won't rise to full volume and it will have a soggy texture.

If the cake is baked too long, the crust will be too brown and hard and the cake will be dry.

22-13. Testing cakes for doneness. To test a cake for doneness, check its appearance first. It should be nicely browned, at full volume and starting to pull away from the sides of the pan. Tap the top very gently with a finger—it should feel firm but springy.

You can also insert a wooden pick or a wire cake tester in the center of the cake. If cake particles stick to it as you remove it, the cake is not done. If the tester is clean, the cake is done. Some people, however, feel that this is not a reliable test since crumbs could stick to rough areas on the pick or tester, even though the cake is done.

22-14. Removing baked cakes from pans. (See 20-34, "Removing baked products from pans.")

Generally, cakes must be removed from the pans as soon as

they are removed from the oven, unless the recipe specifies otherwise. If the cake is left in the pan, moisture condenses as it cools and gives the cake a soggy bottom.

Some cakes must cool 5 to 10 minutes in the pan before removing, not long enough for condensation to form but long enough for them to firm slightly so they can be handled easily.

FOAM CAKES

22-15. Ingredients in foam cakes. Foam cakes contain many of the same ingredients as shortened cakes. They give foam cakes many of the same characteristics as they give to shortened cakes.

• *Sugar.* (See 20-21, "Sugar," and 22-4, "Sugar.") Measure sugar carefully. If you use too little sugar, the cake will be tough. If you use too much sugar, the crust will be too brown.

• *Eggs.* (See 20-27, "Eggs as ingredients.") Since eggs comprise the only liquid in most foam cakes, the size of eggs is important. Follow the recipe instructions carefully regarding the amount of eggs to use. If you use poor-quality eggs, the cake may not rise sufficiently. It also won't rise properly if the egg whites are either overbeaten or underbeaten. (See 8-15, "Beating egg whites.")

• *Liquid.* In most foam cakes, eggs are the only liquid used. Some, however, call for small amounts of liquid. If the batter does not have enough liquid, the baked cake will be dry in texture. If too much liquid is used, the cake will have a solid, moist texture and won't rise properly.

• *Flour.* (See 20-1, "Purpose of flour"; 20-2, "Kinds of flour"; and 22-6, "All-purpose vs cake flour.") Too much flour can result in a solid, compact texture.

22-16. Mixing foam cakes.

For angel food and sponge cakes: If you're making an angel food cake, combine the dry ingredients. If you're making a sponge cake, beat the egg yolks until creamy yellow and blend into the liquid and dry ingredients. Beat the egg whites with part of the sugar until stiff. (See 8-15, "Beating egg whites," and 20-8, "Air as a leavening.") Fold the dry ingredients or the batter into the egg whites. (See 20-8, "Air as a leavening.") If you beat the dry ingredients or batter into the egg whites, the cake will have poor volume. If the ingredients are not mixed completely during the folding process, the cake will have streaks in it.

For chiffon cakes: Sift the dry ingredients together into a large bowl. Add the eggs and liquid and beat with a spoon until smooth. Beat the egg whites until stiff. Fold the beaten egg whites into the batter. If the eggs are underbeaten, the cake won't rise properly. It will be compact with an uneven texture. If the batter is underfolded or undermixed, the cake will be coarse and soggy. If the batter is overfolded or over-mixed, the cake will not rise properly. It will be tough with an uneven texture.

22-17. Pans. (See 5-15, "Pan substitutions.") For best re-sults, use the proper size and type of pan. A foam cake is generally baked in a tube pan, which is deep and round with a tube in the center. The tube helps the heat get to the center quickly so the cake bakes evenly.

Most foam cakes must be baked in ungreased pans. (See 20-31, "Preparing pans for baking.") However, occasionally a recipe for a sponge cake or chiffon cake will call for a greased pan.

If you use too large a pan, the crust will be pale and the cake won't rise properly.

If the pan is too small, the batter will overflow and the cake won't rise properly.

If you grease the pan or if the pan wasn't properly washed and contains some grease residue, the cake won't rise properly.

22-18. Baking foam cakes. Follow recipe instructions for time and temperature.

If the oven temperature is too low or the cake is not baked long enough, the crust will be pale. The cake will not rise properly and it will be soggy.

If the oven temperature is too high or the cake is baked too long, the crust will be too brown and tough and the cake will be dry.

A foam cake is done when the top is nicely and evenly browned and the sides start to pull away from the pan.

22-19. Removing cakes from pans. (See 20-34, "Remov-ing baked products from pans.") Follow recipe instructions for cooling the cake and removing it from the pan.

As a rule, a foam cake must be cooled in the pan, which is

inverted during the cooling period. If the pan is not inverted, the cake will fall. If the cake is removed from the pan before it has completely cooled, it will fall.

CAKE MIXES

22-20. Cake mixes. Follow the directions on the package when preparing cake mixes. If you enjoy experimenting, most of the mixes have variations included in the instructions. Stay within the limits of the variations given on the package. Keep in mind that cake mixes are prepared according to specific chemical formulas. If you experiment beyond the variations suggested, you could wind up with a failure.

FROSTING A CAKE

22-21. Frosting a layer cake.
Whatever kind of frosting you use, keep it covered as you work. Moisture evaporating from the frosting can cause a thin crust to form, making it difficult to work.

To frost a cake, brush the crumbs from the surface of the layers. Use a pastry brush or paper toweling. Arrange 4 strips of wax paper on a cake plate. Cover only the edges of the plate, not the center. Place the bottom layer on the center of the plate over the wax paper. If the cake plate is slightly indented and the top of the cake is rounded, turn the layer upside down so the rounded top serves as the bottom of the cake. However, if the cake plate is perfectly flat, place the layer top up.

If the cake is peaked, slice off the peak to make a slightly rounded top. If the cake is lopsided, slice off the higher side to level it.

Use a metal spatula or table knife to spread the frosting. Don't use a sharp knife—you might cut the cake. Spread the filling or frosting evenly over the bottom layer. Place the top layer on top of the filling. Be sure the sides of the layers line up evenly.

Spread a thin layer of frosting over the sides and top of the cake to hold any remaining crumbs. Then spread a thick layer of frosting evenly over the sides, bringing the frosting up over the top edge of the cake. Be sure to fill in any spaces between layers.

Spread the frosting over the top of the cake and blend it in with the frosting on the sides. For an attractive appearance, make designs in the frosting, such as swirls or peaks.

Very carefully, pull the wax paper out from under the cake. Work slowly so you don't remove any frosting from the bottom edge of the cake.

MICROWAVE BAKING

22-22MW. Texture of cakes.

Shortened cakes baked in a microwave oven will have a slightly different texture than those baked in a conventional oven. They will be more moist and less tender.

Foam cakes leavened entirely with egg whites will not bake satisfactorily in the microwave oven because the baking time is too short.

22-23MW. Adapting conventional cake recipes. If you are adapting a conventional recipe to use in the microwave oven, cut down on the amount of liquid and oil. Decrease leavening by one-third.

22-24MW. Cake mixes. Cake mixes bake differently in the microwave oven, depending on the brand. Check the package label for microwaving instructions and follow the directions for best results.

22-25MW. Pan sizes. Because of the speed of baking, microwaved cakes rise higher than normal during baking and then settle down to their normal size. For this reason, you will need pans that are deeper than those used for conventional baking.

If you are using average size pans, fill them a little less than half full. Make cupcakes with the leftover batter.

22-26MW. Use round pans. Cakes cook more evenly in round pans.

If you use a square or rectangular pan, shield the corners with a smooth small piece of foil. Make sure that the foil does not touch any part of the oven interior.

22-27MW. Preparing pans. (See 20-36MW, "Flouring baking pans," and 20-37MW, "Lining baking pans.") If you sprinkle a greased pan very lightly with granulated sugar, the baked cake will come out of the pan more easily.

Moisture tends to condense on the bottom of the baking pan,

giving the cake a soggy bottom. If the cake is to be removed from the pan before serving, line the pan bottom with paper toweling to absorb the moisture. Cool 5 minutes after baking. Turn the cake out and peel the toweling off the bottom.

If the cake is to be cut in the pan, such as a sheet cake, don't line the bottom with paper.

22-28MW. Don't cover cakes. Cakes are baked without cover. However, at the end of the baking period, the top may not be set. To get the top of the cake to set, cover it with plastic wrap and cook on High power for about 30 seconds. If puddles of condensation collect on the surface of the cake, sponge them up with a paper towel.

22-29MW. For even baking. Generally, because of the pattern of the microwaves, the center of the cake will take longer to cook than the edges. For more even baking, make a hollow in the batter in the center of the pan.

To help distribute heat more evenly, place an inverted baking dish on the oven bottom. Place the cake pan on top of the dish to raise the cake.

22-30MW. Rotate cakes during baking. Cakes must be rotated during baking. They will not "fall" when they are rotated. Some cakes may have to be rotated more than once. Follow recipe directions.

Keep in mind that all microwave ovens vary in their cooking patterns. You may have to experiment several times to determine how the cooking pattern in your oven affects baking.

22-31MW. Cooking time. Follow your owner's manual and recipe directions for cooking time. Before adding extra cooking time, allow for carryover cooking.

Overbaked cakes are tough, chewy and hard.

22-32MW. Removing cakes from pans. Cool the cake for a short time, about 5 to 10 minutes, before removing it from the pan. Cool it just long enough for the cake to set but not so long that it sticks to the pan.

22-33MW. Frosting microwaved cakes. Microwaved cakes may be a little difficult to frost. They have a very delicate texture and also lack the crust that conventionally baked cakes have. Work gently so you do not tear the surface.

STORING CAKES

22-34. Cakes with cream fillings. Refrigerate all cakes with cream fillings. Don't allow them to set out at room temperature—harmful bacteria will multiply quickly in the cream filling.

22-35. Cakes without cream fillings. Store in tightly closed containers at room temperatures. Refrigerated cakes stale quickly.

22-36. Freezing cakes. If you want to store cakes for more than a few days, freeze them. See 3-4, "Freezer storage."

Cookies

23-1. Ingredients in cookies. Although there are count-less varieties of cookies, there are six basic kinds: bar, 23-6; drop, 23-7; molded, 23-8; pressed, 23-9; rolled, 23-10; and refrigerator, 23-11.

The ingredients in cookies serve the same basic functions as they do in cakes. See Chapter 20, which describes the general functions of ingredients used in baking and Sections 22-2 to 22-8, which describe the functions of the ingredients in cakes.

Because the dough for most cookie recipes is thick, eggs usually supply the only liquid. The size of the eggs can mean either too much or too little liquid.

As in other baked products, too much flour can cause a tough, dry cookie.

Cookies are made by many different mixing methods, so follow the recipe directions carefully. The mixing method can affect the proportion or kind of ingredients used. If you take shortcuts or change the mixing method, you could have disastrous results.

23-2. Shaping cookies. Make cookies the same shape and thickness so they bake evenly. If some are thin and some thick, the thin ones will be done before the thick ones and will overbrown.

23-3. Pans for cookies. Follow recipe directions for the kind of pan to use and for preparing the pan. Depending on the ingredients in the dough, the pans may have to be greased, greased and floured or left ungreased. Certain types of delicate cookies must be baked on parchment paper.

If the recipe calls for a baking or cookie sheet, use a flat baking sheet with low sides. A pan with high sides deflects the heat and keeps the cookies from browning. The high sides also make it difficult to remove the baked cookies.

Unless the recipe instructs otherwise, place the cookies about an inch apart on the baking pan. This allows room for expansion.

Don't put cookie dough on a hot baking sheet—it will melt and spread. If you do a great deal of baking, you'll find it practical to have more than one baking sheet. If you have only one baking sheet, allow it to cool before you put cookie dough on it.

23-4. Baking cookies. Bake cookies in a preheated oven, following the temperature and time given in the recipe.

Most ovens can accommodate only one baking sheet at a time. Place the baking sheet in the center of the oven. If your oven does not bake evenly, you may have to turn the sheet around during baking so all the cookies will brown evenly.

If you're baking two smaller sheets, arrange them in the oven so there is ample space between the cookie sheets and the walls of the oven for the hot air to circulate. Otherwise, the cookies will bake unevenly. (See 20-32, "Pan placement in the oven.")

Watch cookies closely as they bake. A few extra seconds of heat can overbrown them. Even though you remove the pan from the oven, cookies continue to bake until you remove them from the baking sheet. Overbaked cookies will brown excessively. Underbaked cookies will be pale with a doughy texture.

23-5. Tests for doneness. The following tests can help you determine if the cookies are done:
• Cookies will be delicately browned.
• Press drop and bar cookies lightly with your finger. The imprint of your finger should show slightly.

Follow recipe directions for removing cookies from the baking sheets. Also see 20-34, "Removing baked products from pans." Cool cookies on a cooling rack. If cooled on a solid surface, moisture condenses on the bottoms and the cookies become soggy.

23-6. Bar cookies. Bar cookies, such as brownies, are baked in a square or rectangular pan, just like a cake.

To make bar cookies, mix the ingredients according to recipe directions. If the dough is overmixed, the cookies will have a hard, crusty top.

Spread the dough evenly in the pan. If the dough isn't spread evenly, the cookies will have uneven shapes.

After baking, cool and cut according to recipe instructions. Some are cut while warm but others must be cooled before being cut. If you cut bar cookies while too warm, the cut edges become compact and gummy. Some bar cookies crumble when cut while too warm. Use a sharp knife when cutting bar cookies—a dull knife will tear rather than cut and ruin the shape of the cookies.

Overbaked bar cookies are dry and crumbly.

23-7. Drop cookies. Drop cookies are made by dropping rounded or heaping teaspoonfuls of dough on a baking sheet. A drop cookie should have a rounded, half-ball shape when it is baked.

To make drop cookies, prepare the dough according to recipe directions. If the ingredients are not measured properly so they are in the right proportions, the cookies will spread out rather than hold their shape when baked.

To drop dough on cookie sheet, scoop up a rounded portion of the dough with a teaspoon. With a rubber scraper, push the dough from the teaspoon onto the baking sheet. The dough should be in a mound with a peak. If not, the cookies will spread out rather than retaining a rounded shape. Allow about 2 inches between cookies.

Because of their shape, care must be taken to bake drop cookies evenly. The edges are thin while the centers are thick. Begin testing the cookies a few minutes before the baking time is up.

If the cookies are overbaked, the edges become dark and crusty and the cookies are dry and hard. If you've used the correct time and temperature and the edges are dark and crusty, it's possible the baking sheet is too large for the oven. Next time, try a smaller baking sheet.

If the oven temperature is too low, drop cookies will spread out excessively.

23-8. Molded cookies. Molded cookies are shaped by hand, either rolled into balls or crescents. Sometimes the balls are flattened before baking.

To make molded cookies, prepare the cookie dough according to recipe directions. If ingredients are not measured properly and the proportions are changed, the cookies may be crumbly.

Chill the dough so it can be easily shaped. Roll small pieces between the palms of your hands into balls the size of walnuts or about an inch in diameter. You can also form the dough into small crescents or any other shape specified in the recipe. Press the dough together as you shape the cookies. If not pressed together, the cookies will lose their shape and will be crumbly.

Place the shaped cookies about an inch apart on a cookie sheet. If the cookies are to be flattened, place the balls about 3 inches apart.

To flatten the cookies, use a fork or the bottom of a glass. Dip in flour or granulated sugar to keep from sticking to the dough.

Bake according to recipe directions. If overbaked, molded cookies will overbrown. If underbaked, they will be doughy.

23-9. Pressed cookies. Pressed cookies, such as Spritz cookies, are made by pushing the dough through a cookie press.

To make pressed cookies, prepare the dough according to recipe directions. Ingredients must be measured accurately to make sure the dough is of the right consistency to go through the press. If the dough is too soft, it won't hold its shape. If it's too stiff, it will be difficult to force through the press. Unless the recipe states otherwise, the dough should be at room temperature. If the dough is too cold or too warm, it will not go through the press properly and the cookies will be misshapen.

Force the dough through the cookie press onto a baking sheet. Follow the manufacturer's directions for using the cookie press. If the press isn't used according to directions, the cookies may be misshapen. Allow about a half inch of space between cookies. If the dough is slightly soft, chill it for a short time. However, don't chill it so long that it will be too hard to go through the press.

Bake according to recipe directions. If the oven temperature is too low, the cookies will not hold their shape. Overbaking causes excess browning.

23-10. Rolled cookies. Rolled cookies are made from a stiff dough which is rolled out and cut into different shapes with cookie cutters.

To make rolled cookies, mix the dough according to recipe directions. Chill it so it will roll out more easily. Roll the dough about an eighth of an inch thick on a lightly floured surface. Roll the dough lightly and use as little flour as possible. Excess flour will stick to the cookies and will be visible after the cookies are baked. Excess flour will also make the cookies dry.

Dip the cookie cutter in flour. Shake out extra flour and cut out the dough. Place the cookies on a cookie sheet about an inch apart.

Gather up leftover dough, reroll and cut out. Avoid rerolling more than once. If the dough is rerolled too many times, the cookies will be tough.

Follow recipe directions for baking and removing from the baking sheet.

23-11. Refrigerator cookies. Dough for refrigerator cookies must be chilled before it can be cut.

To make refrigerator cookies, mix the dough according to recipe directions. Shape the dough into a long roll so it can be sliced easily. If the roll is not uniform in size, the cookies will be an irregular shape. Wrap the dough in wax paper and chill until it is firm enough to slice evenly. Chilling time will vary with the kind of dough and the thickness of the roll. Don't slice the roll until it is thoroughly chilled and firm. If it's too soft, it won't slice evenly and the cookies will be misshapen.

Slice evenly with a sharp knife. Don't use a dull knife—it will tear the dough and the cookies will be misshapen.

Place the slices on a baking sheet and bake according to recipe directions.

MICROWAVE BAKING

23-12MW. Cardboard as a baking sheet. Use heavy cardboard covered with wax paper as a baking sheet. Bake cookies until they are set. Allow cookies to cool before removing them from the wax paper.

23-13MW. Shield corners of square pans. If you're using a square or rectangular pan for bar cookies, shield the corners with small pieces of smooth aluminum foil to keep them from overbaking. Don't let the foil touch any part of the interior of the oven.

23-14MW. For even baking. If drop or sliced cookies are to bake evenly, they must be the same shape and size.

To make drop cookies, measure the dough out evenly with a

standard measuring spoon. Fill the spoon and level off the top for an accurate measurement.

Bake bar cookies in a ring mold.

23-15MW. Adapting conventional recipes. If you're adapting a conventional recipe for use in the microwave oven, experiment with reducing the fat, sugar and liquid. Since most cookies have no liquid, you may have to increase the flour slightly rather than reduce the amount of liquid. Decrease leavening by one-third.

23-16MW. Doneness test for cookies. Microwaved cookies will not brown. To determine if cookies are done, check their appearance—they should look dry. Overbaked cookies will start to burn in the center.

23-17MW. Carryover cooking. Complete the carryover cooking time before adding microwave time. This is particularly true of bar cookies.

23-18MW. Crumbly cookies. If the baked cookies are crumbly, try adding an extra egg to the dough the next time you make them.

STORING COOKIES

23-19. Storing cookies. Store crisp cookies in a can or plastic container with a loose-fitting cover, which will allow moisture to evaporate. However, if the weather is humid, the loose-fitting cover will allow moisture to seep into the container. In humid weather, store crisp cookies in a container with a tight-fitting cover.

Store soft cookies in an air-tight container. A slice of apple or other fruit in the container helps to keep the cookies soft.

To store cookies for long periods of time, freeze them in moisture-vapor-proof wrapping. (See 3-4, "Freezer storage.")

Pies and pastries

24-1. Pie crust ingredients. Pie crust is basically a combination of flour, solid fat and water. The proportion of fat to flour is high enough to keep too much gluten from developing. However, enough gluten must develop so you can roll the dough out without tearing it. Gluten is also needed for the structure of the pie crust.

The mixing process forms flakes of fat between layers of gluten. As the pie crust bakes, the fat melts, giving off steam. The steam separates the dough into flaky layers, giving pie crust its characteristic flaky tenderness.

For a flaky, tender pie crust, the ingredients must be thoroughly chilled. If the dough warms up, the fat will begin to melt. The result will be a soft, crumbly crust rather than a tender, flaky one.

Measure the ingredients accurately. Too little or too much of any ingredient affects texture and quality.

Too little fat results in a tough or solid crust. Too much fat makes the crust too tender, one that will fall apart. It will also overbrown.

Too little water makes the dough difficult to handle and roll out. When you do get it rolled out, it may fall apart as you try to handle it. The baked crust will be dry and mealy.

If you use too much water, you'll have a sticky dough that's difficult to roll out. The crust will shrink as it bakes and will be tough and solid.

24-2. Basic pie crust recipe. The following is a basic pie crust recipe for a 2-crust, 9-inch pie:

2 CUPS ALL-PURPOSE FLOUR. Use all-purpose flour. If

you use another flour, such as whole wheat, it will change the texture of the pie crust. In addition, you may have to use less fat because of the fat in whole grain flour.

1 TEASPOON SALT.

2/3 CUP SOLID FAT. The fat must be cold. Don't remove it from the refrigerator until you are ready to mix the crust. Some people feel that leaf lard gives the most flavorful and flaky pie crust. However, you can also use any hydrogenated shortening. Butter and margarine give a more flavorful crust but with a different texture—short and tender, like the texture of cookies. You can also use chicken fat. Pie crust can also be made with oil, but the method differs from the one using solid fat.

4 TO 6 TABLESPOONS ICE WATER. The water must be cold to keep the fat from softening. Note that the amount of water is not specific because flour varies in the amount of water it will absorb, depending on the moisture in the air. (See 21-15, "Amount of flour.")

24-3. Mixing pie crust. Handle the dough with your hands as little as possible. Heat from hands melts the fat.

Some experts advise chilling the mixing bowl and utensils.

Don't wash and rinse equipment in hot water and then use it immediately to prepare pie crust dough. It will still be warm and will melt the fat.

To mix pie crust, sift the flour and salt together into a chilled mixing bowl. Add half the fat to the flour. It's much easier to cut the fat into the flour in two steps rather than trying to cut it all in at once. It also takes less time. With a pastry blender or two knives, cut the fat into the flour until the mixture has the texture of cornmeal. Cutting in the fat keeps tiny particles of fat in the dough, making the pie crust flaky.

Cut in the remaining fat until the particles are the size of small peas. If the second part of the fat is cut in too fine, you'll have a dry, mealy crust.

Add ice water gradually, mixing with a fork. Press the mixture with a fork to form a ball. Don't use your hands. The mixture should be just moist enough to hold together.

When you have pressed the dough together with a fork, gather it with your fingers. Press gently to form a firm ball. Handle the dough as little as possible.

If you undermix the dough when adding water, the dough

will be difficult to roll out. The baked crust will fall apart. If you overmix, overhandle or knead the dough, the crust will be tough and solid, with a pale color. In a 2-crust pie, the bottom crust will be soggy.

24-4. Rolling out pie crust.

To roll out dough, first wrap it in wax paper and chill in the refrigerator for about an hour. Chilling makes it easier to roll out without adding excessive amounts of flour. It also helps keep the fat solid. The dough should be firm but not so hard that you can't roll it out. If you've chilled the dough too long and it's too hard to roll out, let it stand at room temperature for a short time. If you try to roll out a dough that's too hard, it will split.

Use a pastry cloth for rolling dough—it needs less flour than a hard surface. If you don't have a pastry cloth, use a wooden or plastic cutting board. To keep the board from sliding, put a damp dishcloth under it. A pastry stocking on the rolling pin also cuts down on the amount of flour needed to roll out the dough. Flour the work surface and rolling pin lightly. The more flour you add to the work surface, the tougher the pastry will be.

If you're making a 2-crust pie, divide the dough in half. Make the half for the bottom crust slightly larger and roll it out first. Cover the remaining dough so it doesn't dry out.

Center the dough on the work surface. Flatten it gently with the palm of your hand, keeping it as round as possible.

With a rolling pin, roll the dough from the center out in all directions. Roll from the center to the edge of the dough, lift the pin, bring it back to the center and roll again in another direction. Try to keep the dough rolling out as round as possible. Don't roll the pin back and forth. If you do, you'll stretch the dough and when it bakes, it'll shrink.

As you roll, lift and move the dough to keep it from sticking to the work surface. Add a little more flour to the work surface if necessary.

Roll the dough out to about ⅛ inch thick. If it's rolled too thick, the crust will be thick, soft and doughy. If it's rolled too thin, it will overbrown easily. It will also be brittle and will break easily when you try to cut the pie.

If the dough tears or breaks as you roll it out, patch it. (See 24-6, "Patching dough.") Don't reroll it—rerolling makes a tough and solid crust.

24-5. Fitting dough into pie pan. Rolled-out pie crust dough is tender and easily damaged. It must be handled gently and quickly to get it from the work surface into the pie pan. You can use several methods to transfer the rolled dough into the pie pan.

• Fold the dough in half or in quarters. Lift it and place it on one half or quarter of the pie pan. Unfold gently and center it in the pan.

• Use the rolling pin to carry the dough to the pie pan. Place the rolling pin on the edge of the dough closest to you. Lift up the edge of the dough and begin to roll the pin away from you, guiding the dough around the pin as you roll. Wind the dough around the pin loosely. Hold the rolling pin over the edge of the pie pan farthest from you. Unwind the dough gently and let it settle into the pie pan.

Very gently, slide the dough down into the pie pan so it fits down in the area where the bottom and sides meet. Be careful not to stretch the dough or punch a hole in it. If you make a hole, patch it. (See 24-6, "Patching dough.") Let the dough rest a few minutes before filling.

If you're making a pie shell and stretch or overhandle the dough when fitting it into the pan, the shell will shrink as it bakes.

24-6. Patching dough.
To patch pie dough, cut off a piece of rolled dough, either from a spot that has too much dough or from the trimmings. With COLD water, slightly dampen the area to be patched. Apply the patch and press firmly so it sticks. Smooth out the edges with a rolling pin.

24-7. To make a pie shell. If you're making a one-crust pie, finish the pie shell as follows (see 24-1 to 24-5 for preliminary steps):
Trim off the pastry about half an inch beyond the edge of the pan. Use a sharp knife or scissors. Fold the half-inch extension under the crust at the edge of the pan. This makes a double thickness of dough on the edge. Shape the edge to make a design.

24-8. Shaping the edge. Make an attractive design on the edge of the pie by fluting the crust. If you're making a 2-crust pie, fluting the edge is almost essential—it helps seal the edges so juices do not run out.

Although many designs can be made, the two most common are scallops and ridges.

To make a scalloped edge, place the thumb and finger of one hand against the edge of the pie crust on the outside, just at the top of the pie pan rim. With the finger of the other hand, push the dough from the opposite side so you push it between the thumb and finger. Be gentle so you do not break the dough. Repeat the process about an inch apart.

To make ridges, press the flat tines of a fork gently on the edge to make ridges. Work carefully—don't poke the fork through the crust. If you make a hole in the crust, patch it to keep juices from running out.

24-9. Baking a pie shell.

A pie shell must be baked if you use a filling that does not require further cooking, such as pudding.

To bake a pie shell, prick holes in the pie shell with a fork before baking. As the crust bakes, steam forms. The steam may cause the crust to puff up and "blister." The holes allow the steam to escape. Do not prick holes in a pie crust which is to be filled and then baked after filling.

To keep the dough from puffing up as it bakes, you might also fill it with dry beans or peas. Remove the beans or peas a few minutes before the baking time is over. To make the beans or peas easier to remove from the pie crust, line the crust with aluminum foil and then fill with beans or peas. A few minutes before the baking time is over, remove the beans or peas by lifting them out with the foil.

As a rule, a pie shell is baked in a preheated oven at 450°F for about 10 to 15 minutes.

24-10. Soggy crust.

If the filling has a high liquid content, such as pumpkin pie, or if it is a juicy fruit filling, the bottom crust could get soggy. To help prevent sogginess, brush the bottom crust lightly with egg white and prebake in a preheated oven at 450°F for about 5 to 10 minutes. Or brush the unbaked crust with melted butter just before filling.

24-11. Fillings for 2-crust pies.

Fruit is the most popular filling for 2-crust pies. You can use either fresh, frozen or canned fruit. The fruit is usually sweetened and the juice thickened so the filling holds its shape when the pie is cut. Flour, cornstarch and tapioca are most commonly used to thicken fruit pies. (See Chapter 10, "Thickeners.")

Follow recipe directions for the amount of filling to use for a pie. If you have extra fruit left over, don't add it to the filling just to use it up. That little extra could make the filling boil over in the oven as the pie bakes. Use the leftover fruit as a snack or in a fruit salad. You can also freeze it for future use.

24-12. Making a 2-crust pie. (See 24-1 to 24-6 for preliminary steps.)

With kitchen scissors or a sharp knife, trim the extra dough from the bottom crust even with the edge of the pie pan.

Prepare the filling and let it stand in the mixing bowl.

To make the top crust, roll out the second ball of dough. Spoon the filling into the pie crust and spread it evenly. Be careful not to mash the fruit. Wipe off filling that has dropped on the crust on the pie pan rim. It can prevent the pie from sealing properly.

Fold the top crust in half. Place it over half the filled pie and unfold. You will need about a half inch of pastry beyond the edge of the pie crust. Trim off the rest of the dough from the top crust with scissors or a sharp knife.

Lift up the edge of the top crust. Moisten the top of the bottom crust just slightly along the edge with cold water. Press the edge of the top crust firmly to the edge of the bottom crust.

Fold the remaining half inch of the top crust under the bottom crust along the edge. This will seal the two crusts together to keep the juices in. If the edges are not sealed properly, the filling will boil out and run over onto the oven bottom. Press both crusts together by shaping the edge. (See 24-8, "Shaping the edge.")

With a sharp knife, cut about 5 slits in the top crust near the center. The slits allow steam to escape and keep juices from boiling out of the pie and onto the oven bottom. Don't cut the slits near the edges of the pie—if any juices escape, they'll flow over the edges.

24-13. Baking a 2-crust pie. Follow the time and temperature specified in the recipe. Times and temperatures will vary, depending on the ingredients used in the fillings.

Don't line the oven racks with aluminum foil to catch drippings in the event of a boil-over. Lined racks prevent the heated air from circulating, resulting in an unevenly baked pie.

Don't put the pie pan on a cookie sheet to bake—it keeps the heated air from reaching the pie, resulting in uneven or poor baking.

If there's a chance the filling may boil over, put a shallow pan on the rack below the one holding the pie. Allow enough space for air to circulate evenly around the pie.

Preheat the oven when you bake a pie or pie shell. The fat must start to melt immediately. If you put the pie or shell into a cold oven, the crust will not be flaky.

If the oven temperature is too low or the pie is not baked long enough, the crust will be pale and tough. The bottom crust will be soggy.

If the oven temperature is too high or the pie is baked too long, the crust will overbrown and the filling will boil over.

24-14. Test for doneness. Check the color. The crust should be golden brown.

24-15. Leftover dough. Don't discard the trimmings from pie crust—turn them into cookies. Cut them into shapes that handle easily, such as rectangles or squares. Sprinkle with a sugar-cinnamon mixture. Place on an ungreased baking sheet and bake in a preheated oven at 450°F for about 8 to 10 minutes or until lightly browned.

24-16. Cream puffs. The method used to prepare cream puffs is simple but somewhat unusual and must be followed carefully. Cream puffs use steam as a leavening. The batter must be beaten long enough to allow the gluten to become strong and elastic. As the cream puffs bake, the steam expands. The strong, elastic gluten permits the cream puff batter to expand, creating a large cavity inside.

24-17. Mixing cream puffs. The basic ingredients in cream puffs are eggs, flour, salt, sugar (optional), water and butter. The eggs must be at room temperature.

To make cream puffs, mix the water with butter and bring to a boil. Add the flour all at once and stir quickly, continuing to cook. Stir and cook only until the paste is firm and dry—it will not cling to the sides of the pan nor to the spoon. Don't overstir the batter. If you do, it will not puff up when baked.

Remove the pan from the heat and cool slightly for about 2 minutes. Add the eggs, one at a time. Beat each egg into the batter with a wooden spoon until the batter is smooth and glossy. Don't add all of the eggs at one time and expect to beat the batter to the proper consistency. The batter must be beaten long enough to develop the gluten. After you've beaten in the last egg, the batter should be thick enough to stand up in a high mound.

Use a greased baking sheet with low sides or a cookie sheet. Drop a Tablespoonful of batter on the cookie sheet, allowing space between each cream puff for expansion. If you want larger cream puffs, use more batter. Shape the batter into a high mound. If it's flat, the cream puffs will not puff up as much. If the dough is not firm enough to mound up and hold its shape, spoon it into muffin tins. However, soft dough will not give as large a cavity for filling as a firm dough.

24-18. Baking cream puffs. Preheat the oven to 400°F. Bake the cream puffs for 10 minutes at 400°F. This allows the steam to form and puff up the dough. Reduce the oven temperature to 350°F and bake about 20 to 25 minutes longer or until done. Baking at the lower temperature allows moisture to evaporate and firms the structure so the cream puffs hold their shape.

Cream puffs are done when they are nicely browned and firm to the touch.

Cool cream puffs thoroughly before filling.

24-19. Filling cream puffs. To fill cream puffs, cut them in half horizontally. Use a sharp knife—cream puffs are fragile. A dull knife will tear them instead of cutting cleanly. Separate the two halves and remove any damp dough from the inside.

Fill the lower half of the cream puff and top with the upper half. You can use instant pudding, sweetened whipped cream, custard or canned pie filling mixed with whipped cream.

MICROWAVE BAKING

24-20MW. Pies are difficult to bake. Usually, 2-crust pies bake best with a combination of microwave and conventional cooking. See your owner's manual for specific directions.

24-21MW. Frozen uncooked pies. Don't attempt to bake frozen uncooked pies in the microwave oven. The bottom crust will not bake.

24-22MW. Preparing pans. Use a glass pie pan. Grease it to keep the crust from sticking.

24-23MW. Precook the bottom crust. Always precook the

284

bottom crust before adding the filling. Otherwise, the bottom crust will not be done. If the crust puffs up, push it down gently after removing it from the oven.

24-24MW. Frozen pie crust. You can use frozen pie crust as a timesaver. Buy the deep dish crust and don't defrost it. Gently pull the foil away from the crust. If the crust cracks, patch it during baking Place the crust in a glass pie pan. Bake on High power for 1 minute, remove and prick the shell. Patch any cracks. Return to the oven and continue cooking on High power for another 3 or 4 minutes. Fill and bake with the filling.

24-25MW. To add color. Pie crusts do not brown but you can add color in several ways:
• Broil in a conventional oven.
• Sprinkle with a cinnamon and sugar mixture.
• Add yellow food coloring to the water when you mix the pie crust.

STORING

24-26. Short-term storage. Pies and pastries should be refrigerated. Don't let them stand at room temperature.

24-27. Freezing pies. Pies give more satisfactory results if frozen before baking rather than after. (See 3-4, "Freezer storage.")

Index

Numbers given are Chapter-Section numbers, not page numbers. "C" following the Section number indicates the information is for the convection oven only. "MW" following the Section number indicates the information is for the microwave oven only.

A

Adding color to microwaved foods
  pies, 24-25MW
  poultry, 18-28MW
Aluminum foil, use in microwave
  oven, 4-48MW
Angel food cakes. See "Foam cakes"
Arrowroot, 10-22
Au gratin vegetables, 13-21

B

Bacon, in microwave oven,
  17-37MW
Baking
  breads in microwave oven,
    21-27MW to 21-29MW
  cakes, 22-1 to 22-21
  cakes in microwave oven,
    22-22MW to 22-23MW
  cookies, 23-1 to 23-11
  cookies in microwave oven,
    23-12MW to 23-18MW
  cream puffs, 24-16 to 24-19
  fish, 19-17
  fruits, 12-20
  general, 4-23, 20-1 to 20-34
  general, for microwave baking,
    20-35MW to 20-38MW
  pies, 24-1 to 24-15
  pies in microwave oven, 24-20MW
    to 24-25MW
  quick breads, 21-1 to 21-11
  vegetables, 13-19
  yeast breads, 21-12 to 21-26
Baking powder
  general, 20-10
  in cakes, 22-7
Baking soda
  general, 20-10
  in cakes, 22-7
Baking temperature, 20-33
Bar cookies, 23-6
Batters
  kinds, 21-1
  pour batters, 21-2
Beurre manie, 10-6
Beverages in microwave oven,
  15-13MW to 15-15MW
Biscuits
  doneness tests, 21-8
  drop biscuits, 21-5
  mixing, 21-5
  rolled biscuits, 21-7
Bouillon, 16-10
Bouquet garni, 11-18
Boil-over
  general, 6-13
  in microwave oven, 6-19MW
Boiling, 4-2
Braising
  fish, 19-21
  general, 4-7
  meat, 17-20
  poultry, 18-12

Breading food
  for microwave oven, 18-25MW
  general, 4-19
Broiling
  fish, 19-18
  fruits, 12-19
  general, 4-21
  in convection oven, 4-34C
  meat, 17-15
  poultry, 18-9
  vegetables, 13-20
Broth, 16-10
Brown sauce, 10-5
Brown sugar, soften in microwave
  oven, 20-38MW
Browning food in microwave oven,
  4-59MW
Butter
  general, 20-15
  in cakes, 22-3
Butter cakes. See "Shortened cakes"
Buying food
  baking powder, 20-10, 20-12
  canned food, 2-9
  cheese, 7-1 to 7-4
  coffee, 15-1
  cream, 6-2
  eggs, 8-1, 8-2
  fat, 20-18
  flour, 20-1 to 20-3
  for microwave oven, 2-14MW
  frozen food, 2-11
  fruit juices, 12-5
  fruits, 12-1 to 12-4
  general guidelines, 2-8
  grains, 9-5
  meat, 17-1 to 17-6
  meat for microwave oven,
    17-27MW
  milk, 6-1
  packaged foods, 2-10
  pasta, 9-3, 9-4
  poultry, 18-1 to 18-3
  rice, 9-1, 9-2
  salad greens, 14-1
  seafood, 19-1 to 19-7
  seasonings, 11-2
  sweeteners, 20-20 to 20-25
  tea, 15-7
  vegetables, 13-1 to 13-5
  yeast, 20-11, 20-12
  yogurt, 6-3

C

Cake mixes
  general, 22-20

  in microwave oven, 22-24MW
Cakes
  in conventional oven, 22-1 to
    22-21
  in microwave oven, 22-22MW to
    22-33MW
Canned fruits, using, 12-13
Carryover time, 4-41MW
Casseroles, convection oven, 4-32C
Charts
  Equivalents, weights and
    measures, 5-5
  Food equivalents, 5-7
  Freezer storage time, 3-4
  Pan substitutions, 5-15
  Substitutions, food (general), 5-6
  Substitutions, seafood, 19-15
Cheese, cooking
  by conventional methods, 7-7
  in microwave oven, 7-8MW
Cheese, kinds, 7-1 to 7-3
Chicken fat, rendering, 18-15
Chicken livers, in microwave oven,
  18-30MW
Chowders, 16-14, 19-22
Clarifying
  butter, 20-15
  fat, 4-18
  stock, 16-7
Cleaning storage areas, 3-7
Cocoa, 15-12
Coffee, 15-1 to 15-6
Condensation in microwave oven,
  4-53MW
Consomme, 16-10
Containers for microwave cooking,
  4-43MW
Convection oven, 4-25C to 4-35C
Conventional mixing method for
  cakes, 22-9
Cookies
  in conventional oven, 23-1 to
    23-11
  in microwave oven, 23-12MW to
    23-18MW
Cooking
  in dry heat, 4-20
  in fat, 4-12
  in liquid, 4-1
  in moist heat, 4-6
Cooking oil, 20-16
Cooking power, 4-37MW
Corn syrup, 20-24
Cornstarch as a thickener, 10-8 to
  10-10

Index

Covering food in microwave oven,
  4-55MW
Cream
  cooking with, 6-15
  how to whip, 6-16
  kinds, 6-2
Cream puffs, 24-16 to 24-19
Cream soups, 16-13
Creamed mixtures, curdling, 6-12,
  16-13
Crepes, 21-2, 21-3
Curdled milk, 6-12
Custard
  general, 10-16
  in microwave oven, 10-28MW

D

Dark bones and meat in cooked
  poultry, 18-17
Decrease recipe, 5-2
Deep-fat frying. Also see "French
  frying."
  in microwave oven, 4-61MW
Defrosting
  meat, 17-8
  meat in microwave oven,
    17-26MW
  poultry, 18-5
  poultry in microwave oven,
    18-18MW
  seafood, 19-10
  seafood in microwave oven,
    19-25MW
Deglazing meat, 11-21
Degreasing stock, 16-5
Doneness tests
  biscuits, 21-8
  cakes, 22-13
  cookies, 23-5
  cookies in microwave oven,
    23-16MW
  meat, 17-12
  pies, 24-14
  poultry, 18-14
  quick breads, 21-11
  seafood, 19-16
  yeast breads, 21-24
Dried fruits
  cooking, 12-17
  serving, 12-14
Drop cookies, 23-7
Drying in microwave oven, 4-62MW
Drying salad greens, 14-3

E

Egg sizes, 8-1

Egg whites, beating, 8-15
Egg yolks, discolored, 8-7
Eggs
  as ingredients in baking, 20-27
  as thickeners, 10-14, 10-15
  cooking by conventional methods,
    8-5 to 8-16
  cooking in microwave oven,
    8-17MW to 8-24MW
  in cakes, 22-5
Equivalents
  food, 5-7
  weights and measures, 5-5
"Exploding" food in microwave
  oven, 4-51MW

F

Fat
  clarifying, 4-18
  how to measure, 5-14
  in baking, 20-14 to 20-18
  smoking point, 4-13
Fat in milk, 6-1
"Fell" on lamb, 17-23
Fines herbes, 11-17
Fish. See "Seafood."
Fish odors, 19-14
Flour
  as a thickener, 10-2 to 10-7
  how to measure, 5-14
  in baking, 20-1
  in cakes, 22-6
  kinds, 20-2
Foam cakes, 22-15 to 22-19
Food equivalents, 5-7
Freezer burn, 3-4
Freezing
  cakes, 22-36
  cheese, 7-5
  eggs, 8-4
  general, 3-4
  herbs and spices, 11-5, 11-10
  milk, 6-5
  pies, 24-27
  soup, 16-15
  thickened foods, 10-22, 10-30
French frying. Also see "Deep-fat
  frying." 4-16
Fresh herbs
  drying in microwave oven,
    11-23MW
  general, 11-6 to 11-10
Frosting
  conventional cake, 22-21
  microwaved cake, 22-33MW

Frozen foods, cooking in convection
 oven, 4-31C
Frozen meat, cooking, 17-24
Fruits
 as seasoning, 11-20
 cooking by conventional methods,
  12-15 to 12-20
 cooking in microwave oven,
  12-21MW, 12-22MW
 serving, 12-10 to 12-14
Frying. Also see "Panfrying,"
 "Sauteing," "Stir-frying"
 eggs, whole, 8-11
 omelets, 8-13
 scrambled eggs, 8-12
 vegetables, 13-17

G

Gelatin, as a thickener, 10-17 to
 10-20
Gelatin, unflavored, dissolving in
 microwave oven, 10-29MW
Gluten, 20-1
Grades
 cheese, 7-4
 eggs, 8-1
 meat, 17-3
 poultry, 18-1
Grains, cooking
 by conventional methods, 9-9
 in microwave oven, 9-12MW
Gravy, 10-1 to 10-7, 17-25
Grease fires, 4-17
Ground meat, browning in
 microwave oven, 17-31MW

H

Hard-cooked eggs, 8-6
Hearty main-dish soups, 16-11
Herbs and spices in cooking, 11-11
 to 11-18
High-altitude cooking
 general, 5-3
 in microwave oven, 4-57MW
Holding time. See "Carryover time."
Hollandaise sauce in microwave
 oven, 10-27MW
Home-canned food, processing in
 microwave oven, 4-60MW
Home-canned vegetables, heating
 by conventional method, 13-23
 in microwave oven, 13-35MW
Honey, 20-22
Hot spots in microwave oven,
 4-38MW

I-J
Iced coffee, 15-5
Iced tea, 15-10
Increase recipe
 amount of seasoning, 11-13
 general, 5-2

K
Kneading
 general guidelines, 21-6
 rolled biscuits, 21-7
 yeast dough, 21-17

L
Labels
 cheese, 7-4
 diet food, 2-4
 general, 2-1
 imitation foods, 2-3
 nutrition, 2-2
Lard, 20-17
Leavening agents, 20-7 to 20-13
Legumes, cooking, 13-22

M
Margarine, 20-15
Measuring
 dry measuring cups, 5-9
 general, 5-8
 level vs heaping measurements,
  5-10
 liquid measuring cup, 5-11
 measuring spoons, 5-12
 guidelines, 5-14
Meat, composition of, 17-1
Meat, cooking
 by conventional methods, 17-11 to
  17-25
 in microwave oven, 17-26MW to
  17-37MW
Meat, kinds, 17-2
Meat tenderizers, 17-13
Meringues, 8-16
Metric system, 5-13
Microwave cooking
 baking, general, 20-35MW to
  20-38MW
 beverages, 15-13MW to 15-15MW
 breads, 21-27MW to 21-29MW
 cakes, 22-22MW, 22-23MW to
  22-33MW
 cheese, 7-8MW
 cookies, 23-12MW to 23-18MW
 custard, 10-28MW
 drying fresh herbs, 11-23MW
 eggs, 8-17MW to 8-24MW

fruits, 12-21MW, 12-22MW
general guidelines, 4-36MW to
4-64MW
grains, 9-12MW
gravy, 10-23MW to 10-25MW
meat, 17-26MW to 17-37MW
milk, 6-18MW to 6-20MW
pasta, 9-11MW
pies, 24-20MW to 24-25MW
poultry, 18-18MW to 18-32MW
rice, 9-10MW
sauces, 10-23MW to 10-27MW
seafood, 19-24MW to 19-33MW
soup, 16-16MW to 16-19MW
thickeners, 10-23MW to 10-29MW
vegetables, 13-24MW to 13-35MW
Milk, cooking
by conventional methods, 6-8 to
6-14
in microwave oven, 6-18MW to
6-20MW
Milk, kinds, 6-1
Molasses, 20-23
Molded cookies, 23-8
Muffin, method of mixing, 21-9
Muffins, 21-9 to 21-11

N

Newspapers in microwave oven,
4-56MW
Non-caloric sweeteners, 20-25
Nonfat dry milk
as ingredient in microwave
cooking, 6-20MW
how to use, 6-1, 6-17
Nutrition labels, 2-2

O

Omelets, 8-13
One-bowl mixing method for cakes,
22-10
Open dating, 2-7
Outdoor cooking
general, 4-22
meat, 17-16
Oven frying
fish, 19-20
poultry, 18-11
Overcooked food in microwave
oven, 4-49MW

P

Pan placement
in convection oven, 4-29C
in conventional oven, 20-32
Pan substitutions, 5-15

Panbroiling
general, 4-14
meat, 17-17
Panfrying
fish, 19-19
general, 4-15
meat, 17-18
poultry, 18-10
Pans for baking
how to prepare, 20-31
kinds, 20-30
Pans for convection oven, 4-28C
Pans for microwave oven. See
"Containers for microwave
cooking"
Pancakes, 21-2, 21-3
Pasta, cooking
by conventional methods, 9-8
in microwave oven, 9-11MW
Pasta, kinds, 9-3
Paper towels, use in microwaving,
4-45MW
Pies
by conventional method, 24-1 to
24-15
in microwave oven, 24-20MW to
24-25MW
Pink color in
cooked pork, 17-22
cooked poultry, 18-16
Plastic wrap, use in microwaving,
4-45MW
Poaching
eggs, by conventional method,
8-10
eggs, in microwave oven, 8-23MW
fish, 19-22
fruit, 12-16
general guidelines, 4-4
Potato starch, 10-22
Poultry, cooking
by conventional methods, 18-6 to
18-17
in microwave oven, 18-18MW to
18-32MW
Power failure, 3-5
Preheating oven, 20-33
Pressed cookies, 23-9
Pressure cooker, 4-11
Price per serving, 2-6
Protein foods, cooking, 4-24
Pureed vegetable soups, 16-12

Q

Quick breads, 21-1

Quick loaf breads
  in conventional oven, 21-9 to
    21-11
  in microwave oven, 21-27MW
Quick-mix method for cakes, 22-10

R

Rack position in convection oven,
    4-30C
Recipes, adapting and changing
  baking in microwave oven,
    20-35MW
  cakes for microwave oven,
    22-22MW, 22-23MW
  convection oven, 4-35C
  cookies for microwave oven,
    23-15MW
  experimenting with flavorings,
    20-28
  experimenting with herbs, 11-12
  high-altitude cooking, 4-57MW,
    5-3
  honey as substitute for sugar,
    20-22
  microwave cooking, 4-64MW
  molasses as substitute for sugar,
    20-23
  soy flour in yeast bread, 21-26
  wheat germ in yeast bread, 21-26
  yeast bread rapid mix method,
    21-14
Recipes, how to evaluate, 5-1
Reducing stock, 16-6
Refreezing food
  general, 3-6
  meat, 17-9
Refrigerator cookies, 23-11
Reheating, in microwave oven
  breads, rolls, 21-29MW
  cooked eggs, 8-24MW
  seafood, 19-33MW
Removing baked products from
    pans, 20-34
Rest time. See "Carryover time"
Rice, cooking
  by conventional methods, 9-7
  in microwave oven, 9-10MW
Rice, kinds, 9-1
Rice starch, 10-22
Rising, yeast dough
  by conventional method, 21-18
  in microwave oven, 21-28MW
Roasting
  general, 4-23
  in convection oven, 4-33C

meat by conventional method,
    17-14
meat in microwave oven,
    17-26MW to 17-30MW
poultry by conventional method,
    18-7
poultry in microwave oven,
    18-18MW to 18-24MW, 18-29MW,
    18-31MW, 18-32MW
Roasting in plastic cooking bag,
    4-10
Rolled cookies, 23-10

S

Safety hints
  for microwave oven, 4-63MW
  grease fires, 4-17
Salad dressings, 14-5
Salads
  how to make, 14-6
  molded gelatin, 10-17 to 10-20,
    10-29MW
  parts of, 14-5
Salt
  in conventional cooking, 11-22
  in microwave cooking, 4-58MW,
    13-25MW
  in processed food, 2-12
Sauces
  by conventional methods, 10-1 to
    10-7
  in microwave oven, 10-23MW to
    10-27MW
Sauteing
  fruits, 12-18
  general guidelines, 4-15
  vegetables, 13-17
Scalded milk, 6-10
Salloped vegetables, 13-21
Scorched milk
  in conventional cooking, 6-9
  in microwave cooking, 6-18MW
Scrambled eggs
  by conventional methods, 8-12
  in microwave oven, 8-22MW
Scum on cooked milk, 6-11
Seafood, cooking
  by conventional methods, 19-12 to
    19-23
  in microwave oven, 19-24MW to
    19-33MW
Seasonings in cooking, 11-1 to 11-22
Separating eggs, 8-14
Shellfish. See "Seafood"
Shortened cakes, 22-1 to 22-14

Shortening
  general, 20-17
  in cakes, 22-3
Simmering
  general, 4-3
  vegetables, 13-15
Skin on cooked milk, 6-11
Slow cooker, 4-8
Smoking point of fat, 4-13
Soft-cooked eggs, 8-6
Soup
  by conventional methods, 16-1 to
    16-14
  in microwave oven, 16-16MW to
    16-19MW
Sour milk, 6-14
Spoiled food, cause of, 3-1
Sponge cakes. See "Foam cakes"
Standing time. See "Carryover
  time"
Steaming
  fish, 19-23
  general, 4-9
  vegetables, 13-16
Stewing
  fish, 19-22
  fruits, 12-16
  general, 4-5
  in convection oven, 4-32C
  meat, 17-21
  poultry, 18-13
Stir-frying
  general, 4-15
  meat, 17-19
  vegetables, 13-18
Stock, 16-1 to 16-7
Storing
  baking powder, 20-13
  breads, 21-30
  cakes, 22-34, 22-35
  canned milk, 6-6
  canned seafood, 19-11
  cheese, 7-5
  coffee, 15-2
  cookies, 23-19
  cream, 6-4
  cured seafood, 19-11
  dry storage, 3-2
  eggs, 8-3
  fat, 20-19
  flour, 20-4
  freezer storage, 3-4
  fruits, 12-6 to 12-9
  general guidelines, 3-8
  grains, 9-6

home-dried herbs, 11-9
  leftover cooked vegetables, 13-10
  leftovers, 3-9
  meat, 17-7
  milk, 6-4
  nonfat dry milk, 6-6
  oil, 20-19
  pies, 24-26
  poultry, 18-4, 18-5
  power failure, 3-5
  refrigerator storage, 3-3
  seafood, 19-8, 19-9
  seasonings, 11-3 to 11-5
  soup, 16-15
  stock, 16-8
  sweeteners, 20-26
  tea, 15-7
  thickened foods, 10-30
  vegetables, 13-6 to 13-9
  yeast, 20-13
  yogurt, 6-7
Straining stock, 16-4
Stuffing for poultry
  for conventional methods, 18-8
  for microwave oven, 18-32MW
Substitutions
  food, general, 5-6
  pans, 5-15
  seafood, 19-15
Sugar
  general, 20-21
  how to measure, 5-14
  in cakes, 22-4
  in processed foods, 2-13
Sun tea, 15-11
Sweeteners, 20-20 to 20-25

T

Tapioca, as a thickener, 10-11 to
  10-13
Tea, 15-7 to 15-11
Tearing salad greens, 14-4
Thickeners, cooking with
  by conventional methods, 10-1 to
    10-22
  in microwave oven, 10-23MW to
    10-29MW
Time, cooking in microwave oven,
  4-40MW, 4-44MW, 4-50MW

U

Unit pricing, 2-5

V

Vegetables as seasoning, 11-19
Vegetables as thickeners, 10-21

Vegetables, cooking
  by conventional methods, 13-12 to
    13-23
  in microwave oven, 13-24MW to
    13-35MW

W

Waffles, 21-2, 21-4
Wax paper, use in microwave oven,
  4-45MW
Waxy rice flour, 10-22
Water, weight of, 20-6

White sauce
  by conventional method, 10-4
  in microwave oven, 10-23MW to
    10-25MW

X-Y-Z

Yeast
  how to use, 21-14
  kinds, 20-11
Yeast breads
  by conventional method, 21-1 to
    21-26
  in microwave oven, 21-28MW
Yogurt, 6-3

Notes

Notes